URBAN POLICY IN TWENTIETH-CENTURY AMERICA

URBAN POLICY in TWENTIETH-CENTURY AMERICA

EDITED BY

ARNOLD R. HIRSCH
AND
RAYMOND A. MOHL

RUTGERS UNIVERSITY PRESS
NEW BRUNSWICK, NEW JERSEY

HOUSTON PUBLIC LIBRARY

Library of Congress Cataloging-in-Publication Data

Urban policy in twentieth-century America / edited by Arnold R.
Hirsch and Raymond A. Mohl.
    p.   cm.
  Includes bibliographical references and index.
  ISBN 0-8135-1905-5 (cloth)—ISBN 0-8135-1906-3 (pbk.)
  1. Urban policy—United States. I. Hirsch, Arnold R. (Arnold
Richard), 1949-   . II. Mohl, Raymond A.
HT121.U72 1993
307.76′0973—dc20   92-9429
                                                   CIP

British Cataloging-in-Publication information available

Contents

Preface

DURING Spring semester 1990, the History Department of the University of New Orleans invited Professor Raymond A. Mohl of Florida Atlantic University to conduct a seminar in urban history. The department was working in conjunction with the College of Liberal Arts and the College of Urban and Public Affairs (CUPA) to launch a new, interdisciplinary Ph.D. program in urban studies. The seminar provided an opportunity to introduce a select group of University of New Orleans history and urban studies graduate students to the field through the views and experiences of an eminent senior scholar.

Even before Mohl's arrival in New Orleans, we started planning a lecture series to accompany the seminar. With the generous support of the University of New Orleans, the College of Liberal Arts, and CUPA, David R. Goldfield, Sam Bass Warner, Jr., Carl Abbott, and Michael B. Katz delivered invited public addresses. This book represents the fruits of their efforts, as well as the research and writing undertaken by Ray Mohl while in residence, and the revision of some of my own thoughts that resulted from our interaction.

From the beginning, we focused on American urban policy. Although it was impossible to anticipate the world-shaking events of 1991, it was clear that the cold war was winding down, that numerous domestic problems demanded increasing thought, and that U.S. cities, particularly, needed considerable attention. The lectures and, subsequently, the chapters in this book were never intended to articulate a new reform program or, in any precise way, advocate a particular agenda. They are, however, designed to stimulate thought on the current plight of American cities, reflection on the character of past policies and practices, and public discussion of broad issues of general concern.

The "urban crisis" that erupted during the 1960s, and was dismissed by Richard Nixon during the 1970s, remained beyond the scope of concerted political action in the 1980s, even as conditions (especially in a number of older, industrial American cities) deteriorated. After a brief flirtation with an activist federal approach that lasted perhaps not much more than a single generation (from the New Deal to the Great Society), the national government sounded retreat and disengaged from urban America, leaving the cities to wither or weather the market forces that were deemed the final arbiters of their fate.

The federal withdrawal was both intellectual and political, and neither retreat occurred overnight. Clustered around the problems of physical revitalization (i.e., urban renewal) and social reconstruction (i.e., human renewal), federal initiatives from the beginning faced daunting obstacles. Indeed, given the long view, what appears exceptional is not the current lack of federal concern, but rather the flurry of activity that encompassed the middle third of the twentieth century. Born under the extraordinary pressure of the Great Depression, the application of national power to specifically urban problems was extinguished as the final embers of the riotous 1960s smoldered and cooled in the early years of the 1970s. The physical, structural rebirth of U.S. cities remained confounded with a growing racial dilemma that rendered the most complex problems more difficult still.

The very intractability of America's urban problems lent weight to the critiques of those who scoffed at the notion that human agency, through political action, might successfully lighten the burdens borne by city dwellers. Even the earliest programs that targeted the declining postwar urban core—slum clearance, redevelopment, and the host of initiatives that went under the rubric of urban renewal—drew criticism while still in their infancy.

Martin Anderson in *The Federal Bulldozer: A Critical Analysis of Urban Renewal, 1949–1962** offered a classic, conservative critique that, in many ways, was a harbinger of the resistance that dogged even the discussion of reform during what was supposed to be its heyday. Looking at the early fruits of urban renewal, Anderson claimed, accurately, that the program was noteworthy more for cutting a destructive swath through many of the older U.S. cities than for any positive accomplishments, that the poor and the black populations bore disproportionate burdens in its implementation, and that its beneficiaries— generally well-to-do people and a handful of developers—were not the properly designated recipients of the government largess intended to arrest the decline of urban America.

Where Anderson's ideology overran his data, however, was in his conclusion that the unforeseen consequences of urban renewal resulted from a soft-headed, soft-hearted program of social reform that pushed the federal government into usurping private market prerogatives to the detriment of those the program was intended to help. "Experts," intellectuals, and self-righteous (not to mention self-serving) politicians became Anderson's primary foils, and the violated private market remained, for him, the salvation of the misguided. What Anderson failed to see, however, was that urban renewal, de-

*(Cambridge, Mass.: MIT Press, 1964).

spite its rhetoric of public concern, was never intended as a program of social reform and that it leapt from precisely those private sources he wished to entrust.

Confusing rhetoric with reality, Anderson portrayed the federal government as an unwanted intruder in the private sphere when it was nothing more than a draftee enlisted in a series of local agendas. Those commercial, industrial, institutional, and real estate interests whose fates remained tied to the postwar inner city recognized that government powers (particularly that of eminent domain), subsidies, and assistance (especially the dedication of public housing for relocation purposes) were imperative to overcome the threshold obstacles impeding redevelopment. The facade of social reform provided additional political support and assured the cooperation of those bureaucrats and activists, largely survivors and supporters of the New Deal, whose assistance remained critical. Social reform itself, however, never amounted to more than an anticipated by-product, if that, to the program's architects. Hardly representing the usurpation of private market forces, slum clearance and urban renewal epitomized their articulation and certainly during the 1950s and early 1960s did not embody an unfettered social conscience freely enacting its will.

At bottom an attempt to short-circuit more far-reaching measures deemed too "socialistic," redevelopment and renewal stood as necessary compromises pushed by metropolitan America's primary corporate actors. As attempts to reconcile market forces, private initiative, and the use of public resources deemed necessary for urban salvation, they proved halting and inherently contradictory efforts that not only failed to deliver on their social promise, but provided the ammunition for critics such as Anderson who took the rhetoric surrounding the programs at face value. Rather than documenting the foibles of "do-good" big government, however, these early stabs at urban reconstruction simply demonstrated that public powers in private hands could not be reasonably expected to deliver the greatest good for the greatest number.

Contemporaries, however, saw only the destruction and heard nothing more than the hollow words. "Liberals" abhorred the damage done to inner-city neighborhoods, particularly as blacks bore disproportionate burdens and white ethnics witnessed the rending of their communal ties. "Conservatives" excoriated the purported social agenda of the new federal presence, the expense of these novel initiatives, and the obvious failure of the programs to meet their stated, or even sub-rosa, objectives. Attacked from all sides, redevelopment and renewal were jettisoned after a twenty-year romp across the urban landscape.

What remained was the unresolved tension displayed by those market forces and actors that both demanded and conditioned federal intervention. The result, particularly in the 1970s and 1980s, was a series of recurring scandals in the Department of Housing and Urban Development as private interests that were unburdened by the weight of any social agenda milked programs that, by design, were ripe for exploitation. Making the best of a bad situation, the critics of federal intervention drained every drop of economic and political advantage that could be had from agencies that, as they averred, simply proved the government's inevitable propensity for wasteful and inefficient bumbling.

Efforts directed at the human side of the urban equation, the move toward social reconstruction exemplified by the War on Poverty and the Great Society of the late 1960s, attracted similar criticism even if there was less consensus on their unrelievedly negative effect. Critics such as Edward C. Banfield espoused a brand of neo–Social Darwinism by the 1970s that emphasized the timelessness of the problems involved (an ahistorical approach dressed in the garb of historical analysis); dismissed the problem of race; and seemed to sigh at the folly of those who could not help making things worse by trying to make them better.[†] Others, such as Charles Murray, whose *Losing Ground: American Social Policy, 1950–1980* became the bible of the Reagan administration, made explicit the contradictory corollary that granted the federal government an infinite capacity for evil while denying that it had the power to do anything positive at all.[‡]

However, in the end the exertion of federal authority was more a political problem than an intellectual one. The conservative reaction that set in after the riots of the 1960s heralded the persistence of intractable urban, economic, and racial problems did not simply pare the resources futilely aimed at the Democratic party's favorite targets in a pinch-penny counterstroke. Rather, that reaction redirected the flow through programs that encouraged new development and Cold War–driven defense budgets to the booming Sunbelt and, through the innovation of revenue sharing, to the suburbs. The national Republican ascendancy that followed hard upon the civil rights movement tied itself to the economic and demographic transformation of post–World War II America, cashing in on majoritarian racial sentiment and the shifting of geographical centers of power. The "benign neglect" of minority problems in the wake of the superheated 1960s,

---

[†]Edward C. Banfield, *The Unheavenly City Revisited* (Boston: Little, Brown, 1974).
[‡]Charles Murray, *Losing Ground: American Social Policy, 1950–1980* (New York: Basic Books, Inc., 1984).

then, represented more than a desire for peace. It became the necessary precursor to an era of the redistributionist policies congenial to a conservative political agenda and the bridge to more blatant antiminority appeals during the 1980s.

If the "neo-conservative" reaction occasionally displayed incompatible assumptions (the federal government has been alternately blamed for being powerless to enact positive change and for succeeding so well that future engagement is unnecessary), the "liberal" response has been even more incoherent. Failing to agree on the sources or the nature of the problems involved, there is certainly no consensus on proposed approaches. Internal debates over the merits of race-specific or race-neutral remedies, the role of "culture" in perpetuating current difficulties, and the continuity or discontinuity of urban and minority experiences have no fruitful end in sight. Further burdened by a continued reluctance to discuss the most painful and sensitive issues freely, openly, and frankly, those who see themselves supporting a "progressive" agenda still need to confront the worst excesses and mistakes of the previous reform era. They do, however, possess a sense of urgency and the perception that something must be done.

The end of the cold war, the recession of the early 1990s, and questions regarding America's stature and quality of life all call for a period of self-assessment. Stocktaking and the search for new directions seem appropriate. If, despite the wishes of some, the mere passage of time has proven inadequate as a solution to the problems of entrenched poverty and social injustice, the extra measure of pain meted out in the eddies of the American economy has similarly failed as an "incentive" equal to the task it has been assigned. Indeed, global trends and their effect on life in the United States highlight the need to reinterpret the causes and consequences of the current state of affairs and to reexamine the proper sphere and content of government policy. Let the debate be renewed.

ARNOLD R. HIRSCH

Contributors

Carl Abbott is Professor of Urban Studies and Planning at Portland State University. He is the author of numerous books, including *The New Urban America: Growth and Politics in Sunbelt Cities*, rev. ed. (Chapel Hill: University of North Carolina Press, 1987); *Portland: Planning, Politics, and Growth in a Twentieth-Century City* (Lincoln: University of Nebraska Press, 1983); and *Urban America in the Modern Age: 1920 to the Present* (Arlington Heights, Ill.: Harlan Davidson, 1987).

David R. Goldfield is Robert Lee Bailey Professor of History at the University of North Carolina at Charlotte. He is editor of the *Journal of Urban History* and author of *Cotton Fields and Skyscrapers: Southern City and Region, 1607–1980* (Baton Rouge: Louisiana State University Press, 1982); *Promised Land: The South since 1945* (Arlington Heights, Ill.: Harlan Davidson, 1987); and *Black, White, and Southern: Race Relations and Southern Culture, 1940 to the Present* (Baton Rouge: Louisiana State University Press, 1990.

Arnold R. Hirsch is Professor of History and Urban Studies at the University of New Orleans and Chair of the Department of History. He is the author of *Making the Second Ghetto: Race and Housing in Chicago, 1940–1960* (Cambridge, England: Cambridge University Press, 1983) and co-editor of *Creole New Orleans: Race and Americanization* (Baton Rouge: Louisiana State University Press, 1992).

Michael B. Katz is Professor of History and Chair of the Department at the University of Pennsylvania. He is the author of many books, including *The Irony of Early School Reform: Educational Innovation in Mid-Nineteenth Century Massachusetts* (Cambridge, Mass.: Harvard University Press, 1968); *Poverty and Policy in American History* (New York: Academic, 1983); *In the Shadow of the Poorhouse: A Social History of Welfare in America* (New York: Basic Books, 1986); *Reconstructing American Education* (Cambridge, Mass.: Harvard University Press, 1989); and *The Undeserving Poor: From the War on Poverty to the War on Welfare* (New York: Pantheon, 1990).

Raymond A. Mohl is Professor of History at Florida Atlantic University. He is the author of *Poverty in New York, 1783–1825* (New York:

Oxford University Press, 1971); *The New City: Urban America in the Industrial Age, 1860–1920* (Arlington Heights, Ill.: Harlan Davidson, 1985); and *Steel City: Urban and Ethnic Patterns in Gary, Indiana, 1906–1950* (New York: Holmes and Meier, 1986). He has also edited *The Making of Urban America* (Wilmington, Del.: Scholarly Resources, 1988) and *Searching for the Sunbelt: Historical Perspectives on a Region* (Knoxville: University of Tennessee Press, 1990).

Sam Bass Warner, Jr., is Jack Meyerhoff Professor of American Environmental Studies at Brandeis University. He is the author of *Streetcar Suburbs: The Process of Growth in Boston* (Cambridge, Mass.: Harvard University Press, 1962); *The Private City: Philadelphia in Three Periods of Its Growth* (Philadelphia: University of Pennsylvania Press, 1968); *The Urban Wilderness: A History of the American City* (New York: Harper and Row, 1972); *Province of Reason* (Cambridge, Mass.: Harvard University Press, 1984); and *To Dwell Is To Garden: A History of Boston's Community Gardens* (Boston: Northeastern University Press, 1987).

URBAN POLICY IN TWENTIETH-CENTURY AMERICA

1

RAYMOND A. MOHL

Shifting Patterns of American Urban Policy since 1900

As BIG-CITY mayors grimly gathered in August 1991 at the annual U.S. Conference of Mayors, it seemed clear that urban America faced difficult times ahead. Crime, violence, drugs, unemployment, poverty, and homelessness have plagued U.S. cities for too many years, tearing at the human fabric of urban life. Decades of neglect and physical decay have undermined the urban infrastructure, as sewers, streets, bridges, public housing projects, and transit systems crumble, break down, and fall apart. Schooling, health care, social services, and environmental protection have deteriorated badly; deterioration was especially pronounced during the conservative Reagan years when federal financing for such programs was slashed. A half century of suburbanization has sucked the life out of the central cities, most of which currently house a disproportionate share of the nation's low-income, black, Hispanic, and new immigrant population. Much of the urban economy has shifted to the periphery as well, leaving behind entire communities devastated by unemployment, underemployment, poverty, and dependency. Although the bill for social services has skyrocketed, the urban tax base has eroded. Consequently, some smaller cities, such as Bridgeport, Connecticut, and Chelsea, Massachusetts, have already gone bankrupt, whereas larger cities like New York, and Philadelphia teeter on the edge of insolvency. Rising expenses and falling revenues, the National League of Cities has asserted, will ultimately force many other cities into a financial "death spiral."[1]

Significant shifts in urban policy making over the past two decades have produced distinctive patterns of social disinvestment. The traditional relationship between the cities and the federal government, first established during the New Deal era of the 1930s and strengthened during the Great Society years of the 1960s, has all but disintegrated. Despite periodic assertions about the desirability of a national urban policy, presidential administrations from Richard Nixon to George Bush have encouraged the steady reduction and elimination of programs established during the 1960s. Many other costly responsibilities have been shifted to state and local governments. The 1990–1992 national economic recession, which was marked by massive layoffs of public and private-sector employees and huge cutbacks in social services and public works, brought concerns about the American city dramatically to the forefront of discussion once again. Few disagreed that an effective urban policy was needed—a policy that addressed the multiple needs of cities and their citizens. Yet ideological and political conflicts seemingly immobilized the policy making process.

Progressive Era

Debates about the place of the city in American life are nothing new in the 1990s. For many decades, journalists and novelists, reformers and preachers, politicians and businesspeople have been mulling over the effects of urban life. "The problem of the twentieth century will be the city," religious reformer Josiah Strong predicted in his 1898 book *The Twentieth Century City*. Strong was mostly concerned about political corruption, uncontrolled immigration, and the inability of Christian morality to restrain rampant materialism. However, some writers and reformers of the progressive era had a more optimistic outlook on American urban life. For political reformer Frederic C. Howe, the city was "not only the problem of our civilization, it is also the hope of the future." In typical progressive fashion, Howe optimistically argued that through economic regulation, social programs, and political education the cities could banish the poverty, social disorder, and political corruption that shaped and dominated urban life in the industrial era. Despite their divergent viewpoints, both Strong and Howe offered a program—an urban policy of sorts—for the American city during a period of explosive growth.[2]

Progressive-era reformers focused on the city, and with good reason. During the industrial explosion of the late nineteenth century, urban America anchored the process of economic growth and material progress that came to characterize the nation. However, the rapid rise of an urban and industrial civilization imposed immense costs. Euro-

pean immigrants and native-born rural migrants poured into the industrial cities in search of economic opportunities. Overcrowded and
run-down housing conditions typified the working-class districts of
most cities. Competitive capitalism tended to exploit the new industrial workers, who were as yet unprotected by labor unions or governmental regulation. Environmental safeguards, social services, and
public health measures were primitive and weakly developed. Meanwhile, cities expanded in haphazard and disorderly ways, with little
planning or control. Municipal governments of the time, especially
those in the big cities dominated by political machines, often encoun-
tered difficulties or demonstrated incompetence in managing urban
growth. The American industrial city was a huge, unregulated, economic growth machine, its evolution shaped primarily by market
forces that provided both the source of its strengths and the cause of
its most serious problems.[3]

The political reformers of the early twentieth century—such as
Josiah Strong and Frederic C. Howe—advocated a disparate set of
urban policies, hoping to impose order and control on the American
city. The federal government was not yet active in addressing urban
issues. Thus, the urban reformers worked mostly within the arenas
of municipal and state government or through private social agencies and reform organizations. The progressive movement of this
period comprised a diverse set of causes, impulses, and programs.
Reform coalitions formed, disbanded, and reformed, depending on
the issue; conflict and disagreement just as often split and divided
reformers and reform organizations. Evangelical moral reformers,
for instance, were mostly interested in attacking the twin evils of
the machine boss and the corner saloon—the sources of corruption,
criminality, booze, and vice. Many political reformers sought to modernize the structure of city government, replacing the politicized
mayor and ward system with the seemingly more accountable and
more efficient city manager or commission form of municipal rule.
Social reformers advocated improvements in education, recreation,
housing, working conditions, and social welfare. Still other reformers concentrated on achieving higher levels of economic regulation,
consumer protection, or social insurance. City planning emerged
during this period, with its focus on reorganizing the urban environment through park planning, landscape architecture, building regulation, and land-use zoning. Municipal engineers were active in most
cities, applying technological advances to the building of such necessary infrastructure systems as sewers, water supply, electricity, and
public transit.[4]

These urban reformers achieved varying degrees of success. Purity reformers succeeded in abolishing the saloon with the passage of the prohibition amendment to the U.S. Constitution in 1918. Although the largest cities such as New York and Chicago successfully resisted the structural reformers, the city manager form of municipal government was adopted in more than four hundred cities by 1930—mostly small or medium-sized cities with predominantly native-born populations. Social reformers almost everywhere were successful in implementing at least some aspects of their diverse, people-oriented programs. By the 1920s, the principles of city planning were widely accepted, and the municipal engineers had long been indispensable as builders of the modern city.[5]

Urbanization and Policy in the 1920s

Despite some important reform successes, especially at the state and local level, urban policy making of the progressive era remained a disorganized, haphazard, and ineffective process that often came too late and provided too little to ensure long-term civic improvement. Indeed, the problems confronting urban America had intensified by the 1920s with continued rapid growth. The 1920 census revealed that, for the first time, more than half of the American people lived in urban areas. By 1930, New York City's population approached an astonishing 7 million. Chicago's population soared by 25 percent during the 1920s, reaching almost 3.5 million by the end of the decade. Three other major cities—Philadelphia, Detroit, and Los Angeles—also grew rapidly, in some cases dramatically, and ranged between 1.2 and 1.9 million people. Moreover, the mass European immigration of the industrial era had brought a dizzying array of ethnic diversity to urban America. By 1920, for instance, just more than 36 percent of New York City's huge population was foreign born. Immigrants also composed 20 percent or more of the population of such diverse big cities as Boston, Philadelphia, Chicago, Detroit, Pittsburgh, Cleveland, Milwaukee, Minneapolis, San Francisco, Los Angeles, and Seattle, among others. Restrictive legislation curbed mass European immigration by the mid-1920s, but urban America confronted the challenges of absorbing and acculturating the vast numbers of newcomers who had arrived in earlier years.[6]

Racial diversity also became a prominent feature of the American city during the 1920s. Before 1920, most cities in the Northeast, Midwest, and West had small black populations, because blacks were heavily concentrated in the rural and urban South. During World War I and after, labor shortages in the industrial heartland stimulated a powerful migration of southern blacks to the urban Northeast and Midwest. Unaffected by the new immigration restrictions, Mexicans also were attracted to industrial and agricultural jobs in the United States during the 1920s. Cities in California, Texas, and the Southwest were on the receiving end of a new Mexican migration, but large colonies of Mexican immigrants also emerged as far away as Omaha, Denver, Minneapolis, Chicago, and Detroit.[7] As a consequence of these labor migrations of the 1920s—numbering about nine hundred thousand Mexicans and nine hundred thousand blacks—race relations increasingly intruded to the forefront in the cities. The newcomers from the American South and from Mexico sought housing, employment, education, and political power in the "Jim Crow" society of urban America. Official racial policies, such as school segregation and racial zoning, along with "unofficial" discrimination in housing, hiring, and voting became standard urban practices.[8] Racial and ethnic tension increased throughout the 1920s, as reflected in the national resurgence of the Ku Klux Klan.[9] The vicious race riots in East St. Louis and Houston in 1917, in Philadelphia in 1918, in Chicago, Washington, D.C., and elsewhere in 1919, and in Tulsa in 1921, served as unfortunate harbingers of things to come.[10]

Other important urban shifts were observable during the 1920s, as well. The centrifugal drift of population intensified during the decade, facilitated by the popularity of the automobile, the promise of suburbia, and the prosperity of the middle class. The automobile was a particularly powerful agent of urban change, pushing out the boundaries of metropolitan regions and permitting suburban commuters to live in distant fringe areas. Motor vehicle registration tripled during the 1920s, climbing dramatically to about twenty-seven million cars and trucks by 1930. Downtown traffic jams and heavy congestion during commuter rush hours became commonplace. Urban policy makers and planners were forced to accommodate the automobile, which increasingly appeared to be the mode of transportation preferred by those who could afford it. Thus, city planners and politicians concentrated on street development and highway building, seeking to alleviate traffic congestion and make the downtown more accessible to commuters and shoppers. Cities such as Detroit, New York, Philadelphia, and Chicago were beginning to plan for "superhighways" as early as the 1920s. A standardized system of traffic control was implemented nationwide by the end of the decade, incorporating improved street design and uniform traffic rules, signs, signals, and lights. The automobile had already begun to assert its supremacy over the modern city.[11]

Mass adoption of the car culture in the 1920s had its costs. Ridership on the nation's electric streetcar systems peaked in 1923 at almost sixteen billion individual trips. However, these mass transit systems soon languished and ultimately disappeared as the popularity of motor vehicles surged. Public perceptions that streetcars cluttered the streets and slowed automobile traffic contributed to the demise of mass transit, as did the assumed flexibility and comparative cheapness of the newly popular bus systems. The aging streetcar systems were poorly maintained, ineffectively regulated by public agencies, and often badly mismanaged. Municipal governments generally accepted the new automobile technology as an improvement over older forms of mass transit. The automobile industry played an important role in the decline of mass transit, as well. Beginning in the mid-1920s, through a series of subsidiary companies, General Motors began buying financially strapped streetcar systems and substituting buses for electric streetcars. By the end of the 1940s, as one study has noted, General Motors "had participated in the elimination of over a hundred electric transit systems in forty-five cities, including New York, Los Angeles, Philadelphia, St. Louis, and Baltimore." The quick death of the nation's electric streetcar systems clearly resulted from deliberate urban policy choices that had long-term consequences for American cities.[12]

If the automobile shaped urbanism and urbanization during the decade of prosperity, so also did city planning. Widely accepted and institutionalized by the 1920s, city planning had become an integral aspect of urban policy making. Planning promised cities that were more orderly, more efficient, and more beautiful. Consequently, hundreds of cities adopted zoning ordinances and established planning commissions by the mid-1920s. Dozens of cities drew on the expertise of such well-known planning consultants as Harland Bartholomew and John Nolen in crafting comprehensive city plans to guide future urban development. In the conservative business climate of the 1920s, however, few of these plans went much beyond accommodating the automobile, modernizing the street layout, revitalizing the business district, decorating the downtown with civic plazas and public art, and facilitating business growth and real estate development. In many cities, planning simply became a tool used by businesspeople's leagues and committees to create new urban space for commercial and industrial development. Unlike in Europe, where housing had always been incorporated within wider planning conceptions, the United States had no tradition of planning for the poor population. There was little room for housing, neighborhood revitalization, and improvement of slum conditions in the comprehensive city plans of the 1920s. This should not be surprising, because most planners during this period worked for people who had power, money, and authority, and the urban policy that resulted from the planners' work reflected those interests. As historian Charles Beard put it in 1927, "Two decades of city planning added up to little more than some civic plazas and boulevards that made it easier for businessmen to drive to work."[13]

The automobile and the highway networks built in the 1920s pushed the suburban periphery to new and distant limits. In the industrial era, many cities extended their governing authority and recaptured suburbanizing population through ambitious annexation policies. By the 1920s, however, suburban communities were successfully fighting annexation, leaving rapidly expanding metropolitan areas politically fragmented. It became increasingly clear, at least to some thinkers and writers, that urban America needed metropolitan and regional approaches to questions of political governance, economic development, city planning, and social life. The Regional Planning Association of America (RPAA), founded in 1923 by Lewis Mumford and other planning activists, exemplified the effort to counter the decentralizing urban pattern. Rather than accepting unregulated metropolitan sprawl as inevitable, RPAA proposed the building of entirely new, self-supporting communities of fifty thousand people on the outer edges of the metropolitan region, surrounded by greenbelts free of any development. RPAA made some modest efforts to build such small, self-contained communities at Sunnyside Gardens in New York City and at Radburn in New Jersey. However, the one major attempt to implement regional planning in the 1920s—the New York Regional Plan—sought instead to build new transportation links that would facilitate continued suburbanization coupled with enhancement of the urban core. Mumford and the RPAA planners attacked the New York Regional Plan as a sellout to central-city business interests. Nevertheless, the plan formed the basis of transportation and recreation facilities built over the next few decades by New York's chief public works planner and power broker, Robert Moses. Aside from disputes among planners, the multiplicity of municipalities that sprawled across every large metropolitan area and the jealously guarded prerogatives of suburban communities impeded effective regional planning in the 1920s. Regional planning and metropolitan government remained a visionary dream awaiting future implementation.[14]

Depression and New Deal Eras

The Great Depression of the 1930s had a severe effect on American cities. Municipal payrolls were trimmed as a consequence of tax deliquencies and increasing relief costs, and many cities defaulted on debt payments or filed for bankruptcy. Massive unemployment brought poverty, dependency, homelessness, and despair to middle-class urban America for the first time. By the end of 1931, for example, more than 800,000 New Yorkers went without work, whereas in Chicago the unemployed numbered more than 625,000. Factory closings, job layoffs, mortgage foreclosures, and evictions became commonplace. Banks foreclosed on the homes of almost 300,000 people in 1932 alone. In New York, Chicago, and other cities, thousands of tenants organized to prevent landlords from carrying out eviction notices, while councils of the unemployed staged marches and demonstrations demanding relief. Several million homeless migrants tramped the nation or rode the rails in boxcars in search of work, while uncounted thousands slept in municipal lodging houses or lived in makeshift "Hoovervilles" that blighted the urban landscape. On a single day in January 1931, 85,000 New Yorkers waited in breadlines at churches and shelters for free meals. The resources of private social agencies, emergency relief committees, and settlement houses were insufficient to cope with the magnitude of the Great Depression. The breadline and the soup kitchen had become ubiquitous urban institutions. By the time Franklin D. Roosevelt was inaugurated as president in 1933, big-city mayors were demanding federal help for urban America.[15]

In the face of unprecedented need, an urban lobby emerged to press the case for a national program of urban assistance. The National Municipal League, an outgrowth of the progressive era, and the newly formed U.S. Conference of Mayors served to focus these lobbying efforts. Detroit Mayor Frank Murphy and New York Mayor Fiorello LaGuardia were especially effective in establishing the Conference of Mayors and forging new links between Washington, D.C., and the cities. Franklin D. Roosevelt's New Deal had something for everyone, and many new programs dealt directly with urban problems. To some extent, Roosevelt himself had an anti-urban bias, as reflected in New Deal programs for subsistence homesteads and greenbelt towns. However, many influential New Dealers, including former social workers such as Harry Hopkins and Frances Perkins, responded positively to the agenda of urban mayors and city planners. Equally important,

Roosevelt's political coalition incorporated huge segments of the urban electorate, including especially working-class whites and blacks. New Deal programs for unemployment and work relief, public works, and low-cost public housing, in particular, significantly affected the American city.[16]

Although it did not offer a fully developed urban policy, the New Deal initiated a dramatically different relationship between the cities and the federal government—an activist and interventionist approach that produced quick results. The Federal Emergency Relief Administration, created in May 1933, provided instant work relief to millions of unemployed urbanites. The Civil Works Administration (CWA), a temporary work-relief agency created during winter 1933–1934, put more than 4 million people to work on a vast array of local projects. CWA bypassed state agencies and for the first time provided direct federal assistance to municipalities. Somewhat later, work-relief efforts were consolidated in the Works Progress Administration (WPA), which had, one historian has noted, "a distinctly urban flavor." Agencies such as CWA and WPA supplied funding for the construction of water and sewer systems, parks and recreational facilities, airports, subways, bridges, and, according to one recent estimate, more than 500,000 miles of streets and 110,000 public buildings in American cities. Urban mayors quickly seized upon all of these programs, not only to provide jobs for the unemployed, but to rebuild their cities.[17]

The work-relief agencies were complimented by the Public Works Administration (PWA), which generally focused on large-scale public works projects such as center-city and harbor redevelopment, slum clearance, and housing projects. After 1937, the United States Housing Administration assumed the public housing functions of PWA. These New Deal housing and public works efforts encouraged urban governments to think about long-term planning objectives. The PWA projects, for example, had to be integrated into coherent planning frameworks, thus rejuvenating local city planning boards and arming them with newfound legitimacy and authority. To acquire federal funding for public housing, which amounted to 90 percent of project costs, urban communities had to establish local housing authorities for purposes of planning and administration. In addition, dealing directly with the federal government in these new ways forced the cities generally to centralize, streamline, and modernize their governmental operations. In these ways, the New Deal not only provided substantial funding for urban redevelopment and housing, but stimulated urban planning and more efficient local management practices.[18]

Not all New Deal programs affected cities positively. Local control and implementation of many programs often meant that some groups benefited more than others. Widespread racism translated into discrimination against blacks in job and housing programs. Some building projects disrupted or destroyed black and working-class white communities. New Deal financing for urban highway construction paved the way for increased suburbanization and the consequent decline in urban mass transit. Real estate interests and builders turned many New Deal projects to their own advantage.[19]

Similarly, massive federal funding for work and relief tended to strengthen the urban political machines, which Franklin D. Roosevelt relied on for electoral support. Urban benefits were not evenly distributed—some cities and regions got more than their share. In Louisiana and Georgia, for instance, where state Democratic organizations run by Huey Long and Eugene Talmadge were hostile to the Roosevelt administration, federal New Deal bureaucrats shut down or cut off funding for programs affecting New Orleans and Atlanta. In Memphis, where the Ed Crump machine firmly supported the New Deal politically, local programs were often flush with federal funding. The arrival of federal aid made the urban political picture exceedingly more complex than ever before.[20]

Despite these mixed outcomes, the New Deal cemented a new relationship between the cities and the federal government. Although its urban policies were piecemeal rather than systematic, the New Deal forced city governments to create planning and housing agencies that had policy-making implications. Most important, perhaps, from a policy and planning standpoint was the work of the National Resources Board ([NRB]; later renamed the National Resources Planning Board [NRPB]), whose urbanism committee came closer to articulating a national urban policy than any other New Deal agency. In an influential 1937 report entitled *Our Cities: Their Role in the National Economy,* the NRB urbanism committee laid out a complete urban policy agenda. Among other things, the NRB report advocated a permanent program of public works, national industrial and transportation planning, extensive slum clearance and public housing programs, and federal support for crime prevention. Recognizing that suburbanization had pushed the metropolitan region far beyond central-city boundaries, NRB argued the need for greater home rule and for metropolitan government. In addition, the NRB report advocated a cabinet-level Department of Urban Affairs to promote national urban planning. None of these goals was achieved during the New Deal era, but the NRB agenda established important public policy objectives for the future.[21]

World War II

During World II, significant new urban patterns began to emerge, especially in federal–city relations. Mobilization and war production stimulated the nation's industrial economy. Military and defense spending promoted urban expansion, especially in the South and Southwest, where the federal government built dozens of new air bases, naval bases, and military training facilities. To a certain extent, the links between militarism and urbanism dated back to 1919, when the main U.S. naval fleet was shifted from the Atlantic to the Pacific Ocean, touching off competition among San Diego, Los Angeles, and San Francisco for federal military facilities. In the 1920s and 1930s, California's largest cities developed important symbiotic alliances with the federal military establishment. World War II multiplied these relationships throughout the South and the West—the region now labeled the Sunbelt. Florida, California, and Texas especially benefited from federal military and defense spending during the war years.[22]

A massive migration of military and private-sector defense manufacturing workers occurred during the war. The wartime economy pulled more than five million people from rural states and from some older industrial areas to "newer war-industry centers," especially in the southwestern and Pacific Coast states. More than five hundred thousand people moved to the San Francisco Bay Area between 1940 and 1945, for example, whereas other centers of shipbuilding, aircraft production, and defense manufacturing grew apace. A regional relocation of the black population also occurred during the war years, as news of industrial job opportunities in the Northeast, Midwest, and West filtered through the rural South. These wartime migrations posed intense problems of housing and social services for the cities. Moreover, black migration and consequent competition for jobs and housing brought racial tensions boiling to the surface once again, as race riots broke out in New York City, Detroit, and Los Angeles. War overseas was accompanied by unanticipated migration, change, and conflict at home.[23]

Federal involvement in urban policy making intensified during the war. The federal government became actively involved in local communities through new wartime agencies such as the Office of Civilian Defense (OCD) and the Office of Community War Services (OCWS). These agencies funneled federal money to rapidly growing war-industry communities for schooling; playgrounds and recreation; child-care centers; medical facilities; and programs for sanitation, housing, public health, conservation, and rationing. Taken together, OCD and OWCS represented a vast community-organization effort in support of the war, but this effort also translated into a variety of urban social services programs funded by the federal government. Moreover, through additional wartime agencies such as the Division of Defense Housing Coordination and the National Housing Agency, the federal government stimulated the provision of low-cost housing for defense workers. In the Oakland, California, area, for instance, federal agencies built more than thirty thousand public housing units accommodating about ninety thousand war workers and their families. Almost twenty thousand units of defense housing went up for shipyard workers in Vanport and Portland, Oregon, and another fifteen thousand war-housing units were built in the Washington, D.C., area. Despite fierce opposition from the real estate industry, public housing programs for defense workers were expanded dramatically during the war years.[24]

Urban policy also was shaped during the war by NRPB, the successor agency to the New Deal's NRB. Like its predecessor, NRPB had ambitious goals, amounting to the complete postwar redevelopment of the American city. Through planning, public housing, metropolitan consolidation, and federal–local cooperation, NRPB hoped to link economic and social development with the physical rebuilding of urban America. These expansive ideas proved too visionary, or perhaps too socialistic, for a conservative Congress embattled with an aggressive executive branch. In 1943, Congress killed NRPB, cutting off promising urban policy initiatives. Nevertheless, World War II involved the federal government in urban policy on a vast scale.[25]

Changing Urban Patterns, 1945–1990

In the half-century since the end of World War II, American urban patterns have shifted dramatically. Pent-up housing demand and rising postwar prosperity stimulated a suburban residential boom after 1945, typified by the enormous Levittown development of 17,400 single-family tract houses in suburban Long Island.[26] Consequently, population massively spilled out into the sprawling suburban fringe that, by 1970, had more residents than the central cities. Equally important, the Sunbelt cities of the South and West began growing at an astonishing rate after 1945, whereas the aging industrial cities of the Northeast and Midwest began to suffer a long downward spiral in population.[27] As suburbia and the Sunbelt beckoned middle-class and working-class whites, southern blacks moved into the old urban cores—about 5 million blacks making the trek North and West between 1940 and 1970. In addition, after the 1965 amendments to the Immigration and Nationality Act, immigrants from Latin America, Asia, and the Caribbean began following blacks into the declining central cities.[28] As a result of these demographic shifts, much of urban America was abandoned to the blacks, the poor, and the new immigrants. By the 1980s, social scientists suddenly discovered the presence of an enormous urban underclass whose life prospects had been dangerously diminished by the failure of social policy and collapse of such urban institutions as the public schools. By 1990, minorities had become a majority in 51 of the nation's 200 largest cities.[29] Since the 1940s, then, the American city has been reshaped by the suburban shift, the growth of the Sunbelt, the new black migration, and third-world immigration. These four massive migrations have confronted urban policy makers with difficult and persistent issues of race, ethnicity, and class.

As the urban population structure began to shift after 1945, powerful forces of change began to redefine the urban economy. First, the process of deindustrialization had already gotten underway by midcentury. Over the next thirty years, much of the nation's basic manufacturing shifted to nonmetropolitan areas in the Sunbelt South and West, or to lesser developed nations such as Mexico or South Korea. Similarly, as several scholars have demonstrated in an important study, *The Rise of the Gunbelt* (1991), the enormous military and defense spending of the cold war era was heavily channeled to the southern and western perimeter of the nation. For the old industrial cities, deindustrialization and the military remapping of America translated into huge losses in manufacturing employment and the shutdown of factories, shops, and mills. As early as 1955, white-collar, professional, and service workers outnumbered blue-collar and industrial laborers, and the trend intensified quickly over the next several decades. The postindustrial service economy arrived quite early in the postwar era.[30]

A second important shift in the economic structure also was becoming evident by midcentury. By the 1950s, central-city businesses had begun following the white middle class to the urban periphery. The dynamic of change began with the decentralization of retailing in the late 1940s, as downtown department stores set up shop in the new suburbs. By the mid-1950s, even the fully enclosed suburban shopping mall had made its first appearance. The enthusiastic adoption of the drive-in automobile culture and the rapid expansion of the highway network accelerated the process. In particular, construction after 1956 of the interstate highway system facilitated the seemingly endless expansion of the metropolitan fringe. The now ubiquitous shopping malls, the high-rise office complexes, and the campuslike industrial parks that engulf the suburban freeway interchanges across the nation give an amorphous but nevertheless familiar shape to this "outer city." As Joel Garreau has suggested in his recent book, *Edge City: Life on the New Frontier* (1991), this new pattern has come to represent "the essence of urbanism" in America today.[31]

Postwar Urban Policy, 1945–1960

The dramatic demographic and economic shifts that shaped the postwar American city were barely anticipated in 1945. As they looked to the future, big-city mayors, urban planners, and downtown businesspeople and realtors seemed primarily interested in massive programs for central-city redevelopment. "The time has come to rebuild our cities," architect Louis Justement contended in his 1946 book *New Cities for Old*—a view that was widely shared at the time. The housing stock and the infrastructure of most American cities had been built quickly and often shoddily during the industrial era. The problems of deteriorating housing, blighted neighborhoods, and urban decay had been only partially addressed during the New Deal era. Clearing inner-city slums was on the agenda of most postwar mayors, planners, and developers. Moreover, the arrival of the automobile demanded permanent alterations in the street systems that had been designed initially for the horsecar city. Thus, the urban lobby sought to expand the federal–municipal partnership for purposes of large-scale urban redevelopment, central-city revitalization, and transportation planning.[32]

Downtown landowners and business groups were especially interested in the modernization of the central business districts. In the late 1940s and 1950s, they often carried out their own extensive private redevelopment efforts, such as the well-known Pittsburgh Renaissance.[33] Some states encouraged redevelopment of central-city areas during the 1940s by conveying the power of eminent domain to private-sector firms. In New York City, for instance, the Metropolitan Life Insurance Company used such authority to acquire an eighteen-block land parcel on Manhattan's Lower East Side for an enormous nine thousand-unit high-rise apartment complex of thirty-five buildings called Stuyvesant Town.[34] Downtown business interests also worked hard for passage of the Taft-Wagner-Ellender bill, which provided federal aid for urban redevelopment, mortgage and insurance incentives for the housing industry, and some public housing. When the bill eventually passed in 1949, it was the urban redevelopment provision that had the greatest immediate effect, whereas the public housing thrust of the legislation lagged.[35]

Business activism played a significant role in postwar urban redevelopment. However, federal policy initiatives have had much to do with the changing shape of metropolitan America after 1945 as well. Federal mortgage and tax policies, for example, essentially subsidized the suburban housing boom for middle-class and working-class whites. Subsidized and tax-deductible mortgages made dream houses in the suburbs affordable for millions of urban families. At the same time, federal property-appraisal policies facilitated inner-city *redlining* by banks, mortgage companies, and federal housing agencies, thus discouraging investment in inner-city communities. The redlining, initiated in the 1930s by the Federal Housing Administration (FHA) and the Home Owners Loan Corporation and later adopted by the Veterans Administration, virtually guaranteed the decline and eventual decay of entire neighborhoods. Discriminatory practices at the local level—racial zoning, racially restrictive covenants, "gentlemen's agreements" among realtors—supplemented the redlining of the lending agencies, with similarly negative consequences for the long-term physical well-being of urban America.[36]

Although public housing programs had promising beginnings in the New Deal era, relatively little was accomplished in fulfilling that promise in the postwar years. The public housing sector in the United States has always been weakly developed. In the progressive era, most social reformers were reluctant to promote government-built housing, preferring instead to regulate the private housing market through building codes and the like. New Deal public housing initiatives were viciously attacked by private interests as "socialistic," and by the 1950s, the real estate industry had organized a nationwide propaganda campaign against public housing. The 1949 urban redevelopment legislation authorized 810,000 new public housing units over the next 6 years, but by 1960, only 320,000 had actually been built. In reality, considerably more housing was demolished under the redevelopment provisions of the 1949 law than was built under the public housing provisions.[37]

Even where public housing was built in the postwar era, the ubiquitous high-rise apartment blocks that resulted quickly turned into new vertical ghettos. Typically, the enormous Pruitt-Igoe housing project in St. Louis won architectural awards when it was built in the 1950s.

Within two decades, this high-rise icon of architectural modernism had become virtually unlivable and was dynamited to the ground—all thirty-three, eleven-story buildings. Housing projects in Newark, Chicago, and other cities eventually suffered a similar fate.[38] By the end of the 1950s, some of the most fervent supporters of the concept of public housing had become the severest critics of the massive high-rise projects that went up during that decade. Cost cutting in construction, inadequate maintenance, the depressing institutional quality of the projects, the racial policies of FHA, and the social costs of neighborhood destruction and relocation all virtually guaranteed the quick physical deterioration of public housing. Moreover, because most public housing was concentrated in the central cities, federal policy essentially "worked to keep the poor in place," discouraging them from moving to the suburbs. Meanwhile, the simultaneous rapid expansion of residential subdivisions on the garden city model relied heavily on the underpinning of federal mortgage insurance, tax policies, and highway building programs. In a variety of ways, then, federal housing policies substantively contributed to endless suburban sprawl, but did little for the low-income people trapped in the decaying central cities. Governmental reluctance to push too deeply into public housing has meant that most of the inner-city poor residents have been abandoned to the private housing market and to the slumlords.[39]

Federal urban redevelopment and transportation policies had other consequences as well. Landmark congressional legislation of 1949 and 1954 paved the way for central-city urban renewal—long a goal of downtown businesspeople, landowners, and politicians. The Urban Land Institute, a lobby group for the urban real estate industry, had been promoting plans for slum clearance and urban rebuilding since the late 1930s. The institute wrote early drafts of the urban renewal legislation that Congress ultimately supported in 1949.[40] The new legislation armed urban authorities with the power of eminent domain, facilitating the destruction of "blighted" housing and run-down factory districts and permitting the assembly of large land parcels suitable for redevelopment. However noble the aim, the results of urban redevelopment proved less than fully satisfying. The experience of most cities demonstrated that urban renewal and slum clearance often masked a program of black removal. When low-income housing was built in renewal areas, residential densities often doubled or trebled. Big-city central business districts were rebuilt and modernized under the aegis of urban renewal legislation; look-alike glass and steel office towers transformed the urban skyline everywhere. However, the public housing and planning provisions of the urban renewal legislation were never fully implemented.[41]

Federal transportation policies, especially the building of the interstate highway system after 1956, had equally contradictory consequences for urban America. Urban business and political interests had fastened on inner-city expressways as the salvation of the deteriorating urban cores. Combined with downtown parking garages, high-speed freeways would ease urban traffic congestion and attract suburbanites to downtown areas for business, entertainment, and shopping. That was the theory, at least. In reality, the urban interstates speeded the economic decentralization and population dispersal to the suburbs that had already begun after World War II. Moreover, construction of urban freeways resulted in extensive housing destruction and community displacement. Black communities, in particular, were uprooted in virtually every big city to make way for the new urban traffic arteries.[42]

The destruction of inner-city neighborhoods as a consequence of highway construction and urban renewal had wide-reaching effects. The pace of public housing construction was too slow to accommodate those displaced by government redevelopment projects. Some federal programs, such as interstate highway building, did not require relocation housing for people dislodged in the name of progress. Consequently, dislocated blacks began moving into nearby white neighborhoods where rents were low and housing prices affordable. In many cities, slumlords and shady real estate operators managed the process of relocation and neighborhood "transition," as blacks moved into newer, "second ghetto" communities. This process, which occurred on a large scale between 1945 and the 1960s, was filled with racial conflict and tension. Not surprisingly, it also speeded the suburban dispersal of the white population.[43]

Rise and Decline
of Urban Policy, 1960–1980

The urban renewal and highway building of the 1950s—with all of their social consequences—provided the backdrop for new urban policy initiatives in the 1960s. The suburban and Sunbelt migrations had already begun to affect dramatically the demographic structure of the older industrial cities of the Northeast and Midwest. White flight from the urban cores was matched by intensified black in-migration from the South. The emergence of a national civil rights movement after the mid-1950s coincided with these urban changes.

Amidst the cultural complexity of the 1960s, the ghetto riots of Watts, Harlem, Newark, Detroit, Miami, and Washington, D.C., among others, drew new attention to the cities. The nation, the mass media suddenly discovered, was in the midst of a great "urban crisis" demanding governmental response.[44]

To a certain extent, the social liberalism of the John F. Kennedy–Lyndon B. Johnson years elaborated and embellished the programmatic experimentalism of the New Deal era. The War on Poverty and the Great Society rejuvenated the social optimism of old progressives such as Frederic C. Howe and New Dealers such as Harry Hopkins. However, the sweeping social policies of the 1960s also incorporated significant new innovations. The Johnson administration, for instance, was fully committed to civil rights, which had not been true of earlier presidential administrations. Contemporary social science research on economic development, poverty, families, schooling, juvenile delinquency, and the "welfare problem" provided the stimulus for many new programs designed to break what was termed at the time the "cycle of poverty." Architects of the Great Society, such as Sargent Shriver, sought active community involvement in every phase of these new antipoverty efforts. The community action programs (CAPs) that consequently sprang up throughout the nation gave an entirely new dimension to urban policy making and implementation. These innovative approaches characterized the social policy of the mid-1960s.[45]

The Great Society reached high tide between 1964 and 1966. President Johnson drew on his masterful political skills in creating a liberal consensus and guiding through Congress his multidimensional program for social reform, material progress, and equal opportunity. A great new flood of social legislation flowed out of Washington, D.C., seeking to address problems of poverty, unemployment, education, housing, medical care, urban planning, environmental protection, public health, social welfare, legal services, and civil rights. In particular, the Economic Opportunity Act of 1964 created specialized, urban-based social agencies such as Head Start, Job Corps, Neighborhood Youth Corps, and VISTA (Volunteers in Service to America). The Model Cities demonstration program provided funding for comprehensive planning and redevelopment in specifically targeted urban neighborhoods. Through CAPs, ordinary urban citizens were urged to participate in local policy-planning efforts. Federal grants were awarded to encourage urban governments to cooperate on metropolitan-area problems that often crossed municipal boundaries. Special commissions were established to study housing, race relations, and urban problems. A new cabinet-level Department of Housing and Urban Development (HUD) was created to strengthen and give focus to urban reform programs. As President Johnson put it in 1965 in an important message to Congress on urban problems, these varied programs were "all part of an effort to build the great cities which are at the foundation of our hopes for a Great Society."[46]

Urban policy initiatives were undertaken on a vast scale during the Johnson administration. After decades of relative neglect, urban America captured national attention. However, the optimism generated in the early days of the Great Society was short lived. Some Great Society programs, such as Model Cities, were overambitious but underfunded; as a former FHA official put it, "Its short life was rocky, filled with confusion, and darkened by the inevitable contradictions between big promises and small results." Local policy disputes, "bureaucratic resistance to change," and an overall lack of coordination undermined the effectiveness of many other Great Society programs. Low-income housing programs were badly mismanaged by FHA and manipulated by urban real estate brokers and speculators. CAPs often pitted neighborhood leaders against urban politicians and agency staffers charged with administering social programs. The poverty program emphasized individual opportunity, but it did little to create new employment or redistribute wealth. The expanding welfare system soon came in for heavy criticism—from the left as manipulative of poor people and from the right as wasteful and morally bankrupt. Even supporters of the antipoverty campaign were critical: as one welfare bureaucrat noted in 1967, "The welfare system is designed to save money instead of people and tragically ends up doing neither." Nevertheless, the poverty program did achieve some significant success in pulling fifteen million American families above the official poverty line by 1968. In the final analysis, however, inadequate funding, confusion in goals, local political battles, and difficulties in administration ultimately undermined many Great Society programs.[47]

After 1965, American military involvement in Vietnam increasingly pushed the domestic social policy of the Great Society aside. The political controversy and social strife generated by the war in Southeast Asia quickly undercut the centrality of urban policy in the late 1960s. More important, perhaps, Richard M. Nixon came to the presidency in 1969 with a conservative domestic agenda. Nixon and his Republican successor, Gerald Ford, had little sympathy for the expansive and expensive urban programs of the Great Society era. By the early 1970s, the "urban crisis" was declared to be over, despite plenty of evidence to the contrary. As Stephen E. Ambrose noted in his recent biography of Nixon, the president gave the order to his aides to "flush Model Cities and the Great Society along with it." The Model Cities

program was terminated in 1973. Nevertheless, Nixon's record on the
cities reflected new thinking and took unexpected turns.[48]

The concept of a "New Federalism" shaped Richard Nixon's urban
and domestic policies. The free-spending liberalism of the Great Society era had to be curbed, Nixon contended, but so also did the excessive involvement of the federal government in state and municipal
affairs. Nixon hoped to reverse the growth of federal power and responsibility, but at the same time promote stronger, more effective
local governments. Official thinking about cities during this period
was also powerfully shaped by Nixon's urban affairs adviser, Daniel P.
Moynihan. A Democrat of conservative inclination who had earlier
worked in the Johnson administration, Moynihan had a surprising
degree of influence on urban and social policy during the Nixon years.
He had already worked out a set of guiding principles for a national
urban policy before joining the Nixon administration in January
1969. Moreover, he assumed the leading role in Nixon's Urban Affairs
Council, established by the president early in 1969 to coordinate urban programs and policy. As a consequence of Moynihan's influence,
Nixon's urban policy reflected a curious amalgam of older programs
cut or redesigned, along with many new innovations based on the
New Federalism model.[49]

Heading President Nixon's agenda for the cities was *revenue
sharing*—a program discussed by economists through the 1960s, proposed by Nixon in 1969, and ultimately enacted by Congress in
1972. Designed to replace many categorical federal grants, the new
program redistributed federal funds to states and communities with
minimal spending restrictions. The earlier urban renewal and Model
Cities programs, by contrast, were loaded with conditions, restrictions, and bureaucratic red tape. Revenue sharing, it was believed,
would restore power and decision making to local communities,
where political conservatives thought it belonged. The new program
called for community development block grants allocated on the basis of a community's population size, poverty level, and housing
needs. Revenue sharing became linked to the idea of community
redevelopment, which soon emerged as a central thrust of urban
policy in the Nixon–Ford era.[50]

The Nixon administration also initiated a number of other innovative programs aimed at urban America. Under Moynihan's prodding,
Nixon supported a fundamental welfare reform. The so-called Family
Assistance Plan (FAP) provided for a guaranteed annual income of
sixteen hundred dollars to poor families with children, but included
as well work incentives designed to break the cycle of welfare dependency. Described by Moynihan as "a quantum leap in social policy,"

FAP was attacked both by the Republican right-wing and welfare advocacy groups, and in 1971 the program was defeated in Congress.[51] Other urban innovations of the Nixon administration were put into place with the Housing and Community Development Act of 1974, which reflected Nixon's essential approach to urban policy. This legislation provided new revenue sharing block grants for water and sewer systems, for neighborhood development, and for rent supplements to poor people in private housing. Other legislation provided funding for urban mass transit systems and for employment training. Another Nixon initiative offered federal mortgage guarantees to private "new town" developers. Richard Nixon opposed the wide-ranging urban agenda of Lyndon Johnson's Great Society on general principles. In contrast, the Nixon administration pushed a coordinated set of programs designed to extricate the federal government from the urban scene and, at the same time, provide new discretionary funding for local governments and incentives for the private housing market and development activities.[52]

Despite these new approaches, the problems of the cities seemed as deeply entrenched as ever. The New Federalism had some powerful negative consequences for urban America. Building new towns in the suburbs, for instance, did little to improve life in the declining central cities. Revenue sharing and sewer construction grants actually provided new levels of federal support for suburban expansion. As a 1973 Brookings Institution study noted, revenue sharing was "an inefficient means of dealing with the special plight of large cities because much of the money will be distributed among suburban governments that are not facing critical fiscal problems." Severe cutbacks in federal spending on social programs and human resources coincided with revenue sharing. Local officials gained greater financial autonomy through revenue sharing, but the flow of revenue sharing dollars never compensated for the loss of many categorical federal programs. Even the much-touted FAP would have done relatively little, because the income floor of sixteen hundred dollars per family was well below the official poverty line. Consequently, the older central cities faced a deepening financial crisis through the 1970s. The rising costs of poverty-related social programs, city services, infrastructure maintenance, and municipal payrolls simply were not matched by new federal funding. The widely publicized fiscal collapse of New York City in 1975 and of Cleveland in 1978 stemmed from the policy decisions and economic imbalances of the 1970s. In the final analysis, the Nixon and Ford administrations had abandoned the Great Society idea of social engineering and social investment in the city.[53]

The frustrations of urban policy making continued throughout the remainder of the 1970s. President Jimmy Carter initially asserted a strong commitment to America's cities. In the first year of his presidency, for instance, Carter made a well-publicized visit to a devastated, abandoned, and burned-out South Bronx neighborhood. The junked automobiles and massive piles of rubble in garbage-strewn empty lots reflected, one writer noted, "a mountain range of failure." With the television cameras rolling, Carter intimated that the South Bronx could be "turned around," that new urban policy initiatives, especially public–private cooperative efforts for economic development, might salvage the nation's inner-city slums. However, the South Bronx tour was nothing more than a media event, and little ever came of Carter's promised national urban policy.[54]

Indeed, the metropolitan study panel of Carter's Commission for a National Agenda for the Eighties essentially wrote off the aging industrial cities with their devastated economies, entrenched social problems, and low-income and low-skill populations. The commission's position was based on the economic and demographic transformations that had shaped and reshaped urban America by the 1970s. It was clear by that time, for instance, that the United States was in the midst of a far-reaching transition from an industrial to a technological and service-based economy. Similarly, massive population shifts were underway, as metropolitan area populations increasingly decentralized. Industrial cities such as St. Louis, Detroit, Cleveland, Chicago, Pittsburgh, Baltimore, and Boston suffered population losses ranging from 20 to 50 percent between 1950 and 1980. Deindustrialization wracked the old industrial heartland during those decades, as increasingly obsolescent factories and mills shut down or moved. The dynamic sectors of the urban economy had migrated to the suburbs and the Sunbelt. As the Carter commission scanned the urban scene, this dual economic and demographic transformation was not necessarily a bad thing.[55]

Ultimately, the Carter commission concluded that urban policy could do little to counteract what the free market had produced. The idea of urban renaissance was little more than an illusion that defied "statistical detection." Although some gentrification and residential restoration had occurred in some cities, the more dominant pattern was "the continuing deterioration of living conditions and income levels in central cities." Rather than supporting the urban underclass through "place-oriented" policies, the commission's 1980 report urged urban policies that, among other things, would help low-income people move from the aging central cities to economically vibrant suburban or Sunbelt areas where job opportunities were available. Thus, despite an initial inclination to focus national policy planning on central-city issues, the Carter administration ultimately abandoned urban policy to marketplace forces.[56]

While the national government was reversing decades of federal urban policy in the 1970s, some states began seizing the urban initiative. Several states, from Hawaii to Vermont, enacted growth management legislation in the 1960s and 1970s. Florida's Land Management Act of 1972, for instance, conveyed powerful authority for statewide planning and land-use regulation.[57] In New York State, Governor Nelson Rockefeller began developing state-initiated policy solutions to urban housing and transportation problems in the early 1960s. In 1967, Rockefeller pushed a Metropolitan Transportation Authority through the legislature to finance, upgrade, and coordinate the operation of regional transportation systems in the New York City metropolitan area. In 1968, the Rockefeller administration established an Urban Development Corporation in a major effort to build moderate-cost housing and promote redevelopment in central cities. Other Rockefeller urban policy initiatives focused on welfare reform, job training, narcotics control, law enforcement, and "home rule" for cities. In addition, New York's state government was deeply involved in the rescue of New York City from bankruptcy in 1975.[58]

In Massachusetts, Governor Michael S. Dukakis developed an extensive statewide urban policy during his first gubernatorial term from 1975 to 1978. Along with chief state planner Frank T. Keefe, Dukakis consciously pushed policies to revive the dying economies of the state's older central cities. By executive order in 1977, for instance, Dukakis required all state agencies establishing new offices to locate in older urban downtowns rather than in the suburbs. Through business tax credits and a variety of publicly created development finance agencies, the state provided incentives for private investment in the cities. At the same time, headlong suburban residential and commercial development was reined in. Several agency heads met weekly as a "development cabinet" to establish coordinated urban policy on issues such as mass transit, urban housing, city jobs, and neighborhood development. With congressional help, an urban heritage park was created in Lowell, built around the city's industrial history. Dukakis worked closely with the state's mayors, and pushed his "Massachusetts model" in speeches at the National League of Cities and at the National Governors' Conference. The cities, Dukakis contended, harbored "great opportunities for promoting and achieving many of our national objectives," and for that reason the states needed to become "full partners" in the shaping of national urban policy.[59]

Few states went as far or as fast as Massachusetts in the development of a coordinated urban policy during the 1970s. But the Massachusetts example should alert us to the fact that policies and programs affecting the cities were being made at the state as well as at the national level. As the federal government began disengaging from urban America in the 1970s under Nixon and Carter, the role of the state governments increased in importance.

Reagan Revolution, 1980–1992

The entrepreneurial and free-market tendencies of the Carter administration's urban policy position were reinforced by a similar shift in overall American political values by the end of the 1970s. The conservative drift of the electorate helped account for the election of President Ronald W. Reagan in 1980, but it also explained why urban policy was completely jettisoned in the 1980s. This rejection of urban intervention was spelled out clearly in President Reagan's *National Urban Policy Report* of 1982, which reaffirmed the need to accommodate government action to marketplace forces.[60] Consequently, the federal government disengaged even further from the social interventionist programs of the New Deal and the Great Society—only the social security program remained sacrosanct, as Reagan often assured the elderly. A "social safety net" was promised for those at the bottom of the income scale, but those promises appeared increasingly empty as massive federal cutbacks kicked into place. During the Reagan and Bush years of the 1980s, big-city budgets gradually were decimated as Congress and the administration further choked off the flow of federal dollars. Spending on human services and public works declined dramatically. Urban governments faced entrenched problems that seemingly defied solution: inadequate resources, languishing human and social services, an aging housing stock, a deteriorating infrastructure, and increasing levels of poverty, crime, homelessness, and other social problems. These difficulties, of course, were compounded by the corporate exodus to the metropolitan periphery and the continued suburban flight of the white middle class—both of which badly eroded the urban tax base.[61]

The free-market ideology of the 1980s provided the philosophical underpinning for this federal disengagement from urban America. The political culture of the decade encouraged the view that the big cities and their low-income populations had to be made more socially self-reliant and more economically productive. The economic values of growth and competitiveness, of individualism and productivity, moreover, underlay other federal policies that transformed the nation and its cities during the Reagan years and after. Massive tax cuts for the wealthy beginning in 1981 vastly intensified the income gap between rich and poor, as political analyst Kevin Phillips has persuasively demonstrated in his book *The Politics of Rich and Poor* (1990). Combined with enormous military and defense spending under Reagan, the tax cuts stimulated huge and unprecedented federal budget deficits, as well. The rollback of many types of federal regulation, and especially the banking deregulation of 1983, gave free and virtually unhindered reign to bankers, builders, developers, and other adventurous entrepreneurs. Often with the cooperation of urban government agencies, especially the newly fashionable downtown development authorities, private developers began rebuilding the urban core once again. The free market prevailed. "In the process," as urbanist Robert Wood recently wrote, "the private sector came to dominate the urban development process to an extent rarely seen since the heyday of the 19th century industrial city."[62]

One natural consequence of economic deregulation and commercial overbuilding had emerged by the end of the 1980s. It took the form of massive scandals in the banking industry, in the savings and loans, and in HUD. In the aftermath, it appears that perhaps as much as $500 billion was siphoned out of the banking, savings, and investment system to support overdevelopment on a vast scale. New downtown and suburban office towers soared in the 1980s, conveying the illusion of boom times in the city. The "malling of America" quickened its pace, as new shopping centers sprawled across the urban landscape, especially on the metropolitan periphery. New convention centers, elaborate luxury hotels, waterfront festival marketplaces, even downtown aquariums became trendy ways of luring people back into the city. Lavish housing developments and condominium complexes sprouted throughout Sunbelt states such as Florida, Texas, Arizona, and California.

However, by the early 1990s, the perils of speculation and overdevelopment had become abundantly clear. The commercial vacancy rate in the fifty-six largest American cities averaged around 25 percent by 1991. The glut on the housing market, especially of condominums, produced dramatic declines in housing values. Shopping center development had come to a standstill, because many retail complexes were empty of both shops and customers. The downtown lure of convention centers and marketplaces had not been uniformly successful. Meanwhile, the private developers made off with the enormous profits that flowed from the construction process. The government and the public were left holding the bag—and the bag was empty.[63]

The urban development of the 1980s stood in stark contrast to the crumbling infrastructure and run-down, dilapidated, housing stock of many central-city areas. It is not unusual to find new high-rise office blocks casting long shadows over nearby blighted and ghetto-ized neighborhoods. Two decades of urban policy have focused on free-market mechanisms—urban enterprise zones, private–public partnerships, tax concessions, financial incentives, downtown development authorities—to rebuild the central business districts. The idea was that private investment in the city, with some assist from government, would ultimately have a trickle-down effect on the urban masses. The economic development innovations of the 1970s and 1980s reflected clear policy choices.[64]

The rejection of social investment also represented a deliberate policy choice. Private developers had big incentives to redevelop the urban cores, because most of the risk was taken by the banks, savings and loans, and insurance companies that put up the money, or by the governments that guaranteed the loans. However, few were willing to take similar risks in building housing for low- and moderate-income urban people. As Robert Wood put it succinctly in a 1991 article, "As public policy veered sharply toward encouraging and guaranteeing private commercial investment, it savaged the housing and neighbor-hood programs designed to help cities and their people." The urban policy of the 1980s, in short, led to the construction of downtown office towers and convention centers that no one needed, but ignored the construction of decent housing that millions of low-income people badly needed. The urban policy of the Ronald Reagan–George Bush era produced this sad and perverse outcome.[65]

As the nation moved out of the 1980s and into the 1990s, public awareness of a new, deeper, and more pervasive urban crisis began to emerge—a "second urban crisis." Typically, the nongovernmental 1988 Commission on the Cities, established twenty years after the famous Kerner Commission report on civil disorders, suggested the depth of the contemporary urban problem in its report *Quiet Riots:*

There are "quiet riots" in all of America's central cities: unemployment, poverty, social disorganization, segregation, family disintegration, hous-ing and school deterioration, and crime are worse now. These "quiet riots" are not as alarming as the violent riots of twenty years ago, or as notice-able to outsiders. But they are even more destructive of human life. National security requires renewed human investment if we are to be a stable and secure society of self-esteem. We have the means. We must summon the will.

Clearly, the economic growth policies of the Reagan era had not "trickled down" to low-income neighborhoods of the central cities. The 1988 Commission on the Cities advocated a new national urban policy that would revitalize inner-city schooling, promote job training, reform the welfare system, provide universal health insurance, expand housing programs, and rebuild the urban infrastructure—all under direct White House coordination. Grass roots community organizations had to be empowered, housing integrated, and affirmative action vigorously promoted. "We must," the report concluded, "bring the problems of race, unemployment, and poverty back into the public consciousness, put them back on the public agenda."[66]

Similarly advocating heightened levels of social investment in the city, National Urban League president John E. Jacob urged in a 1990 article the implementation of an Urban Marshall Plan and an Urban Investment Bank that "develops our economic infrastructure, renews our cities and moves people out of poverty." As the 1990–1992 recession deepened, mayors, journalists, and urban interest groups increasingly called for a new urban policy that would put the "peace dividend" to work in rebuilding the nation and salvaging the cities. Television networks presented programs on the troubled cities. Syndicated newspaper columnists such as Tom Wicker, Russell Baker, David Broder, William Raspberry, and Neil Peirce advocated new governmental action to rebuild the urban infrastructure, reform welfare and health care, attack urban problems, and rescue the central cities. Social scientists laid out the framework for new urban policies and programs. The urban crisis was back, and it seemed for real.[67]

Adding powerfully to the sense of cities in crisis were the disturbing events in Chicago and Los Angeles during April and May 1992. A great public works disaster hit Chicago: the Chicago River flooded an abandoned tunnel system beneath the city's business district. With their basements flooded and their computer systems down, and lacking electrical power and elevator service, hundreds of office buildings, hotels, department stores, and smaller shops were forced to close. Chicago's entire central city virtually shut down for several days as a consequence of this massive infrastructure breakdown. The 1992 Chicago flood typified the potential consequences of years of dangerous neglect of urban America's aging insfrastructure. As one public works expert noted, "It's the shape of things to come in America unless we reverse decades of underinvestment that threatens to undermine our cities."[68]

Even more alarming was the rage of racial violence that broke out in Los Angeles at the end of April in the wake of the acquittal of four white police officers charged with beating a black motorist. In a series of events reminiscent of the Watts riot of 1965, which also ignited after a police confrontation in the black community, Los Angeles's racial tinderbox exploded in several days of rioting, burning, shooting, and looting. Only the arrival of the National Guard and several thousand U.S. Army infantry soldiers and Marines brought the conflagration under control. Racial tensions were on the rise elsewhere, too, as long-simmering anger and hostility boiled to the surface in Atlanta, New York, San Francisco, and other cities. The nation, it seemed, was paying the price for two decades of inattention to the human and social needs of the central cities. Race, the *Wall Street Journal* announced as Los Angeles smoldered, was "returning to the front burner."[69]

The Los Angeles riots etched sharply the widely divergent perspectives about the directions of current urban policy. The consensus of postriot journalistic analysis held, as *U.S. News and World Report* asserted, that "urban problems and race relations are getting worse." A wide range of social scientists, big-city mayors, and urban advocates argued the need for a greater commitment of national resources to the cities and their problems. At the White House, however, the Bush administration blamed the Los Angeles riots on the failed social policies of the Great Society years. Shaped by political ideologies, these differing analyses of the urban condition promised to impede effective responses to the new urban crisis.[70]

Thus, the prospect for serious federal initiatives on urban policy seemed dim as the 1990s began. As social scientists Marshall Kaplan and Franklin James indicated in their book *The Future of National Urban Policy* (1990), "The increasing political impotence and economic weaknesses of cities" help to explain why urban policy "no longer . . . generates excitement at congressional hearings." The American city has become just another casualty of the Washington budget battles, and, with the exception of embattled mayors, few politicians appeared to care. Americans, at least those with decision-making power, seemed to have lost their social conscience. Some analysts held out hope for a new cycle of liberalism and social reform, but it was difficult to discern evidence of such a political shift in the midst of the deepest economic recession since the 1930s.[71]

Throughout the twentieth century, urban policy debates often stood at the center of the nation's domestic politics. State and local government moved haltingly to reshape and reform urban life and institutions during the progressive era. In the New Deal years, the federal government first began developing important program and policy links with urban governments on such matters as housing, planning, employment, public works, and social welfare. During the next thirty years, federal urban policy increasingly shaped physical development and social investment in the American city. The Great Society programs of the 1960s, in particular, extensively elaborated the urban initiatives of the New Deal. In urban policy, there was a direct and linear progression from Franklin D. Roosevelt to Lyndon B. Johnson. The Great Society also introduced a number of striking innovations in urban policy.

Since the early 1970s, however, the focus of national urban policy has shifted dramatically. Under the "New Federalism" of first Richard Nixon and then Ronald Reagan, costly social programs were eliminated or turned over to the states and cities. Federal policy makers facilitated private entrepreneurial schemes to salvage the central business districts or build up the outer city. According to a 1990 report from the U.S. Conference of Mayors, "Reagan-era cutbacks have cost the cities $20 billion in federal funding since 1981." Not surprisingly, these policies have produced new levels of urban deterioration and despair—a second urban crisis. Yet, a widely shared skepticism about what government can or should accomplish has tended to impede positive action.[72]

In a very real sense, the central dilemma of the industrial city has reappeared. One hundred years ago, reformers struggled to control rampant economic interests and provide a measure of social justice in urban America. The urban policy battles of the 1990s may not be all that different.

NOTES

1.   Debbie Howlett, "Cities Are in Financial Tailspin," *USA Today,* 9 July 1991, 3A. See also Bill Turque, "Cities on the Brink," *Newsweek,* 19 November 1990, 44–45; Michael deCourcy Hinds, "80's Leave States and Cities in Need," *New York Times,* 30 December 1990, 1, 16–17; Sam Roberts, "More Than Just Another Fiscal Crisis," *New York Times,* 17 November 1991, 18E.

2.   Josiah Strong, *The Twentieth Century City* (New York: Baker and Taylor Co., 1898), 53; Frederic C. Howe, *The City: The Hope of Democracy* (New York: Charles Scribner's Sons, 1905), 280; and, more generally, Frederic C. Howe, *The Confessions of a Reformer* (New York: Charles Scribner's Sons, 1925).

3.   For overviews of the American industrial city, see Blake McKelvey,

The Urbanization of America, 1860–1915 (New Brunswick, N.J.: Rutgers University Press, 1963); Maury Klein and Harvey A. Kantor, *Prisoners of Progress: American Industrial Cities, 1850–1920* (New York: Macmillan, 1976); Raymond A. Mohl, *The New City: Urban America in the Industrial Age, 1860–1920* (Arlington Heights, Ill.: Harlan Davidson, 1985).

4. For early interpretations of this period, see Robert H. Wiebe, *The Search for Order, 1877–1920* (New York: Hill and Wang, 1967), and Samuel P. Hays, *The Response to Industrialism, 1885–1914* (Chicago: University of Chicago Press, 1957). Dozens of more specific studies demonstrate the diversity of the progressive reform impulse. For moral reform, see Paul Boyer, *Urban Masses and Moral Order in America, 1820–1920* (Cambridge, Mass.: Harvard University Press, 1978); James H. Timberlake, *Prohibition and the Progressive Movement, 1900–1920* (Cambridge, Mass.: Harvard University Press, 1963); Mark Thomas Connelly, *The Response to Prostitution in the Progressive Era* (Chapel Hill: University of North Carolina Press, 1980). For the structural reform of city government, see Bradley R. Rice, *Progressive Cities: The Commission Government Movement in America, 1901–1920* (Austin: University of Texas Press, 1977); Martin J. Schiesl, *The Politics of Efficiency: Municipal Administration and Reform in America, 1880–1920* (Berkeley and Los Angeles: University of California Press, 1977); Kenneth Fox, *Better City Government: Innovation in American Urban Politics, 1850–1937* (Philadelphia: Temple University Press, 1977). For an outline of the progressive social reform thrust, see J. Joseph Huthmacher, "Urban Liberalism and the Age of Reform," *Mississippi Valley Historical Review* 49 (September 1962), 231–241; John D. Buenker, *Urban Liberalism and Progressive Reform* (New York: Charles Scribner's Sons, 1973). For city planning, see Stanley K. Schultz, *Constructing Urban Culture: American Cities and City Planning, 1800–1920* (Philadelphia: Temple University Press, 1989); William H. Wilson, *The City Beautiful Movement* (Baltimore: Johns Hopkins University Press, 1989). For a discussion of the effects of municipal engineering and technological innovation, see Martin V. Melosi, ed., *Pollution and Reform in American Cities, 1870–1930* (Austin: University of Texas Press, 1980); Jon C. Teaford, *The Unheralded Triumph: City Government in America, 1870–1900* (Baltimore: Johns Hopkins University Press, 1984); Charles W. Cheape, *Moving the Masses: Urban Public Transit in New York, Boston, and Philadelphia, 1880–1912* (Cambridge, Mass.: Harvard University Press, 1980).

5. For the diverse achievements of progressive reformers, see K. Austin Kerr, *Organized for Prohibition: A New History of the Anti-Saloon League* (New Haven, Conn.: Yale University Press, 1985); Roy Lubove, *The Progressives and the Slums: Tenement House Reform in New York City, 1890–1917* (Pittsburgh: University of Pittsburgh Press, 1962); Allen F. Davis, *Spearheads for Reform: The Social Settlements and the Progressive Movement, 1890–1914* (New York: Oxford University Press, 1967); Dominick Cavallo, *Muscles and Morals: Organized Playgrounds and Urban Reform, 1880–1920* (Philadelphia: University of Pennsylvania Press, 1981); Ronald D. Cohen and Raymond A. Mohl, *The Paradox of Progressive Education: The Gary Plan and Urban School-*

ing (Port Washington, N.Y.: Kennikat, 1979); John F. McClymer, *War and Welfare: Social Engineering in America, 1890–1925* (Westport, Conn.: Greenwood, 1980); Marilyn Thornton Williams, *Washing "The Great Unwashed": Public Baths in Urban America, 1840–1920* (Columbus: Ohio State University Press, 1991); Ernest S. Griffith, *A History of American City Government: The Progressive Years and Their Aftermath, 1900–1920* (New York: Praeger, 1974); Clarke A. Chambers, *Seedtime of Reform: American Social Service and Social Action, 1918–1933* (Minneapolis: University of Minnesota Press, 1963); Roy Lubove, *The Struggle for Social Security, 1900–1935* (Cambridge, Mass.: Harvard University Press, 1968); Morton Keller, *Regulating a New Economy: Public Policy and Economic Change in America, 1900–1933* (Cambridge, Mass.: Harvard University Press, 1990).

6. Urban population statistics are from U.S. Bureau of the Census, *Fifteenth Census of the United States: 1930. Population,* vol. 1, *Number and Distribution of Inhabitants* (Washington, D.C.: U.S. Government Printing Office, 1931), 18; U.S. Bureau of the Census, *Fourteenth Census of the United States: 1920,* vol. 2, *Population* (Washington, D.C.: U.S. Government Printing Office, 1922), 661–665. For the effects of immigration through the 1920s, see John Bodnar, *The Transplanted: A History of Immigrants in Urban America* (Bloomington: Indiana University Press, 1985), and Roger Daniels, *Coming to America: A History of Immigration and Ethnicity in American Life* (New York: HarperCollins, 1990).

7. For black migration from the South, see Daniel M. Johnson and Rex R. Campbell, *Black Migration in America: A Social Demographic History* (Durham, N.C.: Duke University Press, 1981), 57–89; Carole Marks, *Farewell— We're Good and Gone: The Great Black Migration* (Bloomington: Indiana University Press, 1989); Peter Gottlieb, *Making Their Own Way: Southern Blacks' Migration to Pittsburgh, 1916–30* (Urbana: University of Illinois Press, 1987); James R. Grossman, *Land of Hope: Chicago, Black Southerners, and the Great Migration* (Chicago: University of Chicago Press, 1989); Joe William Trotter, Jr., *The Great Migration in Historical Perspective* (Bloomington: Indiana University Press, 1991). For Mexican migration during the 1920s, see Mark Reisler, *By the Sweat of Their Brow: Mexican Immigrant Labor in the United States, 1900–1940* (Westport, Conn.: Greenwood, 1976); Lawrence A. Cardoso, *Mexican Emigration to the United States, 1897–1931* (Tucson: University of Arizona Press, 1980).

8. For race relations, racial zoning, and segregation policies during this period, see Christopher Silver, "The Racial Origins of Zoning: Southern Cities from 1910–40," *Planning Perspectives* 6 (May 1991), 189–205; Barbara J. Flint, "Zoning and Residential Segregation: A Social and Physical History, 1919–1940" (Ph.D. diss., University of Chicago, 1977); Thomas L. Philpott, *The Slum and the Ghetto: Neighborhood Deterioration and Middle-Class Reform, Chicago, 1880–1930* (New York: Oxford University Press, 1978); Kenneth L. Kusmer, *A Ghetto Takes Shape: Black Cleveland, 1870–1930* (Urbana: University of Illinois Press, 1976); Joe William Trotter, Jr., *Black Milwaukee: The Making of an Industrial Proletariat, 1915–1945* (Urbana: University of

Illinois Press, 1985); Raymond A. Mohl and Neil Betten, *Steel City: Urban and Ethnic Patterns in Gary, Indiana, 1906–1950* (New York: Holmes and Meier, 1986), 48–107.

9.   For the Ku Klux Klan in the 1920s, see Kenneth T. Jackson, *The Ku Klux Klan in the City, 1915–1930* (New York: Oxford University Press, 1967); Robert Moats Miller, "The Ku Klux Klan," in *Change and Continuity in Twentieth-Century America: The 1920s*, ed. John Braeman et al. (Columbus: Ohio State University Press, 1968), 215–255; William D. Jenkins, *Steel Valley Klan: The Ku Klux Klan in Ohio's Mahoning Valley* (Kent, Ohio: Kent State University Press, 1990); Leonard J. Moore, *Citizen Klansmen: The Ku Klux Klan in Indiana, 1921–1928* (Chapel Hill: University of North Carolina Press, 1991); Leonard J. Moore, "Historical Interpretations of the 1920s Klan: The Traditional View and the Populist Revision," *Journal of Social History* 24 (Winter 1990), 341–357.

10.   For the racial violence of the period, see Elliott M. Rudwick, *Race Riot at East St. Louis, July 2, 1917* (Carbondale: Southern Illinois University Press, 1964); Vincent P. Franklin, "The Philadelphia Race Riot of 1918," *Pennsylvania Magazine of History and Biography* 99 (July 1975), 336–350; William M. Tuttle, Jr., *Race Riot: Chicago in the Red Summer of 1919* (New York: Atheneum, 1970); Arthur I. Waskow, *From Race Riot to Sit-in: 1919 and the 1960s* (New York: Doubleday, 1966); David Allan Levine, *Internal Combustion: The Races in Detroit, 1915–1926* (Westport, Conn.: Greenwood, 1976); Herbert Shapiro, *White Violence and Black Response: From Reconstruction to Montgomery* (Amherst: University of Massachusetts Press, 1988).

11.   Charles N. Glaab, "Metropolis and Suburb: The Changing American City," in *Change and Continuity in Twentieth-Century America: The 1920s*, ed. John Braeman et al. (Columbus: Ohio State University Press, 1968), 339–437. For automobile registration statistics, see U.S. Bureau of the Census, *Historical Statistics of the United States, Colonial Times to 1957* (Washington, D.C.: U.S. Government Printing Office, 1960), 462. For the effects of the automobile, see Miller McClintock, *Report and Recommendations of the Metropolitan Street Traffic Survey* (Chicago: Chicago Association of Commerce, 1926); Miller McClintock, *A Report on the Street Traffic Control Problem of the City of Boston* (Boston: Mayor's Street Traffic Advisory Board, 1928); "Planning for City Traffic," *Annals of the American Academy of Political and Social Science* 133 (September 1927), 1–249; Howard L. Preston, *Automobile Age Atlanta: The Making of a Southern Metropolis, 1900–1935* (Athens: University of Georgia Press, 1979); Blaine A. Brownell, "Urban Planning, the Planning Profession, and the Motor Vehicle in Early Twentieth-Century America," in *Shaping an Urban World*, ed. Gordon E. Cherry (New York: St. Martin's, 1980), 59–77; Carl Abbott, *Portland: Planning, Politics, and Growth in a Twentieth-Century City* (Lincoln: University of Nebraska Press, 1983), 93–103; David Owen Wise and Marguerite Dupree, "The Choice of the Automobile for Urban Passenger Transportation: Baltimore in the 1920s," in *South Atlantic Urban Studies*, vol. 2, ed. Jack R. Censer (Columbia: University of South Carolina Press, 1978), 153–179; Scott L. Bottles, *Los Angeles and the Automobile: The Making of the*

Modern City (Berkeley and Los Angeles: University of California Press, 1987); Mark S. Foster, *From Streetcar to Superhighway: American City Planners and Urban Transportation, 1900–1940* (Philadelphia: Temple University Press, 1981); Paul Barrett, *The Automobile and Urban Transit: The Formation of Public Policy in Chicago, 1900–1930* (Philadelphia: Temple University Press, 1983).

12. Delbert A. Taebel and James V. Cornehls, *The Political Economy of Urban Transportation* (Port Washington, N.Y.: Kennikat, 1977), 72; Kenneth T. Jackson, *Crabgrass Frontier: The Suburbanization of the United States* (New York: Oxford University Press, 1985), 168–171; Stanley Mallach, "The Origins of the Decline of Urban Mass Transportation in the United States, 1890–1930," *Urbanism Past and Present* 8 (Summer 1979), 1–17; David J. St. Clair, *The Motorization of American Cities* (New York: Praeger, 1986), 32–80; Theodora Kimball Hubbard and Henry Vincent Hubbard, *Our Cities To-day and To-morrow: A Survey of Planning and Zoning Practices in the United States* (Cambridge, Mass.: Harvard University Press, 1929), 219–228.

13. Mel Scott, *American City Planning since 1890* (Berkeley and Los Angeles: University of California Press, 1969), 183–269; Richard E. Foglesong, *Planning the Capitalist City: The Colonial Era to the 1920s* (Princeton, N.J.: Princeton University Press, 1986), 199–257; M. Christine Boyer, *Dreaming the Rational City: The Myth of American City Planning* (Cambridge, Mass.: MIT Press, 1983); Peter Marcuse, "Housing in Early City Planning," *Journal of Urban History* 6 (February 1980), 153–176; Hubbard and Hubbard, *Our Cities To-day and To-morrow,* 130–218. The Beard quotation is from Keller, *Regulating a New Economy,* 183, but see also Charles A. Beard, "Conflicts in City Planning," *Yale Review* 17 (July 1927), 65–77.

14. Jon C. Teaford, *City and Suburb: The Political Fragmentation of Metropolitan America, 1850–1970* (Baltimore: Johns Hopkins University Press, 1979); Roy Lubove, *Community Planning in the 1920s: The Contribution of the Regional Planning Association of America* (Pittsburgh, Penn.: University of Pittsburgh Press, 1962); R. L. Duffus, *Mastering a Metropolis: Planning the Future of the New York Region* (New York: Harper, 1930); Michael Simpson, *Thomas Adams and the Modern Planning Movement: Britain, Canada and the United States, 1900–1940* (London: Mansell, 1985), 119–167; David A. Johnson, "Regional Planning for the Great American Metropolis: New York between the Wars," in *Two Centuries of American Planning,* ed. Daniel Schaffer (Baltimore: Johns Hopkins University Press, 1988), 167–196; Stanley Buder, *Visionaries and Planners: The Garden City Movement and the Modern Community* (New York: Oxford University Press, 1990), 165–180; Daniel Schaffer, *Garden Cities for America: The Radburn Experience* (Philadelphia: Temple University Press, 1982). For the now-classic study of Robert Moses, see Robert A. Caro, *The Power Broker: Robert Moses and the Fall of New York* (New York: Knopf, 1974), but see also Jeanne R. Lowe, *Cities in a Race with Time* (New York: Random House, 1967), 45–109, and Joann P. Krieg, ed., *Robert Moses: Single-Minded Genius* (Interlaken, N.Y.: Heart of the Lakes Publishing, 1989).

15. Raymond A. Mohl, "Poverty in the Cities: A History of Urban Social Welfare," in *The Urban Experience: Themes in American History,* ed. Raymond A. Mohl and James F. Richardson (Belmont, Calif.: Wadsworth, 1973), 117–121; Barbara Blumberg, *The New Deal and the Unemployed: The View from New York City* (Cranbury, N.J.: Associated University Press, 1979), 17; Mark Naison, "From Eviction Resistance to Rent Control: Tenant Activism in the Great Depression," in *The Tenant Movement in New York City, 1904–1984,* ed. Ronald Lawson (New Brunswick, N.J.: Rutgers University Press, 1986), 94–133; Daniel J. Leab, "United We Eat: The Creation and Organization of the Unemployed Councils in 1930," *Labor History* 8 (Fall 1967), 300–315; John F. Bauman and Thomas H. Coode, *In the Eye of the Great Depression: New Deal Reporters and the Agony of the American People* (DeKalb: Northern Illinois University Press, 1988), 38–68; William H. Mullins, *The Depression and the Urban West Coast, 1929–1933: Los Angeles, San Francisco, Seattle, and Portland* (Bloomington: Indiana University Press, 1991); Judith Ann Trolander, *Settlement Houses and the Great Depression* (Detroit, Mich.: Wayne State University Press, 1975); Irving Bernstein, *The Lean Years: A History of the American Worker, 1920–1933* (Boston: Houghton Mifflin, 1960), 287–333.

16. Charles H. Trout, "The New Deal and the Cities," in *Fifty Years Later: The New Deal Evaluated,* ed. Harvard Sitkoff (New York: Knopf, 1985), 133–153; Roger Biles, *A New Deal for the American People* (DeKalb: Northern Illinois University Press, 1991), 207–224; William H. Wilson, *Coming of Age: Urban America, 1915–1945* (New York: Wiley, 1974), 176–196. For the effect of the mayors, see Sidney Fine, *Frank Murphy: The Detroit Years* (Ann Arbor: University of Michigan Press, 1975); Thomas Kessner, *Fiorello H. LaGuardia and the Making of Modern New York* (New York: McGraw-Hill, 1989), 292–314. For the greenbelt towns, see Joseph L. Arnold, *The New Deal in the Suburbs: A History of the Greenbelt Town Program, 1935–1954* (Columbus: Ohio State University Press, 1971); Paul K. Conkin, *Tomorrow a New World: The New Deal Community Program* (Ithaca, N.Y.: Cornell University Press, 1959). For the effect of former social workers such as Perkins and Hopkins on New Deal programs, see William W. Bremer, *Depression Winters: New York Social Workers and the New Deal* (Philadelphia: Temple University Press, 1984). For the New Deal political coalition, see Ruth Werner Gordon, "The Change in the Political Alignment of Chicago's Negroes during the New Deal," *Journal of American History* 56 (December 1969), 584–603; John Mollenkopf, *The Contested City* (Princeton, N.J.: Princeton University Press, 1983); Nancy J. Weiss, *Farewell to the Party of Lincoln: Black Politics in the Age of FDR* (Princeton, N.J.: Princeton University Press, 1983); Gerald H. Gamm, *The Making of New Deal Democrats: Voting Behavior and Realignment in Boston, 1920–1940* (Chicago: University of Chicago Press, 1989).

17. Paul V. Betters, "The Federal Government and the Cities: A Problem in Adjustment," *Annals of the American Academy of Political and Social Science* 199 (September 1938), 190–198; Bonnie Fox Schwartz, *The Civil Works Administration: The Business of Emergency Employment in the New Deal* (Princeton, N.J.: Princeton University Press, 1984); Kessner, *Fiorello H.*

LaGuardia, 294; Trout, "The New Deal and the Cities," 145; Biles, *A New Deal for the American People,* 212.

18. Public Works Administration, *America Builds: The Record of PWA* (Washington, D.C.: U. S. Government Printing Office, 1939); David T. Rowlands, "Urban Housing Activities of the Federal Government," *Annals of the American Academy of Political and Social Science* 190 (March 1937), 83–93; Timothy L. McDonnell, *The Wagner Housing Act: A Case Study of the Legislative Process* (Chicago: Loyola University Press, 1957); Mark I. Gelfand, *A Nation of Cities: The Federal Government and Urban America, 1933–1965* (New York: Oxford University Press, 1975), 23–70; Trout, "The New Deal and the Cities," 137–142.

19. Harvard Sitkoff, "The New Deal and Race Relations," in *Fifty Years Later: The New Deal Evaluated,* ed. Harvard Sitkoff (New York: Knopf, 1985), 93–112; Christopher G. Wye, "The New Deal and the Negro Community: Toward a Broader Conceptualization," *Journal of American History* 59 (December 1972), 621–639; Kenneth T. Jackson, "Race, Ethnicity, and Real Estate Appraisal: The Home Owners Loan Corporation and the Federal Housing Administration," *Journal of Urban History* 6 (August 1980), 419–452; Raymond A. Mohl, "Trouble in Paradise: Race and Housing in Miami during the New Deal Era," *Prologue: The Journal of the National Archives* 19 (Spring 1987), 7–21; Jackson, *Crabgrass Frontier,* 172–230.

20. For Roosevelt's relationships with urban political machines, see Bruce M. Stave, *The New Deal and the Last Hurrah: Pittsburgh Machine Politics* (Pittsburgh, Penn.: University of Pittsburgh Press, 1970); Charles H. Trout, *Boston, the Great Depression and the New Deal* (New York: Oxford University Press, 1977); Lyle W. Dorsett, *The Pendergast Machine* (New York: Oxford University Press, 1968); Lyle W. Dorsett, *Franklin D. Roosevelt and the City Bosses* (Port Washington, N.Y.: Kennikat, 1977); Roger Biles, *Big City Boss in Depression and War: Mayor Edward J. Kelley of Chicago* (DeKalb: Northern Illinois University Press, 1984); William D. Miller, *Mr. Crump of Memphis* (Baton Rouge: Louisiana State University Press, 1964); Roger Biles, *Memphis in the Great Depression* (Knoxville: University of Tennessee Press, 1986); Douglas L. Smith, *The New Deal in the Urban South* (Baton Rouge: Louisiana State University Press, 1988). For a succinct summary of urban political changes in the New Deal era, see Roger W. Lotchin, "Power and Policy: American City Politics Between the Two World Wars," in *Ethnics, Machines, and the American Urban Future,* ed. Scott Greer (Cambridge, Mass.: Schenkman, 1981), 1–50.

21. National Resources Board, Research Committee on Urbanism, *Our Cities: Their Role in the National Economy* (Washington, D.C.: U.S. Government Printing Office, 1937); Gelfand, *A Nation of Cities,* 82–104; John Hancock, "The New Deal and American Planning: The 1930s," in *Two Centuries of American Planning,* ed. Daniel Schaffer (Baltimore: Johns Hopkins University Press, 1988), 197–230.

22. Roger W. Lotchin, "The Metropolitan-Military Complex in Comparative Perspective: San Francisco, Los Angeles, and San Diego, 1919–41," *Journal of* *the West* 18 (July 1979), 19–30; Roger W. Lotchin, *Fortress California, 1910–1961: From Warfare to Welfare* (New York: Oxford University Press, 1992); Gerald D. Nash, *The American West Transformed: The Impact of the Second World War* (Bloomington: Indiana University Press, 1985); Gerald D. Nash, *World War II and the West* (Lincoln: University of Nebraska Press, 1990). Of all the states, Florida received the largest chunk of federal military spending—$1.5 billion—between 1941 and 1945. See David R. Goldfield and Blaine A. Brownell, *Urban America: A History,* 2nd ed. (Boston: Houghton Mifflin, 1990), 339.

23.   For wartime labor migration and urbanization, see Philip J. Funigiello, *The Challenge to Urban Liberalism: Federal-City Relations during World War II* (Knoxville: University of Tennessee Press, 1978), 3–38; J. Frederic Dewhurst and Associates, *America's Needs and Resources* (New York: Twentieth Century Fund, 1947), 43–48; Catherine Bauer, "Cities in Flux," *American Scholar* 13 (Winter 1943–1944), 70–84; Johnson and Campbell, *Black Migration in America,* 101–113. For race relations during World War II, see Harvard Sitkoff, "Racial Militance and Interracial Violence in the Second World War," *Journal of American History* 58 (December 1971), 661–681; Neil A. Wynn, *The Afro-American and the Second World War* (London: Paul Elek, 1976), 60–78; Dominic J. Capeci, Jr., *The Harlem Riot of 1943* (Philadelphia: Temple University Press, 1977); August Meier and Elliott Rudwick, *Black Detroit and the Rise of the UAW* (New York: Oxford University Press, 1979); Dominic J. Capeci, Jr., *Race Relations in Wartime Detroit: The Sojourner Truth Housing Controversy of 1942* (Philadelphia: Temple University Press, 1984); Carey McWilliams, *North from Mexico: The Spanish-Speaking People of the United States* (Philadelphia: Lippincott, 1949), 227–258; Mauricio Mazón, *The Zoot-Suit Riots: The Psychology of Symbolic Annihilation* (Austin: University of Texas Press, 1984).

24.   Funigiello, *The Challenge to Urban Liberalism,* 39–162; Miles L. Colean, *American Housing: Problems and Prospects* (New York: Twentieth Century Fund, 1944), 285–290; Roger W. Lotchin, ed., *The Martial Metropolis: U. S. Cities in Peace and War* (New York: Praeger, 1984); Marilynn S. Johnson, "Urban Arsenals: War Housing and Social Change in Richmond and Oakland, California, 1941–1945," *Pacific Historical Review* 60 (August 1991), 283–308; Stephen J. Diner et al., *Housing Washington's People: Public Policy in Retrospect* (Washington, D.C.: D.C. History and Public Policy Project, University of the District of Columbia, 1983), 169–179; Abbott, *Portland,* 125–145.

25.   Funigiello, *The Challenge to Urban Liberalism,* 163–186; Philip J. Funigiello, "City Planning in World War II: The Experience of the National Resources Planning Board," *Social Science Quarterly* 53 (June 1972), 91–104; John F. Bauman, "Visions of a Post-war City: A Perspective on Urban Planning in Philadelphia and the Nation, 1942–1945," in *Introduction to Planning History in the United States,* ed. Donald A. Krueckeberg (New Brunswick, N.J.: Center for Urban Policy Research, Rutgers University, 1983), 170–189.

26.   For postwar suburban development and population growth, see Jackson, *Crabgrass Frontier,* 231–245; Barry Checkoway, "Large Builders, Federal

Housing Programs, and Postwar Suburbanization," *International Journal of Urban and Regional Research* 4 (March 1980), 21–45; Gwendolyn Wright, *Building the Dream: A Social History of Housing in America* (New York: Pantheon, 1981), 242–261. For the new suburban historiography, see Michael H. Ebner, "Re-reading Suburban America: Urban Population Deconcentration, 1810–1980," *American Quarterly* 37 (1985), 368–381; Margaret Marsh, "Reconsidering the Suburbs: An Exploration of Suburban Historiography," *Pennsylvania Magazine of History and Biography* 112 (October 1988), 579–605.

27. For the emergence of the Sunbelt, see Carl Abbott, *The New Urban America: Growth and Politics in Sunbelt Cities,* rev. ed. (Chapel Hill: University of North Carolina Press, 1987); Richard M. Bernard and Bradley R. Rice, eds., *Sunbelt Cities: Politics and Growth since World War II* (Austin: University of Texas Press, 1983); Raymond A. Mohl, ed., *Searching for the Sunbelt: Historical Perspectives on a Region* (Knoxville: University of Tennessee Press, 1990). For a good summary of the aging industrial cities of the Northeast and Midwest, see Richard M. Bernard, ed., *Snowbelt Cities: Metropolitan Politics in the Northeast and Midwest since World War II* (Bloomington: Indiana University Press, 1990).

28. For continued black migration and third-world immigration, see Johnson and Campbell, *Black Migration in America,* 101–170; George Groh, *The Black Migration: The Journey to Urban America* (New York: Weybright and Talley, 1972); Nicholas Lemann, *The Promised Land: The Great Black Migration and How It Changed America* (New York: Knopf, 1991); David M. Reimers, *Still the Golden Door: The Third World Comes to America* (New York: Columbia University Press, 1985); Alejandro Portes and Rubén G. Rumbaut, *Immigrant America: A Portrait* (Berkeley and Los Angeles: University of California Press, 1990); Elliott Barkan, "New Origins, New Homeland, New Region: American Immigration and the Emergence of the Sunbelt, 1955–1985," in *Searching for the Sunbelt: Historical Perspectives on a Region,* ed. Raymond A. Mohl (Knoxville: University of Tennessee Press, 1990), 124–148.

29. For the urban underclass, see Ken Auletta, *The Underclass* (New York: Random House, 1982); William Julius Wilson, *The Declining Significance of Race: Blacks and Changing American Institutions* (Chicago: University of Chicago Press, 1978); William Julius Wilson, *The Truly Disadvantaged: The Inner City, the Underclass, and Public Policy* (Chicago: University of Chicago Press, 1987); Alphonso Pinkney, *The Myth of Black Progress* (Cambridge, England: Cambridge University Press, 1984); Michael B. Katz, *The Undeserving Poor: From the War on Poverty to the War on Welfare* (New York: Pantheon, 1989), 185–235. For the failure of urban schools, see Jonathan Kozol, *Savage Inequalities: Children in America's Schools* (New York: Crown, 1991); Alex Kotlowitz, *There Are No Children Here: The Story of Two Boys Growing Up in the Other America* (New York: Doubleday, 1991). For the census report showing "majority minority" cities, see Margaret L. Usdansky, "Minorities a Majority in 51 Cities," *USA Today,* 17 September 1991.

30. Bernard L. Weinstein and Robert E. Firestine, *Regional Growth and Decline in the United States: The Rise of the Sunbelt and the Decline of the*

Northeast (New York: Praeger, 1978); Barry Bluestone and Bennett Harrison, *The Deindustrialization of America: Plant Closings, Community Abandonment, and the Dismantling of Basic Industry* (New York: Basic Books, 1982); George Sternlieb and James W. Hughes, *Post-Industrial America: Metropolitan Decline and Inter-Regional Job Shifts* (New Brunswick, N.J.: Center for Urban Policy Research, Rutgers University, 1975); Thierry J. Noyelle and Thomas M. Stanback, Jr., *The Economic Transformation of American Cities* (Totowa, N.J.: Rowman and Allanheld, 1983); James Fallows, "America's Changing Economic Landscape," *Atlantic Monthly* 255 (March 1985), 47–68; Anatole Kaletsky and Guy de Jonquieres, "Why a Service Economy Is No Panacea," *Financial Times,* 22 May 1987, London edition, p. 12. For the role of federal policy in producing regional economic change, see Ann Markusen et al., *The Rise of the Gunbelt: The Military Remapping of America* (New York: Oxford University Press, 1991); Bruce J. Schulman, *From Cotton Belt to Sunbelt: Federal Policy, Economic Development, and the Transformation of the South, 1938–1980* (New York: Oxford University Press, 1991); Andrew Kirby, ed., *The Pentagon and the Cities* (Newbury Park, Calif.: Sage, 1992).

31.   Albert M. Greenfield, "American Merchandisers Told of Danger Which Threatens Business Districts," *Urban Land* 3 (January–February 1944), 4–5; "Office Decentralization: A Challenge the Central City Must Meet," *Urban Land* 9 (October 1950), 1, 3; Homer Hoyt, "The Current Trend in New Shopping Centers," *Urban Land* 12 (April 1953), 1, 3–5; Homer Hoyt, "The Status of Shopping Centers in the United States," *Urban Land* 19 (October 1960), 3–5; Victor Gruen, "The City in the Automobile Age," *Perspectives* (England) 16 (Summer 1966), 45–54; Jackson, *Crabgrass Frontier,* 231–271; Peter O. Muller, *The Outer City: Geographical Consequences of the Urbanization of the Suburbs* (Washington, D.C.: Association of American Geographers, 1976); Robert Fishman, "America's New City: Megalopolis Unbound," *Wilson Quarterly* 14 (Winter 1990), 25–48; Joel Garreau, *Edge City: Life on the New Frontier* (New York: Doubleday, 1991), 4. For the general process of postwar urban change, see also Mark I. Gelfand, "Cities, Suburbs, and Government Policy," in *Reshaping America: Society and Institutions, 1945–1980,* ed. Robert Bremner and Gary Reichard (Columbus: Ohio State University Press, 1982), 261–281; Raymond A. Mohl, "The Transformation of Urban America since the Second World War," in *Essays on Sunbelt Cities and Recent Urban America,* ed. Robert B. Fairbanks and Kathleen Underwood (College Station: Texas A&M Press, 1990), 8–32; Sharon Zukin, "The Hollow Center: U.S. Cities in the Global Era," in *America at Century's End,* ed. Alan Wolfe (Berkeley and Los Angeles: University of California Press, 1991), 245–261.

32.   Louis Justement, *New Cities for Old: City Building in Terms of Space, Time, and Money* (New York: McGraw-Hill, 1946), 3. For similar arguments, see Mabel L. Walker, *Urban Blight and Slums* (Cambridge, Mass.: Harvard University Press, 1938); Robert Lasch, *Breaking the Building Blockade* (Chicago: University of Chicago Press, 1946); S. E. Sanders and A. J. Rabuck, *New City Patterns: The Analysis of and a Technique for Urban Reintegration* (New York: Reinhold, 1946); L. Hilberseimer, *The New City: Principles of Planning* (Chicago: Paul Theobald, 1944).

33. Charles T. Stewart, "The Role of Government in Urban Redevelopment," *Urban Land Institute Bulletin* 2 (February 1943), 3–9; Seward H. Mott, "What Can Be Done to Conserve and Revitalize Our Downtown Business Areas," *Urban Land* 4 (October 1945), 1–4; Seward H. Mott, "The Central City— A Universal Problem," *Urban Land* 9 (June 1950), 2–3; Hal Burton, *The City Fights Back* (New York: Citadel, 1954); Miles L. Colean, *Renewing Our Cities* (New York: Twentieth Century Fund, 1953). For business activism in urban redevelopment generally, see Jon C. Teaford, *The Rough Road to Urban Renaissance: Urban Revitalization in America, 1940–1985* (Baltimore: Johns Hopkins University Press, 1990), 44–81. For the Pittsburgh Renaissance, see Roy Lubove, *Twentieth-Century Pittsburgh: Government, Business, and Environmental Change* (New York: Wiley, 1969).

34. *Urban Land Institute News Bulletin,* 21 July 1941, 1–2; *Urban Land Institute Bulletin* 2 (March 1943), 4; *Urban Land Institute Bulletin* 2 (June 1943), 2; Arthur Simon, *Stuyvesant Town, U.S.A.: Pattern for Two Americas* (New York: New York University Press, 1970); Dominic J. Capeci, Jr., "Fiorello H. LaGuardia and the Stuyvesant Town Controversy of 1943," *New-York Historical Society Quarterly* 62 (October 1978), 289–310; Scott, *American City Planning,* 421–425; Lowe, *Cities in a Race with Time,* 64–65.

35. Richard O. Davies, *Housing Reform During the Truman Administration* (Columbia: University of Missouri Press, 1966); Marc A. Weiss, "The Origins and Legacy of Urban Renewal," in *Urban and Regional Planning in an Age of Austerity,* ed. Pierre Clavel, John Forester, and William W. Goldsmith (New York: Pergamon, 1980), 53–80.

36. Jackson, *Crabgrass Frontier,* 190–230; Charles Abrams, *Forbidden Neighbors: A Study of Prejudice in Housing* (New York: Harper, 1955); Robert C. Weaver, *The Negro Ghetto* (New York: Harcourt Brace, 1948); Rose Helper, *Racial Policies and Practices of Real Estate Brokers* (Minneapolis: University of Minnesota Press, 1969); Robert E. Forman, *Black Ghettos, White Ghettos, and Slums* (Englewood Cliffs, N.J.: Prentice-Hall, 1971); William H. Brown, Jr., "Access to Housing: The Role of the Real Estate Industry," *Economic Geography* 48 (January 1972), 66–78.

37. Lawrence M. Friedman, *Government and Slum Housing: A Century of Frustration* (Chicago: Rand McNally, 1968); Anthony Jackson, *A Place Called Home: A History of Low-Cost Housing in Manhattan* (Cambridge, Mass.: MIT Press, 1976); J. Devereux Bowly, *The Poorhouse: Subsidized Housing in Chicago, 1895–1976* (Carbondale,: Southern Illinois University Press, 1978); Lubove, *The Progressives and the Slums,* 117–184; Wright, *Building the Dream,* 114–134, 220–239; Jackson, *Crabgrass Frontier,* 219–230. For the 1950s campaign against public housing, see " 'Grass-roots' Opposition to Public Housing Has 'Canned' Flavor," *Journal of Housing* 7 (May 1950), 158–160; Leo Goodman, "What Makes the Real Estate Lobby Tick?" *Journal of Housing* 7 (December 1950), 423–427; " 'Canned Campaign' to Kill Public Housing Continues," *Journal of Housing* 8 (January 1951), 9–10. For the conservative attack on urban renewal and public housing that continued into the 1960s, see Martin Anderson, *The Federal Bulldozer: A Critical Analysis of Urban Renewal, 1949–1962* (Cambridge, Mass.: MIT Press, 1964).

38. "Slum Surgery in St. Louis," *Architectural Forum* 94 (April 1951), 128–136; James Bailey, "The Case History of a Failure," *Architectural Forum* 123 (December 1965), 22–25; "The Tragedy of Pruitt-Igoe," *Time,* 27 December 1971, 38; Alex Poinsett, "Countdown in Housing," *Ebony* 27 (September 1972), 60–68; Sally Thran, "Public Housing in Trouble: No Room for the Poor," *Commonweal,* 5 January 1973, 292–293; Jane Holtz Kay, "Architecture," *The Nation,* 24 September 1973, 284–286; A. J. Cervantes, *Mr. Mayor* (Los Angeles: Nash, 1974). For the social problems of Pruitt-Igoe residents, see Lee Rainwater, *Behind Ghetto Walls: Black Family Life in a Federal Slum* (Chicago: Aldine, 1970); William Moore, Jr., *The Vertical Ghetto: Everyday Life in an Urban Project* (New York: Random House, 1969). For an early critique of the enormous high-rise public housing program in Chicago, see the four-part series, Ruth Moore, "Public Housing—Boon or a Bust?" *Chicago Sun-Times,* 3 September 1957, 4 September 1957, 5 September 1957, 6 September 1957.

39. Catherine Bauer, "The Dreary Deadlock of Public Housing," *Architectural Forum* 106 (May 1957), 140–142, 219; Eugene Raskin, "The Unloved City," *The Nation,* 7 February 1959, 119–120; Jane Jacobs, *The Death and Life of Great American Cities* (New York: Random House, 1961), 4–25, 392–404; Friedman, *Government and Slum Housing,* 116–146; Peter Marris, "A Report on Urban Renewal in the United States," in *The Urban Condition: People and Policy in the Metropolis,* ed. Leonard J. Duhl (New York: Basic Books, 1963), 113–134; Chester Hartman, "The Limitations of Public Housing," *Journal of the American Institute of Planners* 29 (November 1963), 283–296; Roger J. Vaughan et al., "Federal Urban Policies: The Harmful Helping Hand," in *Policy Studies Review Annual,* vol. 5, ed. Irving Louis Horowitz (Beverly Hills, Calif.: Sage, 1981), 464–465; Michael Kimmelman, "Urban Planning: What Went Wrong?" *U.S. News and World Report,* 30 March 1987, 76–77; Marc A. Weiss, "Developing and Financing the 'Garden Metropolis': Urban Planning and Housing Policy in Twentieth-Century America," *Planning Perspectives* 5 (September 1990), 307–319.

40. *Urban Land Institute News Bulletin,* 1 June 1942, 2–3; *Urban Land Institute Bulletin* 2 (February 1943), 2–3; *Urban Land Institute Bulletin,* 2 (June 1943), 2–4; Weiss, "The Origins and Legacy of Urban Renewal," 58–63.

41. For urban renewal generally, see M. Carter McFarland, *The Challenge of Urban Renewal* (Washington, D.C.: Urban Land Institute, 1962); James Q. Wilson, ed. *Urban Renewal: The Record and the Controversy* (Cambridge, Mass.: MIT Press, 1966); Jewel Bellush and Murray Hausknecht, eds., *Urban Renewal: People, Politics, and Planning* (Garden City, N.Y.: Anchor Books, 1967). For the rebuilding of the downtowns, see Joe R. Feagin, *The Urban Real Estate Game* (Englewood Cliffs, N.J.: Prentice-Hall, 1983), 64–102; Kenneth Fox, *Metropolitan America: Urban Life and Urban Policy in the United States, 1940–1980* (Jackson, Miss.: University of Mississippi Press, 1985), 79–105; Teaford, *The Rough Road to Urban Renaissance,* 82–121. For an early critique, see Catherine Bauer, "Redevelopment: A Misfit in the Fifties," in *The Future of Cities and Urban Redevelopment* ed. Coleman Woodbury (Chicago: University of Chicago Press, 1953), 7–25.

42.   Mark H. Rose, *Interstate: Express Highway Politics, 1941–1956* (Lawrence: Regents Press of Kansas, 1979); John F. Bauman, *Public Housing, Race, and Renewal: Urban Planning in Philadelphia, 1920–1974* (Philadelphia: Temple University Press, 1987), 79–117; L. P. Cookingham, "Expressways and the Central Business District," *American Planning and Civic Annual* (1954), 140–146; William H. Claire, "Urban Renewal and Transportation," *Traffic Quarterly* 13 (July 1959), 414–422; James Rouse, "Transportation and the Future of Our Cities," *Urban Land* 22 (July–August 1963), 7–10; U.S. Bureau of Public Roads, *Highways and Economic and Social Changes* (Washington, D.C.: U.S. Government Printing Office, 1964).

43.   Arnold R. Hirsch, *Making the Second Ghetto: Race and Housing in Chicago, 1940–1960* (Cambridge, England: Cambridge University Press, 1983); Forman, *Black Ghettos, White Ghettos, and Slums.*

44.   Paul Jacobs, *Prelude to Riot: A View of Urban America from the Bottom* (New York: Vintage Books, 1967); David Boesel and Peter H. Rossi, eds., *Cities under Siege: An Anatomy of the Ghetto Riots, 1964–1968* (New York: Basic Books, 1971). For the "urban crisis," see Mitchell Gordon, *Sick Cities* (New York: Macmillan, 1963); Barry Gottehrer, *New York City in Crisis* (New York: David McKay, 1965); James Q. Wilson, ed., *The Metropolitan Enigma: Inquiries into the Nature and Dimensions of America's "Urban Crisis"* (Cambridge, Mass.: Harvard University Press, 1968); Robert L. Branyan and Lawrence H. Larsen, eds., *Urban Crisis in Modern America* (Lexington, Mass.: D.C. Heath, 1971); Richard A. Cloward and Frances Fox Piven, *The Politics of Turmoil: Poverty, Race, and the Urban Crisis* (New York: Pantheon, 1974).

45.   Michael Harrington, *The Other America: Poverty in the United States* (New York: Macmillan, 1963); Peter Marris and Martin Rein, *Dilemmas of Social Reform: Poverty and Community Action in the United States* (New York: Atherton, 1967); Robert A. Levine, *The Poor Ye Need Not Have with You: Lessons from the War on Poverty* (Cambridge, Mass.: MIT Press, 1970), 44–90; Allen J. Matusow, *The Unraveling of America: A History of Liberalism in the 1960s* (New York: Harper and Row, 1984), 180–271; James T. Patterson, *America's Struggle Against Poverty, 1900–1980* (Cambridge, Mass.: Harvard University Press, 1981), 115–154.

46.   Lyndon B. Johnson, 2 March 1965, *Problems and Future of the Central City and Its Suburbs,* 89th Cong., 1st sess., H. Doc. 99, 10. For Great Society programs generally, see William H. Chafe, *The Unfinished Journey: America since World War II* (New York: Oxford University Press, 1986), 221–246; Gelfand, *A Nation of Cities,* 354–379. For the War on Poverty, see James L. Sundquist, "Origins of the War on Poverty," in *On Fighting Poverty,* ed. James L. Sundquist (New York: Basic Books, 1969), 6–33; Lawrence M. Friedman, "The Social and Political Context of the War on Poverty: An Overview," in *A Decade of Federal Antipoverty Programs: Achievements, Failures, and Lessons,* ed. Robert H. Haverman (New York: Academic, 1977), 21–47; Carl M. Brauer, "Kennedy, Johnson, and the War on Poverty," *Journal of American History* 69 (June 1982), 98–119; Lemann, *The Promised Land,* 109–221. For Model Cities, see M. Carter McFarland, *Federal Government and Urban Problems* (Boulder, Colo.: Westview, 1978); Bernard J. Frieden and Marshall Kaplan, *The Politics* *of Neglect: Urban Aid from Model Cities to Revenue Sharing* (Cambridge, Mass.: MIT Press, 1975); Dennis R. Judd and Rober E. Mendelson, *The Politics of Urban Planning: The East St. Louis Experience* (Urbana: University of Illinois Press, 1973), 118–175. For reports of special commissions on urban issues, see Office of the President, *A Decent Home: The Report of the President's Committee on Urban Housing* (Washington, D.C.: U.S. Government Printing Office, 1968); Office of the President, *Report of the National Advisory Commission on Civil Disorders* (Washington, D.C.: U.S. Government Printing Office, 1968); U.S. Congress, House of Representatives, *Building the American City: Report of the National Commission on Urban Problems to the Congress and to the President of the United States* (Washington, D.C.: U.S. Government Printing Office, 1968).

47. Quotation is from Patterson, *America's Struggle Against Poverty,* 162. See also McFarland, *Federal Government and Urban Problems,* 86; Levine, *The Poor Ye Need Not Have with You,* 91–189; Fox, *Metropolitan America,* 201–205; Marshall Kaplan, *Urban Planning in the 1960s: A Design for Irrelevancy* (New York: Praeger, 1973), 109–118; Brian D. Boyer, *Cities Destroyed for Cash: The FHA Scandal at HUD* (Chicago: Follett, 1973); Chafe, *The Unfinished Journey,* 236–243; Katz, *The Undeserving Poor,* 112–117; Frances Fox Piven and Richard A. Cloward, *Regulating the Poor: The Functions of Public Welfare* (New York: Pantheon, 1971); William Ryan, *Blaming the Victim* (New York: Random House, 1971); James J. Graham, *The Enemies of the Poor* (New York: Random House, 1970); Daniel P. Moynihan, *Maximum Feasible Misunderstanding: Community Action in the War on Poverty* (New York: Free Press, 1969).

48. Carl Abbott, *Urban America in the Modern Age: 1920 to the Present* (Arlington Heights, Ill.: Harlan Davidson, 1987), 125; Stephen E. Ambrose, *Nixon: Ruin and Recovery, 1973–1990* (New York: Simon and Schuster, 1991), 22.

49. Daniel P. Moynihan, "Toward a National Urban Policy," *The Public Interest* no. 17 (Fall 1969), 3–20. See also Daniel P. Moynihan, ed., *Toward a National Urban Policy* (New York: Basic Books, 1970).

50. Walter W. Heller et al., *Revenue Sharing and the City* (Baltimore: Johns Hopkins University Press, 1968); Dennis R. Judd, *The Politics of American Cities: Private Power and Public Policy* (Boston: Little, Brown, 1979), 329–342.

51. Daniel P. Moynihan, "The Crisis in Welfare," *The Public Interest* no. 10 (Winter 1968), 3–29; Daniel P. Moynihan, *The Politics of a Guaranteed Income: The Nixon Administration and the Family Assistance Plan* (New York: Random House, 1973); Vincent J. Burke and Vee Burke, *Nixon's Good Deed: Welfare Reform* (New York: Columbia University Press, 1974).

52. Fox, *Metropolitan America,* 206–220; Judd, *The Politics of American Cities,* 342–348; George M. Smerk, *The Federal Role in Urban Mass Transportation* (Bloomington: Indiana University Press, 1991), 117–141.

53. For the Brookings Institution report, see William A. Caldwell, *How to Save Urban America* (New York: New American Library, 1973), 227–228. For the negative consequences of the New Federalism, see Fred R. Harris and John V. Lindsay, *The State of the Cities: Report of the Commission on the Cities in the '70s* (New York: Praeger, 1972); Joe R. Feagin, *Subordinating the Poor: Welfare and American Beliefs* (Englewood Cliffs, N.J.: Prentice-Hall, 1975), 149–154; Judd, *The Politics of American Cities*, 338–342; Abbott, *Urban America in the Modern Age*, 125–132. For New York City's well-publicized bout with financial disaster, see Roger E. Alcaly and David Mermelstein, eds., *The Fiscal Crisis of American Cities* (New York: Vintage, 1977); Martin Shefter, *Political Crisis/Fiscal Crisis: The Collapse and Revival of New York City* (New York: Basic Books, 1985); William K. Tabb, *The Long Default: New York City and the Urban Fiscal Crisis* (New York: Monthly Review Press, 1982); Robert W. Bailey, *The Crisis Regime: The MAC, the EFCB, and the Political Impact of the New York City Financial Crisis* (Albany: State University of New York Press, 1984). For Cleveland's default, see Todd Swanstrom, *The Crisis of Growth Politics: Cleveland, Kucinich, and the Challenge of Urban Populism* (Philadelphia: Temple University Press, 1985).

54. Jill Jonnes, *We're Still Here: The Rise, Fall, and Resurrection of the South Bronx* (Boston: Atlantic Monthly Press, 1986), 311–323, quotation on 313.

55. President's Commission for a National Agenda for the Eighties, *Urban America in the Eighties: Perspectives and Prospects* (Washington, D.C.: U.S. Government Printing Office, 1980); Roger W. Schmenner, "Industrial Location and Urban Public Management," in *The Prospective City*, ed. Arthur P. Solomon (Cambridge, Mass.: MIT Press, 1980), 446–468; Anthony Downs, "The Future of Industrial Cities," in *The New Urban Reality*, ed. Paul E. Peterson (Washington, D.C.: Brookings Institution, 1985), 281–294; Bluestone and Harrison, *The Deindustrialization of America*.

56. President's Commission, *Urban America in the Eighties*, 29. For a critique, see Thomas Bender, "A Nation of Immigrants to the Sun Belt," *The Nation*, 28 March 1981, 359–361; Thomas Bender, "The End of the City?" *democracy: A Journal of Political Renewal and Radical Change* 3 (Winter 1983), 8–20.

57. John M. DeGrove, *Land, Growth, and Politics* (Chicago: American Planning Association, 1984), 99–176.

58. "New York City: On the Brink," *The Economist*, 24 May 1975, 64–67; "New York: Yes, We Have No Default," *The Economist*, 29 November 1975, 68–69; Robert H. Connery and Gerald Benjamin, *Rockefeller of New York: Executive Power in the Statehouse* (Ithaca, N.Y.: Cornell University Press, 1979), 242–291; Bailey, *The Crisis Regime*, 148–156.

59. Frank T. Keefe, *City and Town Centers: A Program for Growth. The Massachusetts Growth Policy Report* (Boston: Massachusetts Office of State Planning, 1977); Michael S. Dukakis, *Towards a National Urban Policy: A Draft Discussion Paper for the Coalition of Northeast Governors* (Boston: Commonwealth of Massachusetts, September 1977), "great opportunities" quotation on 3; Michael S. Dukakis, *A Proposal to Encourage the States to Become Full Partners in a National Urban Policy* (Boston: Commonwealth of

Massachusetts, January 1978); Frank T. Keefe, "State Development Cabinets: The Massachusetts Experience," unpublished manuscript in author's possession; Charles Kenney and Robert L. Turner, *Dukakis: An American Odyssey* (Boston: Houghton Mifflin, 1988), 104; Michael S. Dukakis, personal interview with Raymond A. Mohl, Boca Raton, Florida, 25 March 1992; Frank T. Keefe, telephone interview with Raymond A. Mohl, 30 March 1992.

60.   U.S. Department of Housing and Urban Development, *The President's National Urban Policy Report, 1982* (Washington, D.C.: U.S. Government Printing Office, 1982).

61.   Peter K. Eisinger, "The Search for a National Urban Policy, 1968–1980," *Journal of Urban History* 12 (November 1985), 3–23. For the Reagan administration's urban policy, see Robert Benenson, "Reagan and the Cities," *Editorial Research Reports* 2 (July 1982), 531–548; Neal M. Cohen, "The Reagan Administration's Urban Policy," *Town Planning Review* 54 (July 1983), 304–315; George E. Peterson and Carol W. Lewis, eds., *Reagan and the Cities* (Washington, D.C.: Urban Institute Press, 1986); Harold Wolman, "The Reagan Urban Policy and Its Impacts," *Urban Affairs Quarterly* 21 (March 1986), 311–335; Frances Fox Piven and Richard A. Cloward, *The New Class War: Reagan's Attack on the Welfare State and Its Consequences* (New York: Pantheon, 1982); Fred Block et al., *The Mean Season: The Attack on the Welfare State* (New York: Pantheon, 1987).

62.   Kevin Phillips, *The Politics of Rich and Poor: Wealth and the American Electorate in the Reagan Aftermath* (New York: Random House, 1990); "Reagan Era a Boon for Wealthiest," *Fort Lauderdale Sun-Sentinel,* 7 January 1992, 3A; Sylvia Nasar, "The 1980s: A Very Good Time for the Very Rich," *New York Times,* 5 March 1992, A1, C13; Robert Wood, "Cities in Trouble," *Domestic Affairs* 1 (Summer 1991), 228. See also Robert Wood, "Present Before the Creation: Lessons from the Paleosoic Age of Urban Affairs," *Journal of Urban Affairs* 13, no. 1 (1991), 111–117.

63.   For these issues, see Bernard J. Frieden and Lynne B. Sagalyn, *Downtown, Inc.: How America Rebuilds Cities* (Cambridge, Mass.: MIT Press, 1989); William Severini Kowinski, *The Malling of America: An Inside Look at the Great Consumer Paradise* (New York: William Morrow, 1985); Michael C. D. Macdonald, *America's Cities: A Report on the Myth of Urban Renaissance* (New York: Simon and Schuster, 1984).

64.   John Helyar, "The Big Hustle: Atlanta's Two Worlds," *Wall Street Journal,* 29 February 1988, 15; Michael deCourcy Hinds, "80's Leave States and Cities in Need," *New York Times,* 30 December 1990, 1, 16; Thomas Morgan, "In the Shadow of Manhattan Skyscrapers, a Society of Shantytowns Grows," *New York Times,* 20 October 1991, 16; Mark Alan Hughes, *Poverty in Cities* (Washington, D.C.: National League of Cities, 1989).

65.   Wood, "Cities in Trouble," 230; John Herbers, "Cities Attract More Offices, Less Housing," *New York Times,* 21 October 1985, 1, 11.

66.   Fred R. Harris and Roger Wilkins, eds., *Quiet Riots: Race and Poverty in the United States* (New York: Pantheon, 1988), quotations on xiii, 184.

67. John E. Jacob, "We Need an Urban Marshall Plan," *Miami Herald,* 14 January 1990, 1C, 4C; Richard C. Wade, "The Reagan Revolution: Much Ado About Nothing Much," *Urban Resources* 5 (Winter 1989), 36; Marshall Kaplan and Franklin James, eds., *The Future of National Urban Policy* (Durham, N.C.: Duke University Press, 1990); Gary Orfield and Carole Ashkinaze, *The Closing Door: Conservative Policy and Black Opportunity* (Chicago: University of Chicago Press, 1991); Ronald Berkman et al., eds., *In the National Interest: The 1990 Urban Summit* (New York: Twentieth Century Fund Press, 1992).

68. Debbie Howlett, "Chicago Flood Was the Tip of the Iceberg," *USA Today,* 29 April 1992, 1A; William Cronon, "Mud, Memory and the Loop," *New York Times,* 2 May 1992, 17.

69. David Lauter and Sam Fulwood III, "U.S. Racial Slumber Ends with a Jolt," *Los Angeles Times,* 3 May 1992, A1, A15–A16; Don Terry, "Decades of Rage Created Crucible of Violence," *New York Times,* 3 May 1992, 1, 17; Jill Abramson et al., "Verdict's Impact: West Coast Uprising Puts National Spotlight Back on Race Relations," *Wall Street Journal,* 1 May 1992, A1. For recent comment and analysis on the state of race relations, see Andrew Hacker, *Two Nations: Black and White, Separate, Hostile, Unequal* (New York: Scribners, 1992); Studs Terkel, *Race: How Blacks and Whites Think and Feel about the American Obsession* (New York: New Press, 1992); Ze'ev Chafets, *Devil's Night and Other True Tales of Detroit* (New York: Random House, 1990).

70. Brian Duffy, "Days of Rage," *U.S. New and World Report,* 11 May 1992, 21–26, quotation on 21; Timothy Noah and David Wessel, "Urban Solutions," *Wall Street Journal,* 4 May 1992, A1, A6; Michael Wines, "White House Links Riots to Welfare," *New York Times* 5 May 1992, A1, A12.

71. Kaplan and James, *The Future of National Urban Policy,* 325–345, 351–367, quotation on 352; Lucia Mouat, "Big-City Mayors Cry Out For Help," *Christian Science Monitor,* 16 November 1990, 4.

72. Bill Turque, "Cities on the Brink," *Newsweek,* 19 November 1990, 44.

2

MICHAEL B. KATZ

Surviving Poverty in Early Twentieth-Century New York City

Hɪꜱᴛᴏʀɪᴀɴꜱ of public policy usually peer over the shoulders of reformers, politicians, and administrators. Because they write about the passage of legislation, the creation of institutions, and the administration of programs, they neglect the clients of policy, who rarely appear in their stories as interesting or complicated as those who design and implement policy on their behalf. Most policy history (including much I have written) remains incomplete because policy takes its meaning from the experience of its clients as much as from the intentions of its sponsors. Viewed from the vantage of a poor widow, an out-of-work expressman, or a fourteen-year-old worried about how his or her mother will pay the rent, early twentieth-century poverty policy appeared different than it did from the offices of New York's Charity Organization Society (COS), the city's Bureau of Dependent Children, a philanthropist's drawing room, or a legislator's desk in the state capital.[1]

This chapter turns the customary angle by reconstructing a bit of the experience of those who survived extreme poverty in the past, sometime with the help of, and often despite, official policy. Let's begin with excerpts from the lives of three of the poorest families in New York City.[2]

Rose Warrington

Rose Warrington was born in Jersey City in 1878. When she was four years old, her parents died, and she went to live with her only relative, a sister in New York City. When Rose was fourteen, her sister also died, and she moved as a servant into the home of an old woman next door. With almost no schooling, illiterate, unable even to sign her name, she remained there until at the age of eighteen she married George Jackson, who worked for the Street Cleaning Department. Together, they had five children, of whom four survived. Suddenly, in 1907, after an illness of only two weeks, George Jackson died of "galloping consumption," leaving only a purse collected by his workmates. Within two years, eager to find a father for her children, Rose married her lodger, Daniel Warrington. Daniel also had been married before. He and his wife had kept a saloon for ten years until his drinking became intolerable and she left him. Now, her former marriage a secret from her neighbors, she lived with another man as his wife. Daniel's drinking cost him work. A talented plumber and, when sober, an excellent, reliable workman, he was fired reluctantly by employers no longer willing to tolerate his periodic sprees.

At first, the Warringtons lived with their four children and an orphaned niece who, Rose thought, corrupted her older daugher Mabel. They added three children of their own. Daniel was not a devoted stepfather, and neighbors and school officials reported the family for neglect to the Society for the Prevention of Cruelty to Children (SPCC), which successfully prosecuted it and sent the children from her first marriage to institutions, leaving her with her children by Daniel: Sadie, John, and her baby, Rose. Whatever his failings as a stepfather, Daniel managed to provide for his family until a prolonged bout of unemployment in 1917. By every indication, too, he was devoted to his wife and children. Nonetheless, depressed about his lack of a job, one morning he went out to look for work and never returned.

Unable to support herself, Rose turned to the COS, which took up her case. Not only did it provide funds itself; it persuaded a local Roman Catholic Church to help the family; and one of its agents tracked down Daniel's relatives, who began to send money anonymously.

When the COS's visitor paid her regular call in December 1918, she found the family had moved. The reason, she discovered, was that Daniel suddenly had returned. Passionately attached to him, Rose accepted his return without question. Together, the family had moved to a nearby but better apartment, and Daniel had begun to support his family once again. When she found them, the visitor reported Rose as "radiantly happy." Self-sufficient now, no longer in need of charity—indeed, Daniel offered to pay back the COS for the help it had given his family—Rose and Daniel treated the visitor cordially and invited her to call for tea whenever she was in the neighborhood. Daniel said that he had left to teach his wife a lesson: she should appreciate him more and not listen to those—meaning his inlaws—who would interfere.

From organized charity's point of view, one problem remained. Despite her denials, the COS suspected Rose and Daniel never had been legally married, and they gave their opinion to the local priest, who visited the couple. Rose was very angry, as she told the visitor when she returned. Rose did not invite the COS to tea again.

Mary O'Brien

Mary O'Brien, born in Ireland in 1865, emigrated to New York when she was 17. She worked as a waitress for four years and then married Patrick Murphy, a stableman, born five years earlier than Mary. Patrick had arrived in New York in 1883, at the age of twenty-three. By 1895, they had five children. Patrick worked steadily at a stable until 1895, when he was laid off because business was bad. His next job lasted only two months. For a while, the family managed to live on the generosity of neighbors until, on the edge of starvation, it applied for charity. A small donation from the Association for Improving the Condition of the Poor (AICP) tided the family over until Patrick found another job, and the family retained its independence for five years. However, between 1900 and 1910, it asked help from the COS on 13 different occasions.

A series of work-related accidents coupled with chronic ill health kept Patrick from work and left his family periodically destitute. In August 1900, a horse stepped on his foot; in May 1903, a horse kicked him; in February 1905, while shoveling snow for the Metropolitan Street Railway, his feet froze; in August 1907, the heat at the Metropolitan Stables prostrated him. Even when uninjured, he suffered from colds and debilitating rheumatism.

Illness and pregnancy eroded Mary's earning power, too, although she often supported her family. Between 1901 and 1905, she gave birth to three more children, one of whom died. She suffered, too, from jaundice, periodic general ill health, menopause, and recurrent depression and discouragements. She found a variety of unskilled jobs, all of which paid badly. She washed towels for four cents a dozen; did five people's wash for seventy-five cents; cleaned part-time in Altman's department store and elsewhere for about two dollars to four dollars a week; served for a time as a housekeeper, taking care of her own and a neighboring tenement for her rent and eight dollars a month in cash; worked at the COS's laundry for eighty cents a day; cleaned hotels and boarding houses from 7A.M. to 9P.M.; and did "day's work," sometimes found by organized charity, which supplied private individuals with cheap, reliable domestic help. The children helped, too, working after school or looking after the baby.

Despite Mary's efforts, the COS remained suspicious of the family. Its representatives could not understand why Patrick did not work. He was, they thought, simply lazy. In 1907, the family's destitution notwithstanding, the COS finally decided to stop all financial aid. Nonetheless, "because of the children," it kept the case open, visiting, advising, and offering help with jobs, medical care, and schools. Its purpose was to goad Patrick back to regular, full-time work. Its visitors knew the price: Mary's exploitation as the family's breadwinner and the destitution of the children.

A few months later, desperate for help, Mary told the COS visitor the secret of why Patrick did not work. When he was a child, he had burned his left hand. Over time, the muscles had contracted, and the hand was almost useless. He had managed fairly well with his right hand until in recent years rheumatism had weakened it. Patrick said he did not often talk about his hand because he feared it would prevent him from obtaining work.

The Murphys suffered from still another problem—their daughter Ann was mentally deficient. As she reached adolescence, the COS visitor began to worry about the consequences of Ann's developing sexuality. The only solution, she felt, was an institution, and she began a long, eventually successful campaign to persuade the Murphys to place Ann in one. In the course of the procedure, the COS managed to alienate the Murphys by usurping their prerogative to apply to the city's commissioner of public charities themselves. When the COS submitted an application for commitment accompanied by a personal, detailed history of the family, even the city's commissioner of public charities objected.

By the time Ann was institutionalized, the two eldest children, who had reached 14, could leave school and take full-time jobs. With Mary working, too, the family could subsist on its own. And so it did, for at least the next decade.

Nellie Park

On the night of March 26, 1904, a great fire burned the Adams Express Company at 59 Broadway.[3] To save his life, Alexander Park, an expressman who worked for American Express, which rented space on the fifth floor (its main building was next door), jumped out a window. Injured from his fall, never able to work again, he received a little help from the St. Vincent de Paul Conference of a local Roman Catholic Church and half pay from American Express. On May 29, 1910, at the age of 34, he died. When Alexander died, both American Express and the Conference at once stopped their payments. With American Express, it was a matter of policy; with the Conference, it reflected the expectation that a combination of insurance and wages from Nellie, Alexander's twenty-six-year-old widow, would support the family. Nellie collected $150 from his life insurance policy with the National Express Employees Benevolent Association and $134.30 from his policy with the Prudential Insurance Company. She spent $168 for his funeral.

Nellie tried to manage on her own, working in a laundry, but the work proved too strenuous and she switched to cleaning offices for six dollars a week. When eye trouble prevented her from working, she pawned her dress to pay for glasses prescribed by a doctor. Alexander had left Nellie with three young children, aged seven, five, and one; three others had died. At this time, a family of four—so students of the cost of living concluded—needed about fifteen dollars or eighteen dollars a week to survive in New York City. Nellie suffered from more than low wages. Alexander's good intentions had left her unusually inexperienced as a housekeeper. Because he had worked nights, he had stayed at home during the day, helping with the housework, marketing, and lifting customary domestic responsibilities from Nellie, whom he had treated "more or less like a child."

Soon, her depleted resources forced Nellie to move to much less expensive rooms, and she depended increasingly on charity, especially the St. Vincent de Paul Society and the Sisters of Mercy, who for a time brought food every day. Unwell, Nellie visited a doctor who reported she had incipient tuberculosis in her left lung. In these circumstances, the COS, which had been called into the case, advised that she and her children, about whose health authorities worried, go to asylums. A devoted mother, Nellie resisted giving up her children, and authorities, calling her "obstinate" and "ignorant," chastised her for refusing to follow good advice. By April 1911, Nellie capitulated. Threatened with eviction, pressured from all sides, she agreed to go to a sanitarium at Otisville with her boy, Daniel, and to commit her children to a Roman Catholic orphanage. Homesick for her children, Nellie left Otisville in October. She had gained fifteen pounds and felt much better. She tried briefly to manage with all her children, but, unable to support them, arranged for the commitment of the two youngest to a Home, where they remained. She and Daniel lived briefly with her sister, whose husband, a waiter earning only eight dollars a week, refused to allow them to stay very long. Undoubtedly, he objected both to the expense and to the fact that his wife and child along with Rose and Daniel all shared one bed.

Nellie went back to laundry work, against all medical advice, and managed without help for four years. She and Daniel lived in a succession of furnished rooms until they found a small, badly ventilated three-room apartment. Daniel was supposed to attend a day camp for youngsters at risk of tuberculosis. Sometimes he went, sometimes he took the carfare and played on the streets. All the authorities concerned with the case considered him not only wild but stupid. They referred, disparagingly, to his "mental condition." They wanted him put in an institution, but Nellie objected.

Whatever authorities thought about his "mental condition," Daniel was a leader among his peers. Youngsters on the street thronged around him to hear his stories. Clever and resourceful, he made more money than any of the other young boys who hung around a local theater selling candy and peanuts. On one election day, he earned fifty cents peddling apples. He also found marginally licit ways of scavenging coal for his mother.

Indeed, Daniel was devoted to his mother, who, in turn, doted on him, despite their frequent quarrels. He sold papers to help her and earned bits of money with which to take her to the movies.

For a variety of reasons, Daniel had never attended school. When he began, his teachers' assessments proved surprising. Daniel, they felt, was intelligent. He worked industriously and performed well. His teachers liked him very much. His health improved, too. He did not, after all, have tuberculosis. Nellie seemed to be managing competently; her apartment always was clean and her clothes attractive. Even though her wages remained wretched, she worked steadily. Still, neither Nellie's independence nor Daniel's improved health, success in school, and devotion to his mother altered the COS's plan for the Park family. It wanted to send Nellie to a sanitarium and Daniel to an institution. When Nellie continued to resist, the COS enlisted a male visitor from the Catholic Big Brothers—a Mr. Gleason. Even he could not convince her. Determined to prevail, Mr. Gleason and the COS looked for further ammunition. When a doctor diagnosed Nellie as tubercular, the COS moved quickly to enlist the SPCC, which prosecuted the case. As part of the proceedings, Nellie underwent still another and more careful examination, which showed she was not tubercular. Nellie "never has had a positive sputum," reported the clinic. The SPCC's officer worried that this finding might undercut the case, but he felt strongly that Nellie was "a menace and . . . unable to care for Daniel as he should be cared for." The court agreed, and committed him to the Mission of the Immaculate Virgin.

When Nellie met the COS visitor one month later, she was indignant. The judge had told her that the COS had "done the whole business" and the SPCC said the same thing. Nellie wanted nothing more to do with organized charity. Nellie's information was right, as the COS's distorted letter to the SPCC describing the history of her case revealed.

Still, eventually, she made her peace with both Daniel's incarceration and the COS. When the visitor met her on the street sometime later, she reported she was managing financially by doing odd bits of sewing and caring for neighborhood women when they gave birth. She appeared, said the visitor, "well satisfied to have Daniel away and seemed rather inclined to follow the suggestion of visitor to take this opportunity to go away and get herself in good condition and perhaps by the time Daniel has graduated from the school and is able to work, that she will be strong and able to care for her family. . . ."

These stories are excerpts from detailed case histories of families in the files of New York City's COS in the late nineteenth and early twentieth century. A little more than two thousand of these cases, from among the original hundreds of thousands, have been preserved. With a sample of them, I am reconstructing the experience of desperately poor people in New York City and placing them in the context of their time and place. With these records, I can describe in detail the lives and family relations of people whose exclusion from customary sources leaves them outside most written history. The records show how families with incomes far below the poverty lines drawn by contemporary researchers managed to survive. They transform them from one-dimensional stereotypes into individuals, struggling, loving, coping, above all, human. Although many common themes run throughout these stories, no one story is typical. Their message, rather, is the individuality, resourcefulness, and resilience of ordinary people. Like the best ethnographies of the present, the *variety* they reveal underscores a crucial lesson for policy. Images of very poor people implicit in public policy and social science too often sketch bleak portraits of populations uniformly disorganized, apathetic, incompetent, and amoral. As a consequence, they miss the variegated patterns of relationships and activities within even the most disadvantaged neighborhoods, the individuality of people and the strategies they deploy to survive their poverty.

Although my reconstruction of the experience of these poorest of New York's families is still in its early stages, major themes have emerged. The rest of this chapter outlines some of them. First, though, by way of background, a few words about the COS itself and a couple of the other agencies that loom large in these stories; and a few comments, too, on the city in which these stories took place.

Wealthy, philanthropic New Yorkers created the COS in 1882 to eliminate fraud and reduce dependency. The COS investigated applicants to other relief societies and offered support and advice through friendly visiting. Modeled on the COS in Britain, it was one of many such agencies founded throughout the country in the same period. By the twentieth century, contrary to its original model, it also gave relief. The COS worked closely with the city's largest relief organization, the AICP, founded by Robert Hartley in 1843. To coordinate their efforts, in the mid-1890s, the AICP and COS established a Joint Application Bureau, which received requests for help and parceled them out to the appropriate society. In 1939, the two organizations joined to form the Community Service Society.[4]

The COS divided New York City into districts, each with its own office headed by a district secretary and staffed by paid visitors or agents. Visitors had authority to offer emergency assistance, but the district committee made decisions about long-term care. Committees, comprising representatives of the principal professions and religious denominations, generally met weekly. The COS central office maintained a registry of cases and performed other functions, including organizing specialized committees to consider city-wide problems. It also sponsored social research and the first social work training in the city.

The SPCC was the other great agency that looms large in these stories. Organized first in 1876 in New York City, it investigated complaints of child neglect and abuse. Its quasi-police powers permitted the SPCC to require the police to investigate complaints, charge parents in court, and request the commitment of children to institutions. It also served a quasi-penal function, incarcerating children held for trial, removed temporarily from their homes, or awaiting institutional placement. Poor people, who feared it, gave the SPCC its popular name, "The Cruelty."[5]

In 1875, New York City stopped giving public outdoor relief to poor people. It still assisted the needy blind, and, until prevented in the 1890s by a successful campaign spearheaded by the COS, it distributed free coal. Nonetheless, the city still contributed large sums to help dependent people. Most of these were spent through institutions. The city operated an almshouse, workhouse, municipal lodging house, and various hospitals. The city's courts assisted families by prosecuting husbands for desertion and nonsupport and by placing children in institutions. Both the city and state paid the fees of children in private orphanages, including ones run by religious denominations. In 1893, one of every thirty-five children in New York City lived in an orphange supported by public funds.[6] Public funds also sustained voluntary hospitals.

Roman Catholic institutions, such as the enormous Catholic Protectory, were the primary beneficiaries of public funding. Through the local chapters of the St. Vincent de Paul Society, Roman Catholics also assisted great numbers of their poor. The United Hebrew Charities, the city's other major relief agency, assisted poor Jews; in 1900 alone, it investigated 31,088 applications for relief, and its employment bureau placed 6,594 people in work.[7]

Many other agencies and charities populated the city with a complex network not described usefully as either public or private. Every year, the COS listed them in its *New York Charities Directory,* which in 1900, excluding the index and advertisements, consisted of about 620 pages that mapped a vast, intricate, complicated terrain to be negotiated by those in need of help.

In no period in the city's history was its negotiation as difficult, for these years spanned a transformation of New York City's demography, economy, and society. Fueled by new immigrants from eastern and southern Europe, the city's population exploded from 2,300,000 in 1890 to 4,766,000 only 20 years later. Among these, Italians, Jews, Romanians, Syrians and others new in large numbers to America remade the population's composition. Throughout these years, nearly 2 of every 3 New York City residents were immigrants or their children. By 1930, 440,000 Italian immigrants lived in New York City. All but 82,000 had arrived after 1901; the growth trajectory of the city's 238,000 Polish and 442,000 Russian immigrants had followed the same pattern. At the same time, industrialization altered the city's economy. New York never became the site of massive manufacturing. Instead, small firms clustered especially in the clothing, printing and publishing, and luxury trades dotted the city with their shops, factories, and sweatshops. Between 1880 and 1910, workers in these industries accounted for 70 percent of the increase in the city's industrial wage earners. Increasingly, too, the city's economy reflected the emergence of large national corporations, which, from their base in Manhattan, coordinated vast operations throughout the country. As always, too, the city remained a center of finance and shipping. Between 1880 and 1910, the number of national manufacturing firms with assets of $1 million or more located in New York City increased more than ten times from 32 to 330.[8]

Although immigrants often clustered together in distinct sections of the city, aside from the lower East Side, New York's neighborhoods remained remarkably diverse. Indeed, social diversity underlay the COS's strategy, which assumed the presence in each of its districts of enough educated and well-off people, knowledgeable about local conditions, to serve on its committees and provide a pool of volunteer friendly visitors. By late in the nineteenth century, only for the lower portion of Manhattan did this assumption prove untenable.[9]

As a microcosm of working-class New York, consider the demography of one tenement that housed Rose Warrington and her family, whose story I sketched earlier. Among the fourteen families crowded into the tenement on Second Avenue just above 125th Street were an Austrian railroad guard, a German widow, an Austrian waiter, an Italian driver, a Hungarian printer, a Russian railway conductor, an Austrian woman who ran a fruit store, an American driver for an express company, a Finnish carpenter, a Finnish stonecutter, an Italian tailor, and an American laborer on the subway. This ethnic diversity and mix of nonindustrial working-class occupations reflected the composition of the neighborhood, with the notable exception of the block of East 127th Street east of Third Avenue, where nearly all the residents were black.[10]

Set within this dynamic, diverse, changing city, Rose Warrington's story and those of the other families assisted by the COS illustrate themes related to four major topics: routes into and out of dependence; family and gender; housing, space, and mobility; and the social construction of moral worth and the social relations of charity.

Consider first the origins of dependence. Families found themselves dependent because of irregular work, accidents, widowhood, illness, and lack of child care. Most cases, in fact, reflected some combination of these factors; as a result, dependence usually was overdetermined. With men, the irregularity of work created more of a problem than their wages. Charity officials thought any steadily employed man, unless handicapped by an exceptionally large number of children, able to support his family. Most working class men, however, could not save enough to survive their recurrent bouts of unemployment. Women, also subject to seasonal unemployment, earned a fraction of men's wages. Alone, even a steadily employed widow rarely could support herself and more than one child. For this reason, organized charity often supplemented widow's wages.

Patrick Murphy's history of accidents, described earlier, was by no means unusual. America experienced the highest rate of industrial accidents in the industrialized world.[11] Accidents were one reason why sickness was so important a cause of destitution; beyond accidents, a host of illnesses plagued poor people. In these years, the worst, of course, was tuberculosis. In 1914 and 1915, New York City's register of tuberculosis patients numbered 35,000, with 22,000 new cases added each year. Of these, 8,918 died. Their care cost public and private sources $687,342.[12] Sickness, in fact, forms a major thread running throughout nearly every family's story. In almost none of them could the family afford to pay for its own medical care. For this reason, free medical care formed a principal component in the relief of dependence, and the authority of professional medicine, delivered through dispensaries, clinics, and hospitals, often shaped the day-to-day experience of the poor.[13]

Poor people moved in and out of dependence. Could we reconstruct them systematically, patterns would look much like the high turnover uncovered by the Michigan Income Panel Dynamics Study in recent years, only the proportions ever needing help would be much higher. Many families experienced recurrent spells of dependence; some stayed in them for a very long time. Almost all working-class families, however, lived, as one writer put it, on the verge of dependence.[14] I use *dependence* rather than *poverty* because most of these families, even when they managed on their own, were poor by any reasonable standards. Indeed, poverty was the normal state for close to half the city's population. Of these, a floating subset could not survive without outside help.

Families emerged from dependence because men found jobs, women remarried, governments granted pensions, or children went to work. Two of these routes require some comment. Early in the century, some women remained eligible for Civil War pensions, extended to surviving family members of Northern veterans late in the nineteenth century. After 1916, a small but significant number of widows received the state's new mothers' pensions. Although small, together with a job such as cleaning offices (an emerging form of employment that fit mothers' schedules), mothers' pensions enabled women with children to survive. Much more common as a route out of dependence, however, was the labor of children. Children left school at 14—if they were reluctant, the COS usually managed to persuade them otherwise—and found jobs. Most of these paid badly, to start perhaps four dollars a week as a messenger to three dollars or four dollars a week in a sweatshop. Still, together with their mothers' wages, children earned enough to assure the independence of their families. With remarkable willingness, most youngsters accepted their role, for which, of course, they paid a heavy price in forgone prospects for mobility. Indeed, many families escaped dependence on the backs of their children.[15]

For the most part, New York's poor lived in nuclear families with few kin relations other than parents and children. Some, especially widows, took in boarders, a practice organized charity viewed with ambivalence. Boarders meant extra income, which could boost a family over the line to independence. Nonetheless, charity officials and reformers thought families and boarders crammed together in congested rooms posed a menace to health and morals. In any event, few stayed very long, and actual household composition frequently shifted.

The behavior of clients' relatives, where it can be traced, usually reflected ambivalence. Certainly, they believed in their moral obligation to assist their needy kin. None of them whose remarks I have read asserted that relatives could lay no claims on each other, but they, too, usually were either poor or on the verge of dependence, afraid that a modicum of help might be misconstrued as the downpayment on regular assistance, fearful of entrapment by an obligation with no clear end. In these circumstances, relatives followed various courses: material assistance, outright refusal, anonymous donations, and the invention of reasons why their kin did not merit their assistance. In practice, they vacillated between these courses, their guilt and fear evident in their inconsistency.

Wives, too, often revealed ambivalence about their spouses. Many, wanting support from reluctant or deserting husbands, unhesitatingly charged them in Magistrate's, later Domestic Relations, Court.[16] Others vacillated. However, like Rose Warrington, all the ones in these stories quickly took back their spouses from sprees, flings, or jail. Whether it was a mark of their affection or a sign of their need for a man's wage often remains unclear, but, whatever their motive, separation clearly was as likely a temporary as a permanent state.

The most intense bonds united mothers and their children, especially sons.[17] The men in these stories often were indifferent husbands, but their sons rarely neglected their mothers. Like Daniel Park, they worked hard to support and protect them, turning over to them with almost no recorded complaints nearly all their wages. Most mothers, in turn, fought fiercely to preserve their families intact. Although many, in the end, found themselves forced by circumstances to commit children to an institution, most did so with the greatest reluctance. Against the advice of organized charity, they resisted, preferring starvation to separation. Whether or not to break up a family persisted, in fact, as one of the most difficult and often debated questions among charity workers and COS district committees.

Institutions mediated family relations. Whatever an institution's official goals, poor people themselves turned it partly to their own purposes. Courts became arenas for the resolution of family conflicts, orphanages temporary shelters for children during times of family crisis, and hospitals sources of nourishment and child care.[18]

Shelter, as well as food, medicine, and clothing, preoccupied New York's poor. Many of their histories read as a long, unsatisfactory search for decent, cheap housing. They moved often, but usually not very far. Evicted because they failed to pay their rent, they moved next door, down the block, around the corner, rarely out of the neighborhood. Their carefully constructed networks of personal assistance, friendship, and credit bound them within narrow spheres, and the expense of carfare meant they could not afford to live far from where they worked.[19]

Landlords were major players in their stories. A good landlord not only kept his or her buildings well repaired, he or she also allowed tenants to run up a bill for back rent. Landlords faced a dilemma: if they ejected tenants whey they failed to pay, they were unlikely ever to collect any part of the rent, nor was it likely that they would fill their rooms with anyone significantly more affluent. Still, if they were too lenient, if they never took action, they could find themselves permanently with no income from their property. The resolution of this dilemma meant calibrating the relation between potential loss and income with care. Individual landlords differed in the way they reached their decisions, as reflected in the amount of time they allowed to pass before they went to the court for an order to evict. But nearly all of them, by permitting some leeway, served de facto as important creditors of the poor.

Within nearly every tenement—and, remember, New York was a city of tenements—landlords hired a housekeeper or "janitress." These women lived rent free in exchange for cleaning the building, showing apartments to prospective tenants, supervising their conduct, and occasionally collecting rent. Their social origins lay in the same class as the tenants themselves. Sometimes they even were clients of organized charity. Indeed, poor widows performed a difficult calculus in deciding whether to accept a post as housekeeper. True, it meant free rent, but how would she buy food? If her children did not work, she would probably lack cash, because most landlords forbade their housekeepers from working off the premises. Housekeepers, moreover, lived with a potentially draining tension. They were at once agents of landlords, the eyes and ears of organized charity, and members of a network of informants about families strung out across the city. Yet, given the similarity in class background, they often empathized with and liked their tenants. Caught between conflicting pulls, housekeepers composed a vast, shifting, marginal stratum within the city's social structure.[20]

Their advice contributed to the evaluation of applicants by organized charity. The question was, Is the applicant worthy? Does the family deserve charity? Drawing the line between the worthy and unworthy poor has remained an insoluble problem. No society has controlled enough resources to meet everyone's needs. The difficulty is defining the boundary, which must always be a social construct, a reflection of judgment and values rather than science and objective evidence.[21]

To organized charity, personal worth rested on behavior, attitude, and class. The three criteria for judging behavior involved sex, alcohol, and truthfulness. Of these, sexual misconduct was the most serious and truthfulness, the least. Charity workers knew that everyone lied a little bit. The problem was to prevent it from becoming excessive. They also accepted, if unwillingly, that most people drank a little. Only when drinking translated into incapacity for work, domestic violence, or an excessive financial drain did COS workers assert their authority. Sexuality was another matter. COS officials defined not just prostitution, but any sex outside marriage, as illicit, and they often pried relentlessly into the behavior of adolescents and young widows.

Readiness to work, willingness to take advice, and gratitude were the three most desirable attitudes. The COS often cut off help to clients because they thought they were lazy or because they refused to take advice. At the same time, they wanted their help accepted with gratitude, for, as a gift, charity always has been partly about deference and reciprocity. Organized charity expected its clients to express their gratitude, and visitors almost always noted when they did.[22] More than any other response, a sense of entitlement, the opposite of gratitude, annoyed charity visitors. Nonetheless, even when it assessed a family as undeserving, the presence of children who were both blameless and vulnerable frequently checked the COS's desire to stop its help. As in the story of the Murphys, which I told earlier, the phrase "because of the children" explained the COS's continued aid to a family about whose character it retained grave doubts. As for class, a few clients had experienced downward mobility. Through bad luck or bad management they had lost wealth and position. Whatever the reason for their fall, their evident gentility always earned them favorable consideration by the COS, despite behavior that would have assigned a client of humble origins to the undeserving poor. Still, assignment to categories of worth remained provisional, and assessments of individual clients frequently reversed during the years they remained under the care and supervision of organized charity.

Two examples illustrate how and why organized charity changed its opinion of families and how the relations among its officials and their clients played themselves out in decisions about whether to give or withhold aid. The stories of Matilda Gehrig and the Brighams show both this protean quality of evaluation and the social relations of charity that they exemplify.

The COS first helped Matilda Gehrig, a worthy Austrian widow with small children, in 1893. By sewing fringe at home, Matilda earned about four dollars a week. Her parents, themselves poor and dependent on her brother, lived in another apartment in the same building. With a little charity and some decent medical care—for Matilda was in the early stages of tuberculosis—she stabilized her income enough to convince the COS, though not others who knew her, that she could manage on her own.

Within a few years, she married Cesar Romero, a gasfitter born in Cuba. Then, in 1898, again a widow, Matilda asked for help once more. By all accounts, Matilda was a meticulous housekeeper and excellent parent, nor could anyone fault her as lazy or question her morals. Still, her health limited Matilda's options by preventing her from taking heavy tasks or working in a laundry. How could she support herself until her children were old enough to work? Although the COS did not have a very good plan, Matilda did. Send her and the children to the country, she urged, where they could rent a whole house for the price of a Manhattan tenement, grow some of their food, and find occasional day's work.

The COS accepted Matilda's plan and set her up in Sussex, New Jersey, where she went to work at once on her vegetable and flower garden. She also had another idea: if the COS would send children to board with her, the fees for their care would allow her to be independent of charity. Matilda seemed an excellent candidate for a foster parent, and the COS began to send her boarders. Her long remarkable letters to the District Office on the progress of her domestic affairs and the condition of her boarders revealed Matilda as a devoted and skilled foster parent. Under her care, the children sent from New York City thrived happily.

One day Matilda's oldest daughter, Louise, working as a maid in a convalescent home, blurted out that her mother had hoarded five hundred dollars of insurance money in a bank. Louise often exaggerated, and her employer did not believe her assertion. Nonetheless, she reported it to the COS. Armed with a potential revelation of such magnitude, the district secretary herself traveled to Sussex to interrogate Matilda. Matilda broke down. Louise had invented the story about the insurance money; the little she had received all had been spent years ago. But Matilda was not a widow. Her second husband was alive.

Romero was deranged. He had abused Matilda and threatened to kill her if she ever left him. Unable to find work in New York as a gasfitter, he had returned with Matilda and the children to Cuba where he had family. Matilda left him there and returned to New York. When she had heard that he had returned, she asked the COS to move her to the country. She had even tried to live with him for two weeks in Sussex, but he was so crazy and abusive she threw him out.

Matilda had feared to tell the COS. If they knew she was not a widow, she thought, they might stop helping her. But her lie lay heavily on her conscience, and she was relieved to unburden herself. Later, she wrote the district secretary a long letter of explanation and apology, begging for understanding and mercy. The COS checked Matilda's story with her husband's best friend, who confirmed it. Romero was a wreck, drifting from one hostel to another, unable to work. Matilda, better off without him, was, for all practical purposes, a widow.

The COS attitude toward Matilda altered perceptibly after its staff learned her whole story. For a while, it continued to send her cash, clothes, and a few boarders, although not as many as she wanted. With the flimsiest of reasons, it decided that Matilda should be able to support herself. With no evidence that she treated the children it sent her with anything other than intelligent, loving care, it ended not only her irregular allowance but her boarders. Matilda pleaded with the district secretary to resume sending children. Without them, she pointed out, her small income could not support her family throughout the winter. The COS remained unmoved; Matilda had joined the undeserving poor.

Unlike Matilda Gehrig Romero, the COS always classified the Brighams as unworthy. Their contact with this native-born family of native New Yorkers began in 1891. At the time, the elder Brighams already were in their sixties. They lived with a granddaughter; their married son with his large family was in the same building. John Brigham, the father, did not seem very bright. He earned a little money stringing tags for ten cents a thousand. His married son was unemployed. Jennie Brigham, John's wife, clearly did not tell the truth; her story of her life varied every time she repeated it. The family, in fact, appeared to be professional beggars who exploited their granddaughter until she died late in 1891. The COS wanted nothing to do with the family, but, again and again, until the second decade of the twentieth century, it could not escape involvement. The reason usually was a request from someone to whom the Brighams had turned for charity, for the Brigham family appeared masters of New York's vast network of potential assistance. During these years John Brigham died, and Jennie's daughter-in-law sent her husband to prison for nonsupport and then left him. None of this changed the COS evaluation. The Brighams, worthless beggars, could support themselves. On June 12, 1911, a COS investigator concluded, "Family consists of woman and son, former aged, latter indolent, irresponsible and both persistent beggars."

Almost one year later, on May 9, 1912, a visitor, looking up another case in the house, stumbled across Jennie Brigham

living on the second floor rear in extreme old age and utter helplessness without care of any kind, without food, covered with vermin and suffering from sores all over her body. The bedding was nothing but rags, strips, and tufts of cotton. One could not even handle them, without its falling into more pieces. The place including the bed and the person was extremely filthy. The cuspidor stood on the stove filled with sputum and tobacco juice, matches etc. The only other occupant at the time of visit, was a cat, whom the old lady said was her only friend; that she had kept her warm. Visitor went out and bought a cotton blanket (49 cents) a pillow slip (8 cents) and a pint of milk (5 cents). Returned and fed her from a spoon about a cupful of the milk slightly heated. Visitor lifted the old lady out of her bed; re-arranged the material and covered it with half the blanket. Laid the old woman in it and covered her with the other half; then added a few of the dirty rags to give sufficient warmth. . . . Visitor then returned to DO [district office]. Reported the case at once and DS [district secretary] notified the Police Department and was told that the case would be removed to a hosp. at once. . . . May 16, 1912, Telephoned the Harlem [Hospital]. Learned that Mrs. B. died May 15 at 2:15 P.M.

NOTES

1. For extended stories from the clients' viewpoints, see Michael B. Katz, "Families and Welfare: A Philadelphia case," chap. 1 in *Poverty and Policy in American History* (New York: Academic, 1983), and Michael B. Katz, "The History of an Impudent Poor Woman in New York City from 1918 to 1923," in *The Uses of Charity,* ed. Peter Mandler (Philadelphia: University of Pennsylvania Press, 1991), 227–246.

2. The surviving COS case records are in the Rare Book and Manuscript Room of Butler Library, Columbia University. In some instances, I have supplemented the case records with material from manuscript censuses, assessment rolls, and insurance maps.

3. *The Express Gazette,* 15 April 1904, 89. My thanks to Stephen R. Krysko, Archivist, American Express Company, for this reference.

4. For the best single overview of the charity organization movement, see

Frank Dekker Watson, *The Charity Organization Movement in the United States: A Study in American Philanthropy* (New York: Macmillan, 1922); for New York, see Lillian B. Brandt, "Growth and Development of AICP and COS: A Preliminary and Exploratory Review" prepared for the Committee on the Institute of Welfare Research, Community Service Society of New York (1942), and Lillian B. Brandt, "The Charity Organization Society of the City of New York 1882–1907," in *Twenty-fifth Annual Report for the Year Ending September 30, 1907* (New York: United Charities Building, 1907).

5.   For useful information on the SPCC, see George K. Behlmer, *Child Abuse and Moral Reform in England, 1870–1908* (Stanford, Calif.: Stanford University Press, 1982); Catherine J. Ross, "Society's Children: The Care of Indigent Youngsters in New York City, 1875–1903" (Ph.D. diss., Yale University, 1977); Linda Gordon, *Heroes of Their Own Lives: The Politics and History of Family Violence, Boston, 1880–1960* (New York: Viking, 1988).

6.   Ross, "Society's Children," 154; *Humanizing the Greater City's Charity: The Work of the Department of Public Charities of the City of New York* (New York: Public Welfare Committee, 1917); *New York Charities Directory* (New York: The Charity Organization Society of the City of New York, 1900).

7.   *New York Charities Directory*, 97.

8.   Statistics and information on New York's development are from David C. Hammack, chaps. 2 and 3 in *Power and Society: Greater New York at the Turn of the Century* (New York: Russell Sage Foundation, 1982); Ira Rosenwaike, chaps. 4 and 5 and appendixes A–C in *Population History of New York City* (Syracuse, N.Y.: Syracuse University Press, 1972); Emanuel Tobier, "Manhattan's Business District in the Industrial Age," in *Power, Culture, and Place: Essays on New York City,* ed. John Hull Mollenkopf (New York: Russell Sage Foundation, 1988), 77–105.

9.   *Fourth Annual Report of the Central Council of the Charity Organization Society of the City of New York* (New York: Charity Organization Society, 1886), 21–22.

10.   *New York State Census, 1915,* Office of the New York County Clerk, 60 Chambers Street, Room 141b.

11.   James Weinstein, "Big Business and the Origins of Workmen's Compensation," *Labor History* 8, no. 2 (Spring 1967), 157; Carl Gersuny, *Work Hazards and Industrial Conflict* (Hanover, N.H.: University Press of New England, 1981), 20, 28.

12.   [Miss Hurlbutt] Association of Tuberculosis Clinics of New York City, "Study of Homes," 18 August 1916, Community Service Society collection, box 162, "Studies—Joint Committtee on Homes" folder, Rare Book and Manuscript Room, Butler Library, Columbia University, typescript.

13.   David Rosner, *A Once Charitable Enterprise: Hospitals and Health Care in Brooklyn and New York, 1885–1915* (New York: Cambridge University Press, 1982); Charles Rosenberg, "Social Class and Medical Care in the United States: The Rise and Fall of the Dispensary," in *Sickness and Health in America: Readings in the History of Medicine and Public Health,* ed. Judith Walzer Leavitt and Ronald L. Numbers (Madison: University of Wisconsin Press, 1978), 151–171.

14. Lillian Brandt, "On the Verge of Dependence," *Charities and Commons* 15 (1905–1906), 462–468. For a summary on the results of the first ten years of the Michigan Income Panel Dynamics study, see Greg J. Duncan, *Years of Poverty, Years of Plenty: The Changing Fortunes of American Workers and Their Families* (Ann Arbor: University of Michigan Press, 1984).

15. Michael B. Katz, *In the Shadow of the Poorhouse: A Social History of Welfare in America* (New York: Basic Books, 1986), 201; Susan Tiffin, *In Whose Best Interest? Child Welfare Reform in the Progressive Era* (Westport, Conn.: Greenwood, 1982), 121–130, 232–237; Roy Lubove, *The Struggle for Social Security, 1900–1935* (Cambridge, Mass.: Harvard University Press, 1968), 91–112.

16. New York City established a separate Domestic Relations Court in 1910. Magistrates also heard complaints involving nonsupport and desertion. See Raymond Moley, *Tribunes of the People: The Past and Future of the New York Magistrates' Courts* (New Haven, Conn.: Yale University Press, 1932), 29.

17. In this sense, relationships between mothers and sons echo those described by D. H. Lawrence, *Sons and Lovers* (New York: Boni and Liveright, 1989).

18. For examples of the transformation of institutional purposes by inmates and their families, see Barbara M. Brenzel, *Daughters of the State: A Social Portrait of the First Reform School for Girls in North America, 1846–1905* (Cambridge, Mass.: MIT Press, 1983), and Allen Steinberg, *The Transformation of Criminal Justice: Philadelphia, 1800–1880* (Chapel Hill: University of North Carolina Press, 1989).

19. The residential patterns in these cases are similar to those described by Gareth Stedman Jones, *Outcast London* (London: Oxford University Press, 1971). For housing in New York during this period, see Roy Lubove, *The Progressives and the Slums: Tenement House Reform in New York City, 1890–1917* (Pittsburgh, Penn.: University of Pittsburgh Press, 1962), and Donna R. Gabaccia, *From Sicily to Elizabeth Street: Housing and Social Change Among Italian Immigrants, 1880–1930* (Albany, N.Y.: State University of New York Press, 1984).

20. No literature exists on housekeepers or janitors. I have arrived at these conclusions from reading the case records.

21. I have dealt with this problem at length; see Michael B. Katz, *The Undeserving Poor: From the War on Poverty to the War on Welfare* (New York: Pantheon, 1990).

22. For the relationship between charity and gratitude, see Jones, *Outcast London,* 253.

3

ARNOLD R. HIRSCH

With or Without Jim Crow: Black Residential Segregation in the United States

Iᴛ ʜᴀs ʙᴇᴇɴ more than a quarter century since the black neighborhood of Watts erupted in a devastating riot that dramatized not only the racial tension in Los Angeles, but the "urban crisis" of the 1960s. If the perceived depth and nature of that crisis have varied with the ebb and flow of changing political currents, then the 1992 eruption of renewed violence and the pall of smoke that again blanketed the burning heart of central Los Angeles in the wake of the acquittal of the police officers accused of criminally assaulting Rodney King make it seem of interminable duration.

In historical terms, however, the rise of the *urban ghetto*—a massive, geographically continuous, isolated place of almost exclusively black residence and institutional life—is a relatively recent phenomenon. Scattered black enclaves and clusters of free people of color, fugitives, and slaves existed on the peripheries and in the less desirable regions of antebellum southern cities, and the Civil War hastened the growth of such areas as refugees from the countryside sought new life in the city. But nowhere in the United States—certainly not in the North nor in the war-ravaged South—could anything remotely resembling the modern ghetto be found by 1880. The emergence of the modern ghetto appeared in three stages, the first occurring in the half century between 1880 and the beginning of the New Deal in 1933. The second, linked to a growing federal presence in urban affairs and evolving sensibilities on race, spanned the three-and-a-half decades between 1933 and 1968. The third, and current, stage encompasses the post–civil rights era and is characterized by persistently high levels of racial segregation despite the legal prohibition of

discrimination and changing economic realities that are gravely altering the fabric of life in urban America.

This pattern stemmed from a series of dramatic demographic shifts.
The movement of black population from rural to urban areas, from
the South to the North, and the rise of the suburbs each played an
instrumental role. Roughly 90 percent of America's blacks lived in
the South when Abraham Lincoln signed the Emancipation Proclama-
tion, and there was little change for nearly a half-century more. A
notable spontaneous migration of southern blacks, however, occurred
between 1879 and 1881 when some sixty thousand caught "Kansas
fever"; and although that did little to alter the overall picture, it did
mark the beginning of a massive black exodus from the rural South.[1]

Rapidly industrializing cities in the North such as New York and
Chicago registered the most spectacular gains in black population.
Between 1890 and 1930, New York's black population increased from
36,000 to 328,000; Chicago's grew from 14,000 to 234,000. These two
metropolitan giants, moreover, were just the vanguard of a much
broader movement.[2] The coming of World War I, the subsequent cutoff
of European immigration, and the northern cities' insatiable demand
for unskilled labor fueled a black migration that continued at an
accelerated pace through the 1920s.[3] By 1940, the South had claimed
only 77 percent of the nation's blacks, and it was poised on the brink
of still greater losses. The mobilization for World War II and the
postwar economic boom later provided an even stronger impetus for
movement, and the largest decennial black outmigration from the
South occurred between 1940 and 1950. Moreover, the flight from the
South continued at high levels for the next twenty years. The mechanization of southern agriculture finally sundered the ties binding the
black masses to the land and, between 1940 and 1970, almost five
million blacks left the region, largely for the cities of the Northeast
and Midwest. When the exodus apparently came to an end in the
1970s, the South's share of America's black population had fallen to
53 percent.[4]

This movement was part of an even larger phenomenon that encompassed the South as well as the North—the urbanization of blacks. In
1880, only 12.9 percent of the blacks in the United States lived in
"urban" areas; 28.3 percent of whites did so. By 1920, a majority of
whites had become urbanized, whereas barely one-third of the black
population could make that claim. In 1950, however, the U.S. black
population became a predominantly urban one, and ten years later,
blacks were more highly urbanized than whites. The underside of this
process was the near disappearance of blacks from agricultural America. Between 1920 and 1981, the black farm population declined by 96

percent, and by 1981, only 1 percent of the nation's 26.5 million blacks could be counted as farm residents.[5]

The twentieth-century movement of blacks from the farms into American cities coincided with a white exodus out of the city to the suburbs. These parallel parades meant that residential segregation has been increasing for most of the modern era. By 1970, Washington, D.C., and Atlanta held black majorities; the next census added Detroit, Baltimore, and New Orleans to that list. At the same time, throughout the post–World War II era, the suburbs of the largest U.S. cities remained overwhelmingly white. New York suburbs were 4.8 percent black in 1960 and 7.6 percent black twenty years later; the Chicago black suburban population stood at 2.9 percent and only 5.6 percent during those same years. Indeed, as late as 1980, an examination of fourteen of the nation's largest cities (those with a black population of at least two hundred thousand) revealed that none of the industrial cities of the Northeast and Midwest had even a 10-percent black suburban population.[6]

There has been some recent change, but its meaning is by no means clear. One finding of the 1980 census is that the 100-year black migration out of the South has been reversed.[7] This does not represent any new massive movement from the North, and simply reflects the continued urbanization of rural blacks and the development of the so-called Sunbelt. U.S. cities and the black presence within them are still growing—it is just that the most significant urban growth of the 1970s occurred not in the tier of northern industrial states that stretches from the Great Lakes to the East Coast, but rather in the South and West.

Perhaps even more significant (if also more ambiguous) is the revelation by the 1980 census that, for the first time, the increased black presence in the suburbs affected the group's overall distribution. In 1970, 58.2 percent of all blacks lived in central cities; the 1980 findings showed a net drop to 55.7 percent.[8] Undoubtedly, thousands of black individuals—part of a growing nonwhite middle class—have been making the traditional trek to suburbia in search of better homes and schools, a more congenial environment, and expanded opportunities. It would be a mistake, however, merely to assume that the black movement of the 1970s and 1980s reflected the white experience of the 1950s and 1960s. In addition, it certainly would be rash to assume that such figures represent the imminent dispersal of densely concentrated inner-city black populations. That the five cities—St. Louis; New Orleans; Atlanta; Washington, D.C.; and Memphis—with the most notable black suburban populations ranging from 10.9 percent to 21.0 percent are all southern metropolises indicates, indeed, that other explanations exist.[9] In these instances, at least, it seems that the recent spurt of metropolitan Sunbelt growth has swept over peripheral black enclaves that bordered the small southern towns of the nineteenth century. Isolated and poor in earlier years, the residents of such areas recently have been subjected to a surrounding flood of white migrants and have found themselves magically transformed into "suburbanites" by the census. That Houston, New Orleans, Memphis, and Dallas all show dramatic proportionate drops in their still significant black "suburban" populations suggests this possibility.[10] It also is likely that some of the black suburbanites detected by the 1980 census are simply those in the vanguard of traditional ghetto expansion as it spills over immobile city boundaries. Black occupation of an older, inner ring of suburbs and the "whitening" of the "exurbs" (those communities added to the fringes of metropolitan areas between 1970 and 1980) points to this possibility.[11]

It is evident, however, that the years between 1880 and 1980 did witness a massive and sustained process of black urbanization. In those same years, racial issues became national in scope. The period also witnessed the emergence and maturation of the modern urban ghetto in the United States. The vast demographic shifts of that century assembled the raw materials that presaged such a development. The actual fashioning of those ghettos, however, was hardly a "natural" process; the decisions of uncounted individuals and institutions— both willful and inadvertent—contributed mightily to that outcome.

The Emergence of the Ghetto

The upsurge in urban black population in the United States meant, universally, an increase in residential segregation. The process began in the postbellum South where blacks frequently represented 40 percent or more of the urban populations. No southern city possessed a single, all-encompassing ghetto, but many towns had multiple clusters of black residents, frequently located on the urban periphery, surrounding a largely white core. Antebellum neighborhoods that contained significant numbers of blacks and their institutional supports (such as churches and schools) and the camps established for the freed slaves during the Civil War often served as the bases for future black territorial expansion. A leading student of southern cities during this era subsequently concluded that, by 1890, separate black and white neighborhoods had "dominated the urban landscape."[12] However, even though the trend toward increasing segregation was unmistakable, some racial mixing still could be found in many of these clusters. Moreover, the pattern of racial separation showed itself most clearly when small units of measurement such as "linear blocks" were used. The vast urban expanses of almost exclusively black settlement that propelled themselves into the national consciousness during the 1960s were twentieth-century northern creations. In the end, nineteenth-century southern ghettoization was limited by economic, technological, and spatial constraints. Not yet feeling the full weight of the industrial revolution, these generally small, compact southern towns lacked the capacity to sort out their populations by either class or race. They continued to display residential patterns characteristic of a race-relations system that demanded close contacts within a hierarchical framework. Social—not spatial—distance governed relationships across the southern color line.

On the eve of the Great Migration of southern blacks, the rapidly industrializing northern cities, proportionately, held infinitesimal black populations.[13] Generally, as was the case in the South, they lived in scattered clusters. With the gradual and then the accelerated increase in black population that characterized the years between 1880 and 1930, however, a rapid progression toward larger, more densely compacted black neighborhoods became evident. The process proceeded most noticeably and quickly in the region's metropolitan giants: New York and Chicago. Other northern cities—Philadelphia, Detroit, Cleveland, and Pittsburgh, for example—followed at their own pace, but all proceeded in the same direction; in every case, blacks gathered first in blocks, concentrated their residences in small clusters, and shared their larger neighborhoods with whites. As early as the 1890s in Chicago, however, the trend toward increasing segregation and white movement out of these areas of black concentration was clear. Indeed, in compiling measures of residential segregation (indexes of dissimilarity) in ten northern cities between 1910 and 1930, Karl and Alma Taeuber discovered a marked, dramatic increase in the separation of blacks and native whites in every case. Using an index of dissimilarity where the value zero represented perfect integration (each block possessed a proportional share of blacks and whites) and 100 signified total segregation (each block contained only whites and blacks, but not both), they found that the segregation indexes ranged between 44.1 and 66.8 in 1910, and that they ballooned to a low of 61.4 and a high of 86.7 by 1930 (those numbers represent the minimum percentage of nonwhites who would have to move to achieve complete integration).[14]

The forces behind the rapid separation of blacks and whites were many, and not all were related to race. The overwhelming majority of black southern migrants, for example, was poor, and the brute facts of economic life greatly restricted the housing opportunities available to them. Poor people clustered in poor neighborhoods with others like themselves. However, if economic realities alone operated, the poor of all backgrounds and colors would share the same areas. Such was not the case. Whites of literally dozens of nationalities did mix in the streets of U.S. cities, but blacks increasingly found themselves excluded from those neighborhoods. The cultural cauldrons of urban America did produce identifiably "ethnic" colonies, but the most recent scholarship has convincingly demonstrated that the immigrants' communities were nowhere homogeneous, and that their "ghettos" were temporary way stations that oversaw the ultimate dispersal— not the increasing concentration—of their residents.[15]

Another partial explanation can be found in the argument that at least some of the clustering was voluntary, that it represented an expression of cultural affinity and that these strangers in a strange land sought neighbors of like backgrounds to ease their transition into urban, industrial America. There is something to this, but, again, the comparison with European immigrants is instructive. The "new" immigrants from southern and eastern Europe who flooded America at the turn of the twentieth century sought the solace of ethnic familiarity and built institutions and evolved behavioral patterns to preserve and sustain their cultures. In time, though, their narrowly ethnic institutions eroded everywhere, and their behavior adapted to the opportunities and choices America had laid before them. They dispersed residentially, and if the desire for "community" remained strong, they later found that the telephone and the automobile could overcome the need for geographical proximity. As powerful as their cultures and desires were, they could not withstand the lure of "Americanization."[16]

The "cultural affinities" of the blacks, however, have never been put to the same test. During the initial period of ghetto formation, blacks—whatever their economic status—lacked the same choices (residential and otherwise) that had been laid before the immigrants and their children. In the absence of such free choice, any conclusions concerning the degree of "voluntary" black segregation must necessarily remain speculative and, potentially, misleading. Any assumption that centripetal forces within the black community outweighed external pressures in producing the degree of residential segregation that was visible by the Great Depression is dangerously off target.

A final, crucial complex of "nonracial" factors, however, involves the timing of both the black migration and the economic development of the cities that received the blacks. The technological advances and mechanized production associated with industrialization gave rise to the modern corporation, mass markets, and large-scale economic enterprises that altered the face of urban America. Combined with the rapid accumulation of wealth, the seemingly acute visibility of alarming class, ethnic, and racial differences, and the appearance of mechanized forms of mass transit, the specific effects of these technological advances and mechanized production led to the rapid specialization of urban land use. It was not simply that blacks were being separated from whites, but that industrial districts were being kept separate from commercial ones, and that both of those existed apart from the purely residential areas that appeared. The residential areas were divided not only by race, but by class, ethnicity, and the age of the residents as well. Economic and technological advances permitted urbanization on a scale never before possible. The preindustrial *walking city*—a compact settlement that could be crossed easily on foot and contained all manner of residents and enterprises side by side— was no more.[17]

Even here, though, the pattern of black settlement within the context of the industrial revolution was unique. If job location and class status determined the residential choices of most urban workers, then race, not occupation, was still the best predictor of black residence. If Irish shoemakers lived closer to German shoemakers than their ethnic brethren by the early twentieth century, then the black shoemaker could still be found in an emerging all-black ghetto. Industrialization permitted a greater degree of segregation (of all kinds) than was heretofore possible; however, the economic imperatives and technological possibilities of that process affected blacks in a distinctive manner.[18] "Nonracial" forces could not have produced the extreme levels of segregation in evidence by the Great Depression.

Other forces were at work that were not themselves products of malicious racial intent, despite the racist context of the age.[19] Local conditions and what can perhaps best be called historical "accidents" further conditioned the development of these embryonic urban ghettos and provided the peculiar twists that, ultimately, must be examined in each individual case. Two examples should suffice to illustrate the point.

In Chicago, several small black enclaves on the near South Side were devastated by a fire in 1874 that forced their resettlement. The survivors moved farther south and consolidated themselves into what became the core of Chicago's famous "Black Belt." The coming of the World's Columbian Exposition in 1893 also contributed as speculators purchased South Side property and hastily erected cheap rooming houses, apartments, and hotels for the tourists along the major transit arteries leading to the fair. The closing of the exposition and the onset of the grim depression that gripped the nation in the mid-1890s left the speculators holding thousands of costly vacancies. The location of these accommodations along South State Street and Michigan and Wabash avenues, their proximity to the existing black settlement, the simultaneous arrival of large numbers of southern black migrants, and the unavailability of "black" housing elsewhere led to the emergence of a major black colony.[20]

In New York, land speculation also played a similar role in the appearance of the nation's best-known black metropolis, Harlem. Located eight miles from city hall, Harlem remained a "village of shanties and huts" throughout the mid-nineteenth century. A burst of growth triggered by New York's modernizing economy led to Harlem's annexation in 1873, and between 1878 and 1881, three elevated railroad lines extended as far north as 129th Street. Speculators who had earlier followed the tracks of New York's horsecars sparked a frenzy of development until the bubble of inflated land values popped from 1904 to 1905. Those who erected apartments in advance of anticipated railroad extensions found themselves with unrentable vacancies, and even after mass transit provided access, property owners found a glut of accommodations producing the same effect. Enterprising black real estate agents, especially Philip A. Payton and his Afro-American Realty Company, stepped into the soft market and capitalized on the massive turn-of-the-century black migration to New York and the forced relocation of those blacks who had been displaced by rapidly expanding commercial districts. They provided a steady income to the desperate white property owners from whom they leased buildings and facilitated the turnover to black occupancy. By 1920, Harlem's midsection was predominantly black, and the stream of southern migrants completed the transition before the decade was out.[21]

Such rapidly developing poor black neighborhoods produced a host of social problems, and even the attempts to alleviate them further solidified the emerging pattern. Progressive reformers did not ignore the needs of an urbanizing black population, and although their numbers included those who fully supported the color line, there were those who chafed under its restrictions. None, however, had the inclination or the power to challenge it. Settlement houses in working-class neighborhoods, thus, catered to their surrounding immigrant communities, and—whether the impetus came from the immigrants themselves or a sympathetic staff—they usually discouraged black participation in their programs. Those houses set up to serve blacks generally did so on a segregated basis in predominantly black blocks or neighborhoods. The provision of their social services attracted and held more black settlers and discouraged continued white residence around them. Even attempts at reform consequently accelerated and reinforced the move toward residential segregation. That situation did not change in the years after World War I. Housing "reformers" and community planners in the conservative 1920s almost invariably diverted resources and attention from the poor population, worked within the color line, and aggravated the tendencies toward segregation and deterioration that characterized black neighborhoods.[22]

Despite these pressures and forces, however, many blacks—especially those in the developing middle class—made frequent, repeated attempts to move beyond the confines of identifiably "black" neighborhoods. They were rebuffed not by invisible, impersonal, or anonymous forces, but by the overwhelming application of explicitly racial restrictions that reflected the desires of the dominant white majority. No other group had to face such an onslaught; it was the distinguishing characteristic that separated the black ghetto from the ethnic slum.[23]

The first club often picked up in the battle to maintain the homogeneity of white neighborhoods involved the use of legal restrictions and attempts to enlist the power of the state. With southern cities feeling the first wave of black migration most sharply, it is not surprising that the movement for legalized residential segregation appeared as part of the the broader surge of turn-of-the-century Jim Crow legislation. The movement of a black lawyer and his schoolteacher wife into a white Baltimore neighborhood in 1910 triggered the movement to pass racial zoning ordinances that would racially segment American cities. Baltimore's ordinance, which served as a model, was soon succeeded by similar laws in Norfolk, Ashland, Roanoke, and Portsmouth, Virginia; Winston-Salem, North Carolina; Greenville, South Carolina; and Atlanta, Georgia. Between 1913 and 1916, racial zoning laws were adopted by Louisville, St. Louis, Oklahoma City, and New Orleans. A legal showdown sponsored by the National Association for the Advancement of Colored People in Louisville resulted in a 1917 U.S. Supreme Court decision (*Buchanan* v. *Warley*) that invalidated such laws. Several attempts were made to resurrect these ordinances in the 1920s in Norfolk, New Orleans, and Dallas; Winston-Salem even made a last-gasp attempt as late as 1940. In each case, however, they were struck down. Almost exclusively a southern approach, these laws were occasionally debated in northern cities such as Chicago, but never passed, save for the lone exception of Ku Klux Klan–controlled Indianapolis in 1927.[24]

Northern cities took a different tack and, indeed, most cities in the wake of *Buchanan* v. *Warley* opted to limit black residential movement through the use of private agreements—racially restrictive covenants. These contracts prohibited property owners from selling or renting their homes to "undesirables." Especially popular between World War I and World War II, these covenants were ultimately used against a wide range of racial, ethnic, and religious minorities. It was always clear, however, that blacks remained the primary targets; in St. Louis, for example, 99 percent of the covenants executed specified blacks alone as the group to be proscribed. When, in the course of city growth and suburban expansion, entire new subdivisions were placed under such covenants, blacks found themselves legally excluded from vast stretches of the urban landscape. Unlike the racial ordinances of the South, the U.S. Supreme Court gave its tacit approval to lower court rulings that held such covenants valid and enforceable in 1926 (*Corrigan* v. *Buckley*).[25]

Informal, unspoken, day-to-day business practices further buttressed such formal, legalistic restrictions and, ultimately, were probably even more instrumental in creating and maintaining the pattern of residential segregation. Local real estate boards and companies acted as so many gatekeepers, steering blacks into all-black areas and preserving the racial homogeneity of white neighborhoods. Even in a city such as Milwaukee, with its comparatively small black population, real estate agents supplemented a network of restrictive covenants (90 percent of the plats filed after 1910 contained some restrictions banning the sale of property to blacks) with "gentlemen's agreements" not to rent or sell to blacks outside a "sharply delineated area." Where black numbers were far more substantial, as in Chicago, local real estate boards were more outspoken. There, in 1917, the Chicago Real Estate Board acknowledged the need to provide more black housing, but hoped to prevent "promiscuous" sales by advising its members first to fill in existing areas of black concentration and then furnish accommodations only in blocks contiguous to the ghetto. The St. Louis Real Estate Exchange went even further. It simply established "unrestricted colored districts" in which property might be transferred to blacks and declared the rest of the city "off limits" to them. If any blacks should press their interest in purchasing property in white neighborhoods, they almost invariably ran up against the reluctance of financial institutions to provide the capital for such transactions. The private sector in the North, whose pressures were brought to bear on embryonic black industrial concentrations, accomplished what the southern public sector, facing long-established, substantial black communities, could not.[26]

Before the Great Depression, the private housing industry's position on race was perhaps best exemplified by Nathan William MacChesney, a lawyer for the National Association of Real Estate Boards (NAREB) and author of a widely accepted text on real estate law. Not only did MacChesney draft a model restrictive covenant for general use (blacks alone were singled out in the document as they were in his text), but he also added to the NAREB code of ethics an amendment in 1924 that prohibited the introduction of "members of any race or nationality" into neighborhoods where they threatened property values. He also subsequently drafted a model real estate licensing act (one eventually adopted by thirty-two states) that permitted state commissions to revoke the license of any agent who violated the NAREB code—and the failure to discriminate on racial grounds now constituted a breach of professional ethics. A NAREB publication, *Fundamentals of Real Estate Practice* (1943), summarized the housing industry's attitude toward those blacks who pursued the American dream:

The prospective buyer might be a bootlegger who could cause considerable annoyance to his neighbors, a madam who had a number of Call Girls on her string, a gangster who wants a screen for his activities by living in a better neighborhood, a colored man of means who was giving his children a college education and thought they were entitled to live among whites. . . . No matter what the motive or character of the would-be purchaser, if the deal would instigate a form of blight, then certainly the well-meaning broker must work against its consummation.[27]

Supplementing the activities of real estate agents and leaders who refused to facilitate black purchases in white areas were the actions taken in the neighborhoods themselves. Local improvement associations conducted covenant-writing campaigns, tried to inculcate a sense of communal solidarity, and frequently served as vehicles for those rallying against the black "invasion" of their neighborhoods. When pressed, they exerted considerable social pressure on those within their reach and intimidated both potential white sellers and black buyers if all else failed.[28]

Ultimately, however, violence served as a last resort that underscored the general determination to confine the growing black population. The racial tension generated by demographic change and the strains accompanying World War I culminated in a series of racial explosions in 1919. Between April and October 1919, at least twenty-five cities and towns suffered serious rioting that produced more than one hundred fatalities. Violence, it seemed, dogged the black movement from the country to the city, striking both New Orleans and New York in 1900; Atlanta in 1906; Springfield, Ohio, in 1904; and Springfield,

Illinois, in 1908. The eruption of East St. Louis, Illinois, in 1917 was a harbinger of what the postwar years had to offer. The worst urban rioting of 1919, in chronological sequence, struck Charleston; Longview, Texas; Washington, D.C.; Chicago; and Omaha. Although many racial factors contributed to the violence, the confrontation over housing was an important component in many cases, and in the single worst conflagration—the Chicago riot where thirty-eight people died and more than five hundred were injured—it was a central issue.[29]

The 1919 Chicago riot itself occurred within the context of a broader wave of housing-related violence. Between July 1, 1917, and March 1, 1921, fifty-eight homes were bombed—an average of one bombing every twenty days for nearly four years—by those people who were trying to restrict black areas of residence. Invariably, homes owned by blacks in fringe or "white" areas were targeted, as were the homes and offices of the real estate agents (white and black) who handled such properties. Under the cover of the riot itself, white gangs roamed the edges of the "Black Belt," committing, according to the state commission that investigated the riot, "premeditated depredations" against black individuals and property found outside the popularly conceived boundaries of the ghetto. In but a single case, nine black families in the 5000 block of Shields Avenue had their homes vandalized and torched by such mobs; blacks were driven out of the area, and it was twenty-eight years before anyone sold or rented a home on that block to blacks again. In 1947, when another black family moved to that street, it took but one week for them to find their garage mysteriously ablaze. The "chilling effect" of such actions was manifest; there was no more direct method of declaring certain white neighborhoods off limits to blacks.[30]

If Chicago represents perhaps an extreme example, it was by no means alone. Cleveland also experienced attacks by white gangs on black homes during the World War I era, beginning in 1917 and continuing through the 1920s. The violence directed at blacks who attempted to move into suburban or outlying areas was especially brutal, and when one such victim appealed to the mayor of Garfield Heights for help, he was told simply that "colored people had no right to purchase such a nice home." With the metropolitan frontier guarded by well-to-do people, black citizens of Cleveland also found their housing choices restricted by the presence and hostility of inner-city ethnics who jealously patrolled their own "turf."[31] Detroit similarly experienced house bombings in 1917, saw such attacks escalate in spring 1919, and found them "frequent" occurrences in the 1920s. The most publicized incident of the decade arose when Detroit physician Ossian Sweet and his family repelled a white mob from their doorstep by shooting into it; Sweet was tried for murder, and it took Clarence Darrow to get him off.[32]

Once a substantial black presence and the pattern of segregation had been established, additional forces came into play. In the North, particularly, city after city created dual housing markets, one for whites and another for blacks. Given the rapid increase in the number of urban blacks and the limited housing made available to them, their market was characterized by scarcity. The cost of black housing rose sharply, and nonwhites not only had to pay more than whites for equivalent quarters, but also had to devote a proportionately greater share of their incomes to housing. Large units were divided into numerous small ones, and a host of urban problems—particularly those related to poverty, overcrowding, and high population densities—appeared in aggravated form. From the late 1920s to the late 1940s, the dual housing market, the cost of black housing, restrictive covenants, and a severe housing shortage stabilized ghetto borders; modest Depression-era population increases and more substantial war-related ones were simply, and necessarily, absorbed within them. The appearance of post–World War II suburban alternatives for whites, however, ended the shortage, destabilized the inner-city racial frontier, and transformed the dual housing market into a powerful engine that promoted neighborhood change. Ghetto building proved profitable. The blacks' pent-up demand for new accommodations, the increased ability of many to pay for them, and the higher prices they could be charged produced a massive postwar movement of central-city blacks who rushed into the vacancies left by suburban-bound whites. The postwar era consequently witnessed the rapid expansion and reconstitution of new ghetto boundaries. It was this second wave of black migration after 1940, this second era of ghetto formation, that produced the vast geographical concentrations of urban blacks that generated the "long, hot summers" of the 1960s.[33]

The establishment of substantial, segregated urban black communities also gave rise to economic, social, and political forces within those communities that had a vested interest in their persistence. Whether black businesses catering to a concentrated black clientele, ministers tending their flocks, or politicians shepherding their voters, clearly the ghetto of the early twentieth century produced among its leaders many who would view the dispersal of urban blacks only with misgivings, and some that, at times, depended on the ghetto's very creators for their own sustenance. However, the ghetto also produced more than a claque of self-serving manipulators or the "tangle of pathology" that has long been associated with it. It was also a self-sustaining institutional and cultural entity that nourished the social and intellectual networks that made the flowering of a Harlem Renaissance possible. Furthermore, it provided the personal freedom that permitted blacks to organize, coalesce, and pursue their own strategies in coping with modern America. Ideologically, the movements for self-help, race pride, and black nationalism found a natural home in the black metropolis. Although certainly in no way responsible for the rise of the ghetto, blacks had quickly pushed roots down into the fresh soil of these new communities and were very much a part of them. Alone, the forces emanating from within these increasingly complex black settlements could not determine the future development or expansion of the northern ghetto; but, they rendered less clear the choices confronting urban blacks after World War II and weakened the resistance to outside forces that assured the continued segregation of a greatly enlarged black presence.[34]

The Ghetto Sustained

That American cities achieved an exceptionally high degree of racial segregation and maintained those levels throughout the post–World War II period seems beyond dispute. The Taeubers' formulation of indexes of dissimilarity for more than one hundred cities revealed increasing segregation between 1940 and 1950, and a seeming reversal of that trend between 1950 and 1960.[35] There is little question that residential segregation continued until 1950, but the apparent reversal from 1950 to 1960 merits a second look. Given the historical pattern of ghetto expansion, the lower segregation indexes found in 1960 might well have indicated nothing more than the temporary mixture of border areas and new black provinces in an age of rapid white flight from the central city. Ghetto boundaries were being redrawn after nearly two decades of relative stability; the statistical snapshot taken by the census in 1960 caught that process in full motion. Indeed, these cities were not desegregating in the 1950s—they were expanding their ghettos.

There is also a problem in trying to make a single, sound generalization about the residential tendencies of all blacks on the basis of studies that encompassed literally hundreds of cities and metropolitan areas. That is true of the Taeubers' work as well as later examinations of the 1970 census. The towns included in such studies were of varying ages and sizes, and some—especially those caught in the broad net cast by the scrutiny of literally all American standard metropolitan statistical areas (SMSAs) in 1970—included infinitesimal black populations. Equal consideration of all cities regardless of size or the proportion of their black populations, reveals a detectable move away from the intense segregation found at midcentury. This was especially so in smaller metropolitan areas with small black populations; segregation levels dropped sharply in such places. An examination of large concentrations of blacks, however, reveals a very different picture.

The 1980 census counted fourteen major American cities with black populations of at least 200,000. Geographically, they represented a fair sample spread across the North (New York, Chicago, Detroit, Philadelphia, and Cleveland); the South (Houston, New Orleans, Memphis, Atlanta, and Dallas); the border states (Washington, D.C., Baltimore, and St. Louis); and the West (Los Angeles). Together, these metropolitan giants contained nearly 10.4 million blacks, or approximately 40 percent of all blacks in 1980. An examination of the indexes of dissimilarity for these major population centers revealed consistently high levels of segregation between 1940 and 1980 that were fiercely resistant to change.

Between 1940 and 1950, ten of these fourteen cities increased their levels of racial segregation (see Table 3.1). The four exceptions included Chicago and Cleveland, whose extraordinarily high indexes dropped to 92.1 and 91.5, respectively, seemingly because they simply had nowhere else to go; Detroit and Washington, D.C., registered minute decreases, from 89.9 to 88.8 and from 81.0 to 80.1, respectively. For all fourteen cities, the segregation indexes ranged from a low of 79.9 (for Memphis) to a high of 95.0 (for Chicago) in 1940, and from 80.1 (for Washington, D.C.) to 92.9 (for St. Louis) in 1950. The figures for 1960 show something of a reversal: eight cities display decreases in segregation and six show increases. The changes were so slight, however, that the range for all the cities remained virtually unaltered, with a low of 79.3 (for New York) and a high of 94.6 (for Dallas). The same held true for 1970. Central-city indexes constructed by Annemette Sorensen, Karl E. Taeuber, and Leslie J. Hollingsworth, Jr., managed to detail marginal declines in segregation for all fourteen urban areas during the 1960s by ignoring the suburbs. Still, the range of indexes remained remarkably stable, with a low of 73.0 (for New York) and a high of 92.7 (for Dallas) in 1970. Indeed, in 1940, thirteen of the fourteen cities had indexes of at least 80.0, and four were more than 90.0; in 1970, no fewer than eleven were still above 80.0, and four remained higher than 90.0 (see Table 3.1).

The segregation indexes available for both cities and their suburbs in 1970 are not directly comparable with the earlier studies, because they are based on census tracts, whereas the others drew their data

TABLE 3.1

Block-based Indexes of Dissimilarity for Fourteen Cities, 1940, 1950, 1960, and 1970

City	1940	1950	1960	1970
New York	86.8	87.3	79.3	73.0
Chicago	95.0	92.1	92.6	88.8
Detroit	89.9	88.8	84.5	80.9
Philadelphia	88.0	89.0	87.1	83.2
Los Angeles	84.2	84.6	81.8	78.4
Washington, D.C.	81.0	80.1	79.7	77.7
Houston	84.5	91.5	93.7	90.0
Baltimore	90.1	91.3	89.6	88.3
New Orleans	81.0	84.9	86.3	83.1
Memphis	79.9	86.4	92.0	91.8
Atlanta	87.4	91.5	93.6	91.5
Dallas	80.2	88.4	94.6	92.7
Cleveland	92.0	91.5	91.3	89.0
St. Louis	92.6	92.9	90.5	89.3

SOURCE: Annemette Sorensen, Karl E. Taeuber, and Leslie J. Hollingsworth, Jr., "Indexes of Racial Residential Segregation for 109 Cities in the United States, 1940–1970," *Sociological Focus* 8 (April 1975), 125–141.

from city blocks. Tracts are larger units that mask the segregation within them and, thus, yield generally lower indexes of dissimilarity. However, because tract-based indexes exist for both 1960 and 1970, it is still possible to chart the path of change during the 1960s for metropolitan areas as well as the cities themselves.

Over that ten-year period, nine of the fourteen metropolitan areas increased their levels of segregation, four showed slight reductions, and one remained unchanged (Table 3.2). Again, the levels of segregation evident in all the SMSAs remained consistently high (tract-based indexes for the metropolitan areas in 1970 ranged between 73.8 and 91.2). The handful of decreases registered were proportionately smaller than the gains in segregation posted in the majority of cases. In none of the four instances where metropolitan areas lowered their scores was the drop as much as 2.5 percent—indeed, in two of the cases, it was less than 1 percent. In contrast, five of the metropolitan areas with higher segregation scores in 1970 boosted them by at least 4 percent, and four of them did so by 6 percent or more (see Table 3.2).

Perhaps the most startling finding—one that spans both block and

TABLE 3.2

Tract-based Indexes of Dissimilarity for Fourteen Cities and Their Metropolitan Areas, 1960 and 1970

City	1960		1970	
	Central city	**SMSA**	**Central city**	**SMSA**
New York	75.2	74.4	71.6	73.8
Chicago	91.8	91.2	91.0	91.2
Detroit	80.4	87.1	78.2	88.9
Philadelphia	79.0	77.1	76.8	78.0
Los Angeles	85.4	89.2	88.6	88.5
Washington, D.C.	66.4	77.7	72.3	81.1
Houston	80.4	80.4	82.2	78.4
Baltimore	83.0	82.4	84.3	81.0
New Orleans	67.7	65.0	70.9	74.2
Memphis	79.7	72.7	84.4	78.9
Atlanta	83.1	77.1	83.4	81.7
Dallas	88.8	81.2	91.7	86.9
Cleveland	85.6	89.6	86.7	90.2
St. Louis	84.4	85.9	83.8	86.5

SOURCE: Thomas L. Van Valey, Wade Clark Roof, and Jerome E. Wilcox, "Trends in Residential Segregation, 1960–1970," *American Journal of Sociology* 82 (January 1977), 826–844.

tract data, the 1940s and 1950s, as well as the 1960s—was the steady and significant increase in segregation found in the five major southern cities under examination. The tract-based data revealed steadily rising levels of segregation that continued through 1970. Even the more optimistic study by Sorensen and colleagues, however, confirmed that Houston, New Orleans, Memphis, Atlanta, and Dallas were all considerably more segregated in 1970 than 1940, and by 1970, all save New Orleans had registered segregation indexes that topped ninety (see Tables 3.1 and 3.2). The rise of the Sunbelt, the modernization of the South, and the demise of Jim Crow was accompanied by a rapid separation of urban blacks and whites.

Data drawn from the 1980 census compels the conclusion that little has changed. Although the measurable levels of segregation decreased in thirteen of the fourteen cases at hand (New York was the lone exception), the changes were miniscule (the average decline for the four northern cities other than New York was but 2.7 percent). Furthermore, the overall range of the segregation indexes (68.3 to

TABLE 3.3

**Tract-based Indexes of Dissimilarity of Blacks from "Anglos"
for Fourteen U.S. Metropolitan Areas, 1970 and 1980**

City	1970	1980
New York	81.0	82.0
Chicago	91.9	87.8
Detroit	88.4	86.7
Philadelphia	79.5	78.8
Los Angeles	91.0	81.1
Washington, D.C.	81.1	70.1
Houston	78.1	69.5
Baltimore	81.9	74.7
New Orleans	73.1	68.3
Memphis	75.9	71.6
Atlanta	82.1	78.5
Dallas–Fort Worth[a]	86.9	77.1
Cleveland	90.8	87.5
St. Louis	84.7	81.3

SOURCE: Adapted from Douglas S. Massey and Nancy A. Denton, "Trends in the Residential Segregation of Blacks, Hispanics, and Asians: 1970–1980," *American Sociological Review* 52 (December 1987), 802–825.

NOTE: In calculating specifically the index of dissimilarity of blacks from "Anglos," the findings here are not strictly comparable with those cited earlier. However, in providing consistent and comparable figures for both 1970 and 1980, it is possible to chart the course of change over that decade.

[a]Fort Worth was included in these calculations; it was not included in the earlier studies cited.

87.8) appeared at least as high as that generally found in 1930. Nationally, as expected, declines in segregation were greatest in rapidly growing cities with small black populations in the South and, especially, the West. The large ghettos of the slow-growing or declining metropolises in the northern industrial heartland remained nearly as spatially isolated in 1980 as in 1970 (see Table 3.3).

The findings on black suburbanization were similarly discouraging. A 1984 study that embraced 1,600 suburbs in forty-four metropolitan areas concluded that, in the North, blacks have been concentrating in those suburbs that already have a disproportionate share of nonwhites. They have gained access to an inner ring of older suburbs, especially those with high population densities that sit astride central-city borders. In the South, the clear evidence of increasing segregation around Atlanta and Miami appeared exceptional, but the authors found that the decreasing levels of statistical segregation they detected elsewhere in the region reflected nothing more than the white displacement of older black settlements. In short, they saw continuity in the existing pattern of segregation and held little hope that black suburbanization—as it had developed until 1980—represented any significant reversal of that process.[36]

The pattern of black urbanization since 1930 consequently has produced a "second ghetto" that can be distinguished from the "first ghetto" of the World War I era on both quantitative and qualitative grounds. The quantitative measures are astounding—the modern black metropolis simply dwarfs its earlier counterparts. The initial wave of ghetto building produced its largest black colonies in New York and Chicago, each containing 328,000 and 234,000 blacks, respectively, in 1930. By 1980, New York proper held 1.8 million blacks and Chicago had 1.2 million—indeed, the suburbs around these giants held virtually as many blacks in 1980 as the cities themselves did a half-century before. Detroit had more than double and Philadelphia had nearly double the number of blacks that New York had in 1930. Los Angeles, Washington, D.C., Houston, and Baltimore also counted more blacks in 1980 than New York had in 1930. Those cities, as well as New Orleans, Memphis, Atlanta, Dallas, and Cleveland, also, as of 1980, had more blacks than Chicago did at the start of the Great Depression. Although the black exodus from the South around World War I earned the appellation of the "Great Migration," it was the second wave, sparked initially by the mobilization for war in the 1940s and later fueled by the transformation of southern agriculture, that was—in absolute numbers, at least—far more significant.

Given the demographic explosion after 1940, the subsequent areal expansion necessary to contain such enlarged black populations, and the persistence of a high degree of segregation, clearly the emergence of the modern ghetto displayed elements both of continuity and change. There is no question that racial discrimination, for example, currently persists in the private housing market. It has perhaps been moderated by more enlightened popular attitudes, government policies, and—probably most important—by the simple availability of housing as whites continue to abandon the central city for the suburbs. Tensions have always been greatest when blacks and whites competed for scarce supplies, as in the housing shortages that accompanied World War I and World War II. The attempts to restrict black access to new housing by exclusionary improvement associations, zoning practices that regulated lot size and construction, the denial of financing by lenders, and the "steering" practices of real estate agents, however, continue to reinforce prevailing patterns. Indeed, a

1991 survey released by the Urban Institute has indicated that blacks faced discriminatory hurdles 59 percent of the time when purchasing a home; black renters met overt discrimination in 56 percent of their tested encounters.[37]

Another important element of continuity, especially in the immediate postwar period, was the revival of antiblack violence. Between May 1944 and July 1946, whites assaulted forty-six black homes as Chicago replayed its World War I experience; twenty-nine of the attacks involved fire, and at least three people were killed in that reign of terror. Indeed, between 1945 and 1950, some 485 racial "incidents" were reported to the Chicago Commission on Human Relations, and 357 (73.6 percent) involved conflicts over housing. The late 1940s and 1950s also witnessed at least six large-scale riots, involving thousands of participants, that erupted over the black occupation of previously all-white neighborhoods. It is unclear at this point whether the extraordinary level of violence uncovered in Chicago represents an extreme situation or simply reflects its status as one of the nation's most-studied cities. As the 1942 explosion surrounding the Sojourner Truth homes in Detroit and lesser disturbances in St. Louis, New York, Philadelphia, Spokane, and Cincinnati indicate, such attacks certainly occurred elsewhere even if the scale and duration of the disorders remains unclear.[38]

The maintenance of racial segregation after 1930, however, was most notable for the appearance of new forces and new players. The qualitative distinction that separates the second ghetto from the first involves the unprecedented application of governmental power to the turbulent urban landscape. It was particularly the presence of the federal government, beginning in the New Deal, and its collection of often contradictory programs that facilitated the persistence of high levels of residential segregation in the midst of unparalleled urban change.

The federal government never produced anything coherent enough to be called an urban "policy," but it did develop a series of related programs that, in their cumulative effect, greatly accelerated the racial segmentation of metropolitan America and provided official sanction for existing racial patterns. Before the depression, government involvement in the maintenance of residential segregation generally was limited to the spotty judicial enforcement of privately drawn restriction agreements and the localities' brief, unsuccessful fling with turn-of-the-century zoning ordinances. With the emergence of federal supports for the private housing industry, public housing, slum clearance, and urban reveval, however, government took an active hand not merely in reinforcing prevailing patterns of segregation, but also in lending them a permanence never seen before. The implication of government in the second ghetto was so deep, so pervasive, that it virtually constituted a new form of de jure segregation.

Between 1935 and 1950, the federal government displayed an intense color consciousness and insisted on discriminatory practices as a prerequisite for support. Both the Federal Housing Administration (FHA) and public housing began as depression-era programs whose initial value was found in their roles as pump-priming devices designed to get the housing and construction industries moving again. In guaranteeing loans, the FHA's interests did not extend beyond the safety of the mortgages it insured, and in following "sound business principles," it delivered itself into the hands of the private housing industry. NAREB leaders boasted that they placed "hundreds" of "their" people in government service, and their less-than-enlightened racial views soon found their way into FHA manuals. Through FHA, the federal government advocated the use of zoning ordinances and physical barriers to protect the racial stability of the neighborhoods it insured. Most important, it virtually demanded the use of racially restrictive covenants as a precondition before granting loan guarantees, and it declared stables, pigpens, and "inharmonious racial groups" equally objectionable. For the first 15 years of its existence, the FHA *Underwriting Manual,* according to housing expert Charles Abrams, "read like a chapter from Hitler's Nuremberg Laws."[39]

The nation's embryonic public housing program was not subjected to the same kind of leadership, and from the beginning, there were some who saw the program's potential as a tool to clear slums, upgrade urban housing stocks, improve the lives of poor people, and perhaps even undermine existing racial patterns. Initially, however—perhaps as a result of the desire to render the novel federal presence as unobtrusive as possible—public housing was tenanted under the "neighborhood composition guideline." No federal project, in short, was allowed to disrupt the racial status quo; developments in black neighborhoods were occupied by blacks alone, and the same applied to whites; projects in mixed areas, when such could be appropriately located, included both races on a proportionate basis. Equal treatment, in the context of the 1930s, consisted of providing blacks with a "fair share" of the new units, not integration.[40] President Franklin D. Roosevelt's "Black Cabinet," however, as well as some officials in the field (e.g., Elizabeth Wood, executive secretary of the Chicago Housing Authority between 1937 and 1954) did urge the use of public housing to break down residential segregation. Tentative steps in that direction during the war and the immediate postwar years, though, provoked bitterly violent reactions by whites and were quickly abandoned. The result was that two-thirds of the 128 low-rent projects that permitted black occupancy before World War II were wholly segregated developments that accounted for 80 percent of all such units allocated to blacks. There were some exceptions to this picture of federally supported segregated public housing in Marin County, California, and Pittsburgh, and the overall pattern moderated somewhat during the wartime emergency. Public housing, however, offered little challenge to prevailing residential practices and was used more fully to confine blacks in the postwar period. Indeed, data recently drawn on a broad sample of metropolitan areas by Adam Bickford and Douglas S. Massey strongly support the notion that "in the nation's largest cities, public housing segregation appears to be almost universal."[41]

FHA and public housing did more than just countenance racial discrimination until 1950; they facilitated the massive postwar suburban boom, helped strip older towns of their middle classes, and practically assured that thousands of the poorest blacks would remain locked in economically weakened central cities. In adopting systematic methods of appraisal from the Home Owners Loan Corporation, FHA consistently rendered the most favorable judgments on newer, affluent fringe areas or suburbs, whereas black occupancy—by itself, without regard for any other factors—guaranteed any neighborhood the lowest possible rating. The resultant *redlining*—the routine denial of loans in poorly rated areas—disproportionately affected blacks and assured central-city deterioration.[42]

One-half of Detroit and one-third of Chicago were simply excluded from the program by fiat, and after twelve years of operation, there was not a single dwelling unit in Manhattan that had the benefit of FHA coverage.[43] Yet, from the mid-1930s to the mid-1970s, FHA managed to provide $119 billion in home mortgage insurance. Before 1950, 11 million homes were built with the assistance of federal agencies that "pursued a concerted, relentless, and officially sanctioned drive to keep people living only with their own kind. . . ." Private prejudices were now clothed with public powers. In the 1950s and 1960s, federal assistance continued to flood outlying areas, and half of the suburbs built in those decades enjoyed the benefits of FHA or Veterans Administration financing; they remained overwhelmingly white.[44] The suburbs thus bloomed in the crucial first two decades after World War II, watered and nourished by a freely flowing federal spigot, and yet unburdened for the greater portion of that era by the need to deal equitably in racial affairs.

Such policies and results were not simply matters of antiblack animus. An antiurban bias also informed much of FHA's actions. Narrow lots, multifamily dwellings, rental units, and rehabilitation projects all had great difficulty acquiring FHA insurance, and managed to do so only infrequently, if at all, on terms less favorable than those granted to single detached homes in the suburbs. Potential buyers of row houses in Philadelphia and similar structures in New York and Baltimore, for example, found it impossible to qualify for FHA assistance. Densely populated, economically or racially mixed, and aging neighborhoods, whatever their condition, were devalued and red-lined. The effect, however, was the same as if racial criteria were applied: The federal government invited and underwrote the outward migration of the white middle class and eroded the economic viability of the inner city.[45]

FHA provides only a single—if spectacular—example of federal encouragement and subsidization of white flight. The suburbs themselves would have been unthinkable without the rapid postwar construction of the interstate highway system, and policies that favored the automobile similarly facilitated suburbanization. Future investigations into the selection of highway routes and subsequent neighborhood demolition undoubtedly also will reveal a decision-making process not devoid of racial considerations. Even the tax code, which encourages the abandonment of older, still useful structures and provides appealing deductions for mortgage interest and real estate taxes, rendered the suburbs increasingly attractive. The point is not that the federal government "caused" the decentralization of American cities in any meaningful sense; that process had been going on for a century or more by the time World War II ended. Public policy, however, did gravely affect the pace and nature of that outward movement; the sudden appearance of white suburbs ringing increasingly black-core cities in the past generation must be viewed in the context of federal management and support.

The central city subsequently received its own share of government attention, although it was attention that was inspired, once again, by those who had devalued the core and promoted the decentralization of urban America. As early as the 1930s, NAREB and its affiliated organizations cast covetous eyes on the central city even as they bemoaned its "blight" and "uneconomic" uses. The forced concentration, particularly of inner-city blacks, the dense overcrowding and physical deterioration of most core neighborhoods, and the economic potential of such easily accessible, centrally located areas led the spokespeople of the housing industry to call for government assistance in reclaiming such territories for private development. City leaders, burdened financially by spreading slums and an eroding tax base, found much in the NAREB appeal to recommend itself. In the 1940s, those interests were joined by large downtown businesses, central-city institutions, and major urban

investors who anticipated and feared the massive postwar trek to suburbia. To revitalize and expand their markets, hold their constituencies, and protect their investments, they, too, called for government
aid.[46]

Three basic problems prevented the private interests from acting on
their own. First, there was the problem of acquiring land in large
enough parcels to permit successful redevelopment. The virtual impos-
sibility of concluding negotiations with hundreds of individual landowners, and the certainty of "holdouts," meant that land could only be
assembled through the exercise of the public power of eminent domain.
Second, the most desirable inner-city land sought by developers was
prohibitively expensive and became even more costly after slum clearance and site preparation. Clearly, not only government power, but
subsidies also were required. Third, the people occupying the densely
populated urban heartland had to live somewhere. In the 1930s,
NAREB disavowed all responsibility for those to be uprooted; but in
the severe housing shortage of the 1940s, it was a practical and political problem that could not be ignored. Public housing—if not as social
reform, then as relocation housing to permit private development—
proved to be a partial answer.

A number of cities and states passed their own legislation and
began to attack these problems even before the federal government
got involved; indeed, their actions served as models for the later
federal intervention. New York used a twenty-five-year tax exemp-
tion to entice the Metropolitan Life Insurance Company to build
Stuyvesant Town, an apartment complex on the lower east side that
barred blacks and forced the removal of some ten thousand low-
income people from an eighteen-block area. The Mellon family com-
missioned revitalization studies of downtown Pittsburgh, formed the
Allegheny Conference on Community Development, and similarly
recruited the Equitable Life Insurance Company to begin redevelopment there. It was Chicago, though, and its implementation of the
Illinois Blighted Areas Redevelopment Act of 1947 and related legislation that provided not only for the use of eminent domain to clear
slums, but also devised the "write down" formula that empowered
local governments to pass on the property so acquired to private
developers for a fraction of its actual cost, and provided for relocation housing as well. In each of these features, the Illinois laws
presaged the federal Housing Act of 1949. Not only had private
developers been given new bootstraps, but local, state, and federal
authorities further obliged them by hauling them up two-thirds of
the way. Those who claimed that the subsequent destruction of
cheap housing in a time of shortage and the substitution of office

complexes, luxury apartments, and commercial developments represented a "perversion" of the law were blinded by a rhetorical shroud that expressed concern for poor people and promised a decent, safe, and sanitary dwelling for every American.[47]

The slum clearance and public housing programs that gained momentum after 1949 also contributed to the racial segmentation of American society. Public housing, frequently used simply to free inner-city land for private development, became increasingly identified as a "black" program, used high-rise construction, and resegregated its tenants in already densely populated core areas. Able to accommodate only a fraction of those uprooted by the wrecker's ball, thousands of others sought new homes in transitional areas. If the process of suburbanization created central-city vacancies that facilitated racial succession, redevelopment spurred that movement and accelerated the whites' desertion of the central city.[48]

The movement across the urban racial frontier and redefinition of ghetto borders also led directly to the next phase of the government's postwar revitalization program: urban renewal. Redevelopment had always been closely associated with slum clearance. The semantic shift to "urban renewal" indicated a substantive deemphasis of the concern with slums. A new approach was justified, the National Commission on Urban Problems later concluded, "as a broader design to rebuild the cities." The new legislation placed greater stress on the rehabilitation of existing housing and neighborhoods, rather than on their demolition, and for the first time spoke of preserving still healthy middle-class areas. It was a virtual replay of the shift in mood, emphasis, and resources that characterized the post-progressive, conservative 1920s. Direct benefits did not flow to those who demonstrated the greatest need; instead, the poor were left waiting for indirect benefits to "trickle down" and given "models" to emulate.[49]

The crucial point, however, was that the basic provisions of the federal Housing Act of 1954 that embodied the renewal concept copied those enacted in the Illinois Urban Community Conservation Act of 1953. Largely the product of the University of Chicago and its institutional allies, the "conservation" movement in Chicago aimed to staunch the flow of blacks into the university's Hyde Park community, extend the concept of eminent domain to areas that were not yet slums themselves, and redraw the area's racial geography to suit itself.[50]

Given that genesis (the University of Chicago wanted to create a predominantly white and economically upgraded community), some ramifications of the national program became more explicable. The charges so often leveled at the federal effort—that it neglected the poor population, that it was actually antipoor because of its demolition of low-rent housing and inadequate relocation procedures, that it simply subsidized those who needed aid least, and that it was transformed into a program of "Negro removal"—were hardly evidence of a plan gone awry. These were neither "perversions" of the enabling legislation nor the inevitable, if unforeseen, consequences of bumbling "do-gooders." The results were fully intended and the law did exactly what it was designed to do. Other cities were not compelled to use the law in like fashion, but many did just that. Urban renewal was rooted, in large part, in the desire to control and mitigate the consequences of racial succession.

The urban riots of the 1960s provided the illumination by which the urban renewal program was terminated in the early 1970s. By that time, more than a generation of federal intervention in housing and urban affairs had radically transformed metropolitan America, but only within the limits decreed by the private housing industry and those corporate, institutional, and political interests who designed and implemented the programs. Sometimes derided as showing the futility of social reform, urban renewal was never anything of the sort. Poor people reaped only the benefit of rhetorical preambles and a whirlwind of bulldozers.[51]

Ghetto Persistence
in the Post–Civil Rights Era

If the national government never really attempted to address the housing needs of the urban poor, federal policy did gradually purge itself of racially discriminatory intent. Beginning in 1948, the federal government began a long twenty-year march toward the acceptance of a color-blind stance on housing issues. First came the Supreme Court decision (*Shelley* v. *Kraemer*) that rendered restrictive covenants unenforceable. FHA resisted the court's edict for nearly two years, though, and it was not until December 1949 (and after the application of considerable White House pressure by President Harry S Truman) that the agency announced that it would not insure property covered by restrictive covenants after February 1950. Even that ban, however, served the purpose of alerting developers and encouraged many to hasten their applications for covenant-bound property before the announced deadline.[52]

At most, Truman's persistent prodding in the wake of *Shelley* v.

Kraemer led FHA to take a theoretically "neutral" position on racial matters. His intervention finally forced a reluctant FHA to end its outright refusal to support integrated projects in 1949, but the president declined to go so far as to prohibit federal assistance to segregated developments. FHA simply let the matter rest with each private developer, with predictable results—less than two percent of the housing constructed with federally insured mortgages between 1946 and 1959 was made available to blacks. Executive indifference in the 1950s not only left such FHA practices in force, but led to the virtual gutting of the Race Relations Service of the Housing and Home Finance Agency. One of the stronger voices within the government that promoted racial equality during Dwight D. Eisenhower's administration, according to Charles Abrams, it "degenerated into an official apologist for official acceptance of segregation."[53]

It was more than a decade after *Shelley* v. *Kraemer* before the next step was taken as John F. Kennedy announced in the 1960 presidential campaign that he would end racial discrimination in all federal housing programs with "a stroke of the presidential pen" if elected. Public opposition to open occupancy and political considerations cramped Kennedy's writing style, though, and it took two years before an executive order executed a partial ban that applied only to new housing and exempted homes financed by savings and loan associations that operated under the Federal Home Loan Bank Board. The final steps came in 1964 when the Civil Rights Act ended discrimination in the bestowal of government benefits and in 1968 when the Fair Housing Act extended the prohibition on discrimination to include virtually all housing; the real estate industry, lenders, and advertisers all fell under the sweep of the law.[54]

The government's assumption of a color-blind posture, however, obviously has had little effect on stubbornly high levels of residential segregation, for three reasons. First, it is a policy that is terribly difficult to enforce. There are no centralized levers or buttons to push as there are in education and employment where school boards or large employers can be scrutinized easily. Housing remains in the hands of uncounted decision makers: literally thousands of real estate agents, lenders, buyers, and sellers. It also is doubtful that more rigorous enforcement could have more than a marginal effect on the overall distribution of population. That is because of the second reason: Competing, prior, and contradictory government policies have already accelerated the separation of the races and frozen the pattern in concrete. Third, and most important, a review of the pertinent behavioral literature seems conclusive in detailing the enormous historical burden imposed by the cumulative weight of the first and second ghettos. The evidence is overwhelming that people conduct their housing searches in limited areas; that they are most aware of the housing available near their current residences; and that their existing location is the single most critical factor in determining their new location—and each of these findings seems to hold with even greater force for low-income households, renters, and minorities than others. In short, even in the absence of current discrimination, the overwhelming effect of prior restriction has left a living legacy that stretches into future generations.[55]

In the 1930s and 1940s, the federal government mandated racial discrimination; through the 1950s and much of the 1960s, it permitted bias in both the private and public spheres; in the 1970s and 1980s, it outlawed most forms of such discrimination, but only after a sustained postwar building boom served as a federally supported centrifuge that separated an outer layer of whites from a dense black core. Attempting to end discriminatory practices in housing in the post–civil rights era is not simply a matter of closing the barn door a little too slowly—the horse has not only escaped, but it has gotten into the trailer, moved down the interstate, and been put out to stud in rural pastures.

There is no question that attempts to create a color-blind market under civil rights law have failed. However, the dual market that survived in the post–civil rights era was not the same one that existed twenty or thirty years before. White abandonment of America's central cities has ended much of the scarcity that characterized the earlier black housing market. Housing prices have fallen proportionately, and the "race tax" that elevated costs paid by blacks above those paid by whites for equivalent shelter is not the factor it was a generation earlier. The quality of housing available to blacks also has improved substantially over the past forty years, particularly for the growing middle class. Even the poor have derived some benefits here, and the public housing units occupied by thousands—despite the scandalous conditions endured by many—still represent a net gain over the ramshackle hovels pressed into service by the end of the Great Depression. However, during the same period, homeownership and a suburban life style became the common expectation of the vast middle class where previously they had been luxuries reserved for the wealthy. Gains for blacks were relatively less. Segregation still persists, but currently more alternatives are available for upwardly mobile blacks. White desertion of the central city has opened new neighborhoods, and the black middle class has been quick to respond. One result is the increasing class differentiation currently found within urban black communities.[56] Always present to some extent, the ability of well-to-do blacks to distance themselves from poor people has become much more pronounced in the past decade or two; and spatial distance generally has reflected social, ideological, and political difference as well. The full implications of this movement have yet to be seen.

The flight of the black middle class from the poorest sections of the central city also must be placed in the context of the broader assimilation experience of other migrants to urban America. Before 1950, the most mobile segments of the black middle class were denied the role played by their earlier white ethnic counterparts. As the older immigrant communities dispersed, those who enjoyed some measure of economic success led the movement and eased the transition into the American mainstream for those who trailed them. The recent availability of more decent housing, however, has allowed economically successful blacks to undertake that outward push with different results. One consequence is that, as the indexes of dissimilarity of the largest U.S. cities indicate, this movement is proceeding within the context of continued racial segregation; black economic achievement and material well-being have not heralded the "disappearance" of those "assimilated" blacks as was the case with their ethnic competitors. Interestingly, the existence of ample housing stocks and respectable alternatives to the most impoverished communities apparently have led to a reduction of the pressure placed on white suburban areas. Attempts to promote and manage the integration of such all-white neighborhoods, thus, have not been notably successful because of both continued white resistance and seeming black indifference. White accommodations and integration were valued more, it appears, in times of housing shortage when they were the only alternatives to deplorable living conditions. In part, this phenomenon might reflect a new kind of "voluntary" segregation; it is possible that, finally, the centripetal pull of black "cultural affinities" is being tested and has been found to be more enduring than those of the white ethnics. Given past history, though, it might also simply reflect the judgment that entry into all-white communities is just not worth the risk or aggravation, and it is certainly no longer necessary to achieve a decent standard of living.

A second major consequence of this black middle class movement is that it threatens to leave the poor population behind in large blocks of public housing and deteriorating core areas. The decline in overt racism and the spotty enforcement of antidiscrimination laws have meant little to the poorest blacks. Past practices have had their effect, and institutional, ideological, behavioral, and political legacies continue to hamper efforts—whether internal or external—to alter their lives materially. Their continued segregation, not simply by race, but increasingly by class as well, is characteristic of the third stage in the evolution of America's black urban communities. Rather than being placed in an advantageous position by their more successful representatives, those left behind seem more distant and more isolated from the mainstream than before.[57]

The persistence of racial segregation remains a central feature of urban life in the United States, and unquestionably will remain so for the forseeable future. Unable to alter deeply rooted patterns of segregation, the civil rights era ban on racial discrimination did not affect the hard-core economic problems that continue to plague central cities and their residents. If the ghetto has been gilded for some and escaped by others, it shows no signs of disappearing and, indeed, may now present the dual problems of race and poverty in more concentrated form than ever before.

NOTES

1.   Nell Irvin Painter, *The Exodusters: Black Migration to Kansas after Reconstruction* (New York: Knopf, 1976).

2.   Gilbert Osofsky, *Harlem: The Making of a Ghetto: Negro New York, 1890–1930* (New York: Harper and Row, 1966); Allan H. Spear, *Black Chicago: The Making of a Negro Ghetto, 1890–1920* (Chicago: University of Chicago Press, 1967).

3.   "Push" and "pull" factors are at work during any migration. Some of those forces "pushing" blacks out of the South included the spread of lynching, the sense of racial oppression that accompanied the passage of Jim Crow legislation, changes in southern agriculture, and natural disasters such as flooding and the appearance of the boll weevil. See, for example, Florette Henri, *Black Migration: Movement North, 1900–1920* (Garden City, N.Y.: Doubleday, 1976). Even within that context, one must also allow for human agency and assess migrants as conscious and purposeful actors. See James R. Grossman, *Land of Hope: Chicago, Black Southerners, and the Great Migration* (Chicago: University of Chicago Press, 1989); Joe William Trotter, Jr., ed., *The Great Migration in Historical Perspective: New Dimensions of Race, Class, and Gender* (Bloomington: Indiana University Press, 1991).

4.   Harry A. Ploski and James Williams, eds., *The Negro Almanac: A Reference Work on the Afro-American,* 4th ed. (New York: Wiley, 1983), 446. For the link between the mechanization of agriculture and black movement, see Nicholas Lemann, *The Promised Land: The Great Black Migration and How It Changed America* (New York: Knopf, 1991).

5. Ploski and Williams, *Negro Almanac,* 445–455.
6. Ibid.
7. Ibid.
8. Ibid.
9. Ibid.
10. See Table 3.1.
11. Ploski and Williams, *Negro Almanac,* 453.
12. Howard Rabinowitz, *Race Relations in the Urban South, 1865–1890* (New York: Oxford University Press, 1978), 97–124; see also Don H. Doyle, *New Men, New Cities, New South: Atlanta, Nashville, Charleston, Mobile, 1860–1910* (Chapel Hill: University of North Carolina Press, 1990), and James Borchert, *Alley Life in Washington: Family, Community, Religion, and Folklife in the City, 1850–1970* (Urbana: University of Illinois Press, 1980).
13. The striking percentage increases in northern urban black populations between 1910 and 1920, for example, resulted from the addition of significant, but not overwhelming, numbers of black migrants to existing, modest black communities. Detroit added only slightly more than 36,240 individuals to its black population between 1910 and 1920, but that represented an increase of more than 611 percent; Cleveland added 34,000 to a base of fewer than 8,500, for an increase of nearly 308 percent; Chicago's 65,500 new black residents represented a gain of 148 percent; and New York's increase of 61,400 represented a rise of 66 percent. See Henri, *Black Migration,* 69, and Kenneth L. Kusmer, *A Ghetto Takes Shape: Black Cleveland, 1870–1930* (Urbana: University of Illinois Press, 1976), 10.
14. Karl E. Taeuber and Alma F. Taeuber, *Negroes in Cities: Residential Segregation and Neighborhood Change* (New York: Atheneum, 1969), 54.
15. Olivier Zunz, *The Changing Face of Inequality: Urbanization, Industrial Development, and Immigrants in Detroit, 1880–1920* (Chicago: University of Chicago Press, 1982), 327–398; see also Thomas L. Philpott, *The Slum and the Ghetto: Neighborhood Deterioration and Middle-Class Reform, Chicago, 1880–1930* (New York: Oxford University Press, 1978), 136–144; Humbert Nelli, *Italians in Chicago, 1880–1930* (New York: Oxford University Press, 1970), 23–28; Sam Bass Warner, Jr., and Colin B. Burke, "Cultural Change and the Ghetto," *Journal of Contemporary History* 4 (October 1969), 173–188; John Bodnar, Roger Simon, and Michael P. Weber, *Lives of Their Own: Blacks, Italians, and Poles in Pittsburgh, 1900–1960* (Urbana: University of Illinois Press, 1982).
16. Kathleen Neils Conzen, "Immigrants, Immigrant Neighborhoods, and Ethnic Identity: Historical Issues," *Journal of American History* 79 (December 1979), 603–615.
17. Sam Bass Warner, Jr., *The Urban Wilderness: A History of the American City* (New York: Harper and Row, 1972), 85–112, passim.
18. A lively debate exists between those who emphasize ethnicity in housing choice and those who stress the importance of job location in the nineteenth century; both sides agree, however, that blacks constitute a special case and that their experience differed fundamentally from that of white immigrants.

See Zunz, *Changing Face of Inequality,* 129–176, passim; Stephanie W. Green-berg, "Industrial Location and Ethnic Residential Patterns in an Industrializing City: Philadelphia, 1880," in *Philadelphia: Work, Space, Family, and Group Experience in the 19th Century,* ed. Theodore Hershberg (New York: Oxford University Press, 1981); Theodore Hershberg et al., "A Tale of Three Cities: Blacks, Immigrants, and Opportunity in Philadelphia, 1850–1880, 1930, 1970," in *Philadelphia: Work, Space, Family, and Group Experience in the 19th Century,* ed. Theodore Hershberg (New York: Oxford University Press, 1981); see also Kusmer, *A Ghetto Takes Shape,* 45–47.

19.   See, for example, George Frederickson, *The Black Image in the White Mind: The Debate on Afro-American Character and Destiny, 1817–1914 (*New York: Harper and Row, 1971); John W. Cell, *The Highest Stage of White Supremacy: The Origins of Segregation in South Africa and the American South* (Cambridge, England: Cambridge University Press, 1982); Joel Williamson, *The Crucible of Race: Black–White Relations in the American South since Emancipation* (New York: Oxford University Press, 1984).

20.   Philpott, *The Slum and the Ghetto,* 115–145; David A. Wallace, "Residential Concentration of Negroes in Chicago" (Ph.D. diss., Harvard University, 1953).

21.   Osofsky, *Harlem,* 71–149.

22.   Philpott, *The Slum and the Ghetto,* 273–342. See also Robert B. Fairbanks, *Making Better Citizens: Housing Reform and the Community Development Strategy in Cincinnati, 1890–1960* (Urbana: University of Illinois Press, 1988). Fairbanks certainly would question, or at least qualify, the conclusions drawn here, but his own evidence for Cincinnati in the 1920s seems to support such inferences.

23.   It is precisely that distinction that serves as the major theme of Philpott's *The Slum and the Ghetto.*

24.   *Buchanan v. Warley,* 245 U.S. 60 (1917); Roger L. Rice, "Residential Segregation by Law, 1910–1917," *The Journal of Southern History* 34 (May 1968), 179–199.

25.   *Corrigan v. Buckley,* 271 U.S. 323 (1926); Herman H. Long and Charles S. Johnson, *People vs. Property: Race Restrictive Covenants in Housing* (Nashville, Tenn.: Fisk University Press, 1947). For those covenants that lacked an explicit racial designation but still restricted access to urban property, see Patricia Burgess Stach, "Deed Restrictions and Subdivision Development in Columbus, Ohio, 1900–1970," *Journal of Urban History* 15 (November 1988), 42–68.

26.   Stach, "Deed Restrictions," 56–72; Kusmer, *A Ghetto Takes Shape,* 46; Philpott, *The Slum and the Ghetto,* 163; Joe William Trotter, Jr., *Black Milwaukee: The Making of an Industrial Proletariat, 1915–1945* (Urbana: University of Illinois Press, 1985), 71.

27.   Philpott, *The Slum and the Ghetto,* 190–191; quotation is from Long and Johnson, *People vs. Property,* 58.

28.   Chicago Commission on Race Relations, *The Negro in Chicago* (Chicago: University of Chicago Press, 1922), 115–122; William M. Tuttle, Jr.,

Race Riot: Chicago in the Red Summer of 1919 (New York: Atheneum, 1970), 173–180, 251; Zorita Wise Mikva, "The Neighborhood Improvement Association: A Counter-Force to the Expansion of Chicago's Negro Population" (M.A. thesis, University of Chicago, 1951).

29. For the best discussion on the Chicago riot, see Chicago Commission, *The Negro in Chicago,* and Tuttle, *Race Riot.*

30. Chicago Commission, *The Negro in Chicago,* 122; Tuttle, *Race Riot,* 157–183; Philpott, *The Slum and the Ghetto,* 170–180; Spear, *Black Chicago,* 221–222.

31. Kusmer, *A Ghetto Takes Shape,* 165–172.

32. Zunz, *Changing Face of Inequality,* 373–374; Kenneth T. Jackson, *The Ku Klux Klan in the City, 1915–1930* (New York: Oxford University Press, 1967), 140–141.

33. For profiteering in an earlier era, see Zunz, *Changing Face of Inequality,* 375; for developments after 1940, see Arnold R. Hirsch, *Making the Second Ghetto: Race and Housing in Chicago, 1940–1960* (Cambridge, England: Cambridge University Press, 1983), and John F. Bauman, *Public Housing, Race, and Renewal: Urban Planning in Philadelphia, 1920–1974* (Philadelphia: Temple University Press, 1987).

34. Kusmer, *A Ghetto Takes Shape,* 206–274; Spear, *Black Chicago,* 71–126; Trotter, *Black Milwaukee,* 80–114, passim; August Meier, *Negro Thought in America, 1880–1915* (Ann Arbor: University of Michigan Press, 1963).

35. Taeuber and Taeuber, *Negroes in Cities,* 39–41.

36. Douglas S. Massey and Nancy A. Denton, "Trends in the Residential Segregation of Blacks, Hispanics, and Asians: 1970–1980," *American Sociological Review* 52 (December 1987), 802–825; Douglas S. Massey and Nancy A. Denton, "Suburbanization and Segregation in U. S. Metropolitan Areas," *American Journal of Sociology* 94 (1988), 592–626; John R. Logan and Mark Schneider, "Racial Segregation and Racial Change in American Suburbs, 1970–1980," *American Journal of Sociology* 89 (January 1984), 174–188.

37. Brian J.L. Berry, *The Open Housing Question: Race and Housing in Chicago, 1966–1976* (Cambridge, Mass.: Ballinger, 1979); Joe T. Darden, *Afro-Americans in Pittsburgh: The Residential Segregation of a People* (Lexington, Mass.: Lexington Books, 1973), 42, 47–49, 64–65. The Urban Institute study comprised 3,800 audits using paired white and black or Hispanic testers in twenty-five metropolitan areas. It is also notable that regional variations have virtually disappeared; see *New York Times,* 1 September 1991.

38. Hirsch, *Making the Second Ghetto,* 40–67; Dominic J. Capeci, Jr., *Race Relations in Wartime Detroit: The Sojourner Truth Housing Controversy of 1942* (Philadelphia: Temple University Press, 1984); Charles Abrams, *Forbidden Neighbors* (New York: Harper and Row, 1955); Long and Johnson, *People vs. Property,* 73–85.

39. Mark I. Gelfand, *A Nation of Cities: The Federal Government and Urban America, 1933–1965* (New York: Oxford University Press, 1975), 216–222, passim; Long and Johnson, *People vs. Property,* 72; Charles Abrams, *The*

City is the Frontier (New York: Harper and Row, 1965), 61–63, passim; Kenneth T. Jackson, "Race, Ethnicity, and Real Estate Appraisal: The Home Owners Loan Corporation and the Federal Housing Administration," *Journal of Urban History* 6 (August 1980), 419–452. Even though the emphasis here has been on federal housing policies created in the 1930s, it seems certain that research will reveal other federal programs as well as state and local actions that provided their own support for the ghetto-building process in earlier years. The deliberate use of roads and highways to manipulate or confine racial concentrations is beginning to attract significant investigation. See especially Ronald H. Bayor, "Roads to Racial Segregation: Atlanta in the Twentieth Century," *Journal of Urban History* 15 (November 1988), 3–21, and Chapter 4 in this volume. Whether such discoveries will qualify notions of a second ghetto or compel revisions in periodization remains to be seen.

40. Martin Meyerson and Edward C. Banfield, *Politics, Planning, and the Public Interest* (New York: Free Press, 1955), 121–150; see also Capeci, *Race Relations in Wartime Detroit,* and Philip J. Funigiello, *The Challenge to Urban Liberalism: Federal-City Relations during World War II* (Knoxville: University of Tennessee Press, 1978), 80–119.

41. Funigiello, *Challenge to Urban Liberalism,* 97; Meyerson and Banfield, *Politics, Planning, and the Public Interest,* 134; Long and Johnson, *People vs. Property,* 70–71; Hirsch, *Making the Second Ghetto,* 206, 207, 218, 228–229; Adam Bickford and Douglas S. Massey, "Segregation in the Second Ghetto: Racial and Ethnic Segregation in American Public Housing, 1977," *Social Forces* 69 (June 1991), 1034.

42. Jackson, "Race, Ethnicity, and Real Estate Appraisal," 419–452.

43. Gelfand, *A Nation of Cities,* 123, 217.

44. Jackson, "Race, Ethnicity, and Real Estate Appraisal," 419–452; Abrams, *The City is the Frontier,* 62.

45. Jackson, "Race, Ethnicity, and Real Estate Appraisal," 419–452.

46. Marc A. Weiss, "The Origins and Legacy of Urban Renewal," in *Urban and Regional Planning in an Age of Austerity,* ed. Pierre Clavel, John Forester, and William W. Goldsmith (New York: Pergamon, 1980), 53–80; Gelfand, *A Nation of Cities,* 112–115.

47. Gelfand, *A Nation of Cities,* 129, 212; Roy Lubove, *Twentieth-Century Pittsburgh: Government, Business, and Environmental Change* (New York: Wiley, 1969); Hirsch, *Making the Second Ghetto,* 100–134, passim.

48. For a detailed examination of this process in one city, see Hirsch, *Making the Second Ghetto.*

49. Ibid., 271.

50. Ibid., 135–170, 268–275.

51. The use of the results of urban renewal to discredit government intervention and, apparently, all such efforts at "reform" is carried to its greatest polemical lengths in Martin Anderson, *The Federal Bulldozer: A Critical Analysis of Urban Renewal, 1949–1962* (Cambridge, Mass.: MIT Press, 1964). The "lessons" thus learned are repeated in Jon C. Teaford, *The Rough Road to Renaissance: Urban Revitalization in America, 1940–1985* (Baltimore: Johns Hopkins University Press, 1990).

52. Jackson, "Race, Ethnicity, and Real Estate Appraisal," 419–452; Gelfand, *A Nation of Cities*, 220–221; Abrams, *The City is the Frontier*, 62–63; Clement E. Vose, *Caucasians Only* (Berkeley and Los Angeles: University of California Press, 1959); *Shelley* v. *Kraemer*, 334 U.S. 1 (1948).

53. Abrams is quoted in Gelfand, *A Nation of Cities*, 221.

54. Ibid., 341–342; Nathan Glazer, *Affirmative Discrimination: Ethnic Inequality and Public Policy* (New York: Basic Books, 1975), 133, 151–152.

55. William A.V. Clark, "Residential Segregation in American Cities," in *Issues in Housing Discrimination: A Consultation/Hearing of the United States Commission on Civil Rights, Washington, D.C., November 12–15, 1985* (Washington, D.C.: U.S. Government Printing Office, 1986), 42.

56. Berry, *The Open Housing Question*, 499–504, passim; William Gorham and Nathan Glazer, eds., *The Urban Predicament* (Washington, D.C.: The Urban Institute, 1976), 119–178.

57. For implications of these developments, see William Julius Wilson, *The Truly Disadvantaged: The Inner City, the Underclass, and Public Policy* (Chicago: University of Chicago Press, 1987), and Alex Kotlowitz, *There Are No Children Here: The Story of Two Boys Growing Up in the Other America* (New York: Doubleday, 1991).

4

RAYMOND A. MOHL

Race and Space in the Modern City: Interstate-95 and the Black Community in Miami

In 1956, at the urging of President Dwight D. Eisenhower, the U.S. Congress authorized funding for an interstate highway network linking major metropolitan areas. The massive interstate construction effort, which got underway in the late 1950s and the early 1960s, set into motion a vast process of urban change. Mostly completed by the early 1970s, the interstate highway system has had a powerful and shaping effect on modern urban America. Within metropolitan areas, the interstates linked central cities with sprawling postwar suburbs, facilitating automobile commuting while undermining what was left of inner-city mass transit. The wide ribbons of concrete and asphalt stimulated new downtown physical development, but soon spurred the growth of suburban shopping malls, office parks, and residential subdivisions as well. At the same time, the interstates tore through long-established inner-city residential neighborhoods in their drive toward the city cores. Huge expressway interchanges, cloverleafs, and on–off ramps created enormous areas of dead and useless space in the central cities. The bulldozer and the wrecker's ball went to work on urban America, paving the way for a wide range of public and private schemes for urban redevelopment. The new expressways, in short, permanently altered the urban and suburban landscape throughout the nation. The interstate system was an enormous public works program, but it is currently apparent that freeway construction had vast and often negative consequences for the cities. As historian Mark I.

Research for this chapter was supported by the Florida Atlantic University–Florida International University Joint Center for Environmental and Urban Problems.

Gelfand has suggested, "No federal venture spent more funds in urban areas and returned fewer dividends to central cities than the national highway program."[1]

Almost everywhere, the new urban expressways destroyed wide swaths of existing housing and dislocated people by the tens of thousands, uprooting entire communities in the name of progress. According to the 1969 report of the National Commission on Urban Problems, some 330,000 urban housing units were destroyed as a direct result of federal highway building between 1957 and 1968. In the early 1960s, according to the U.S. House Committee on Public Works, federal highway construction dislocated an average of 32,400 families each year. For the years 1965 to 1972, the average number of families displaced was expected to rise to about 37,000 per year. "The amount of disruption," the Public Works Committee conceded in 1965, was "astoundingly large." As planning scholar Alan A. Altshuler has noted, by the mid-1960s, when interstate construction was well underway, it was generally believed that the new highway system would "displace a million people from their homes before it [was] completed."[2]

Dislocated urbanites had few advocates, especially among the highway lobbyists or in the state and federal road-building agencies. As the National Commission on Urban Problems put it, "The position of the Bureau of Public Roads and the State highway departments was that their business was to finance and build highways," and that any social consequences of highway construction were the responsibility of other agencies.[3] However, during most of the expressway-building era, little was done to link the interstate highway program with urban renewal or new public housing construction, or even with relocation assistance for displaced families, businesses, or community institutions. Not surprisingly, the neighborhoods destroyed and the people uprooted in the process of highway building tended to be overwhelmingly poor and black. A general pattern emerged, promoted by state and federal highway officials and by private agencies such as the Urban Land Institute (ULI), of using highway construction to eliminate "blighted" urban neighborhoods and redevelop valuable inner-city land. This was the policy, for instance, advocated by Thomas H. MacDonald, director of the U.S. Bureau of Public Roads (BPR) during the formative years of the interstate system. Combatting blight with highways was also the policy of New York's influential builder of public works projects, Robert Moses. Highway builders and downtown redevelopers had a common interest in eliminating low-income housing and, as one redeveloper put it in 1959, freeing "blighted" areas "for higher and better uses."[4]

The destruction of ghetto housing as a result of highway building, urban renewal, and other redevelopment schemes created a housing crisis for blacks and other low-income inner-city residents in the 1950s and 1960s. In most cities, the forced relocation of people from central-city housing triggered a spatial reorganization of residential neighborhoods throughout urban areas. Rising black population pressure meant that dislocated blacks began moving into neighborhoods of "transition," generally working-class white neighborhoods on the fringes of the black ghetto where low-cost housing predominated. This process of residential movement and change underlay the creation of what historian Arnold R. Hirsch has called, in a study of postwar Chicago, the "second ghetto."[5]

Highways, Housing, and Race in Miami

The building of Interstate-95 (I-95) in Miami provides a good illustration of the complex and occasionally unanticipated social consequences of urban expressway building. One of the major components of the interstate highway network, I-95 stretches from Maine to Florida. In South Florida, the highway parallels the Atlantic coastline and runs through populous Palm Beach, Broward, and Dade counties directly into downtown Miami. Along the way, the new expressway ripped through the center of Overtown, a large black community of at least forty thousand people on the northwest fringes of Miami's relatively small and confined central business district. Expressway construction in the early 1960s wiped out Overtown's main business district, the center of black economic and cultural life in Miami. One massive highway interchange alone destroyed the housing of approximately ten thousand people. Despite official promises, few replacement housing units were built, and those people who were uprooted got little in the way of relocation assistance. Most of those displaced ended up settling in other black neighborhoods in Miami, especially the more distant black community of Liberty City, which in turn began pushing out its boundaries into adjacent white, working-class residential areas. As this process of black removal and resettlement occurred, other large chunks of Overtown territory were taken for parking lots and parking garages, for city and county office buildings, and for other redevelopment purposes. By the end of the expressway-building era, little remained of Overtown to recall its days as a thriving center of black community life, when it was widely known as the "Harlem of the South."

Actually, what happened in Miami during the period of interstate highway construction represented the culmination of thirty years of reorganization and redistribution of urban land on the basis of race. In the early 1930s, most of Miami's black population of about twenty-five thousand was crowded into Overtown (called "Colored Town" at the time) because local policies of racial zoning left few other areas open to black settlement. White business and political leaders, however, were interested in pushing out the boundaries of the downtown business area at the expense of Overtown. In the mid-1930s, New Deal public housing programs provided the first such opportunity. A black public housing project named Liberty Square was built on undeveloped land five miles from the center of Miami. The city's white civic elite conceived of this project as the nucleus of a new black community that might siphon off the population of Overtown and permit downtown business expansion. The availability of federal housing funds mobilized the civic elite, who seized this opportunity to push the blacks out of the downtown area.[6]

Other efforts were under way during the 1930s to achieve the same goal. In 1936, for instance, the Dade County Planning Board proposed a "negro resettlement plan." The idea was to cooperate with the City of Miami "in removing [the] entire Central Negro town" to three newly built "model negro towns" located on the distant agricultural fringes west of Miami. A year later, in a speech to the Miami Realty Board, Coral Gables developer George Merrick proposed "a complete slum clearance . . . effectively removing every negro family from the present city limits." The idea of black removal from the central district died hard, because as late as 1945 civic leaders in Miami were discussing "the creation of a new negro village that would be a model for the entire United States." In 1949, a Miami city political leader offered new plans for black removal from central Miami: the "expansion pressure" of the business district, City Commissioner R.C. Gardner asserted, was "so great that the existing downtown colored section will crumble and give way to modern and beautiful commercial development." These proposals were never implemented, but New Deal housing agencies such as the Home Owners Loan Corporation and the Federal Housing Administration contributed to changing racial patterns. Through their appraisal policies, both agencies redlined Miami's black community and nearby white "transitional" neighborhoods, hastening the physical decay of the inner-city area.[7]

The racial policies initiated in the New Deal era were continued in later years. Until the 1950s, the Dade County Planning Board permitted the gradual and "controlled" expansion of black residential areas. A tacit agreement among city and county officials, real estate developers, and some black leaders designated the northwestern section of

Miami and Dade County for future black settlement.[8] The location of the new public housing project in that area led to the rapid growth and expansion of the black Liberty City community in the 1940s and 1950s. In nearby white working-class neighborhoods on the northern edge of Miami, the number of black residents increased rapidly, especially after bombing incidents in 1951 at an apartment complex on the frontier of white and black neighborhoods that had begun renting to black families. By the late 1950s, the making of Miami's second ghetto was well under way.[9] The advent of the federal interstate highway program in 1956, however, provided a new opportunity to raze the Overtown community and push the dislocated blacks to more distant residential areas on the northwestern fringe of the metropolitan area. At the same time, Miami's white civic leadership perceived the new urban interstate as a massive building project that might stimulate the languishing central business district and permit future downtown expansion and redevelopment.

Origins of the Interstate Highway System

As it emerged in the 1950s, the interstate highway system represented the culmination of a half-century of federal involvement in road building. Early in the automobile era, urban governments began paving city streets for easier automobile transit, but rural roads generally remained unpaved. Consequently, political pressure from agricultural districts and from an organized "good roads" movement led to congressional passage of the Highway Act of 1916, which appropriated federal funds for rural postal roads in communities of fewer than twenty-five hundred people. Increasing automobile registrations, suburban growth, and the rapid rise of intercity trucking further stimulated the good roads movement during the 1920s. Under the Federal Highway Act of 1921, matching federal funds were provided to the states to develop a national system of hard-surfaced highways. During the Great Depression of the 1930s, the federal government expanded its highway-building activities in urban as well as rural areas. Road construction provided large numbers of jobs for unemployed people. Not only did roads stimulate "prosperity on rolling rubber," as one government report suggested in 1939, but "roads put more direct labor per dollar to healthful work than any other major type of construction."[10]

Many states and cities used federal work-relief funds for major highway projects. In New York State, for example, the aggressive public works planner Robert Moses seized this opportunity to build parkways on Long Island, as well as bridges, tunnels, and urban parkways in New York City.[11] Similarly, the urban freeway system in the Los Angeles metropolitan area was initiated in the late 1930s with federal funds from the Works Progress Administration and the Public Works Administration.[12] By the 1930s, it was clear that urban mass transit was on the decline almost everywhere, and that the private automobile had become the preferred means of travel for most Americans. The automobile had become urbanized. Urban planners had come to accept this new and seemingly permanent innovation and began to focus on ways to facilitate traffic flow and eliminate downtown congestion within metropolitan areas—thus the importance of urban freeways.[13]

Other forces were also at work promoting the freeway idea during the 1930s. The automobile industry had a big stake in highway building. Modern highways in cities would permit the industry to tap the potentially huge urban market for automobiles. The industry's lobby groups—the Automobile Manufacturers Association, the Automotive Safety Foundation, the Highway Research Board, and the National Highway Users Conference—consistently argued the necessity for urban expressways during the 1930s and after.[14]

The automobile industry had a hard and practical interest in urban freeways, but the imaginative "Futurama" exhibit sponsored by General Motors at the 1939 New York World's Fair may have had a greater effect, as historian Mark S. Foster has noted, in "stimulating public thinking in favor of massive urban freeway building." Throughout the summer of 1939, in lines that sometimes stretched more than one a mile, five million Americans waited patiently for a glimpse of "the motorways of the world of tomorrow." Created by industrial designer Norman Bel Geddes, Futurama featured modernized expressways speeding traffic through great skyscraper cities at one hundred miles per hour. Bel Geddes envisioned that these free-flowing urban thoroughfares would become part of a "National Motorway System," connecting all cities with populations of more than one hundred thousand. In this exhibit and in his subsequent book, *Magic Motorways* (1940), Normal Bel Geddes linked America's future with the automobile and the freeway.[15]

In another exhibit at the 1939 World's Fair, the Ford Motor Company also gave prominence to urban expressways. In Ford's "City of Tomorrow" exhibit, designer Walter Dorwin Teague presented high-speed expressways "as integral components of future city design." Futurama got most of the publicity, but the Ford exhibit was popular among fair visitors, not least because Teague used real cars to move people on a small-scale elevated expressway and ramp system. The message conveyed by General Motors and Ford was unmistakable: the urban future would be shaped by the automobile and its needs and the expressway would be an integral part of that future.[16]

These expressway visions were popular and exciting, but ultimately it was the federal government that seized the highway-building initiative. Long the chief agency in charge of the government's road-building effort, BPR was officially created in 1919, although the agency's origins actually date to a federal Office of Road Inquiry established in 1893. By the end of the 1930s, BPR was advocating not only urban highways but also an "interregional highway system" linking the nation's metropolitan areas. Several BPR research studies between 1939 and 1944 established the economic importance of urban expressways in the postwar era. Significantly, in view of later developments, these BPR expressway reports linked inner-city highway building with slum clearance and the physical redevelopment and spatial reorganization of the cities. Thomas H. MacDonald, a highway engineer from Iowa who had headed BPR since 1919, became a fierce promoter of such projects within the Franklin D. Roosevelt administration. Symbolizing the BPR's emerging focus on urban transportation and express highways, the agency was shifted from the Department of Agriculture to the newly established Federal Works Agency (FWA) in the federal administrative reorganization of 1939.[17]

Despite considerable infighting between urban and rural legislators and interest groups, the Federal Highway Act of 1944 represented a victory of sorts for MacDonald and BPR. The new legislation authorized establishment of a national system of interstate highways, not to exceed forty thousand miles, linking the nation's major cities. Because of wartime constraints on the American economy, the Federal Highway Act of 1944 did not appropriate any funds for highway construction. However, the outlines of the interstate highway system were laid down at this early date, if only on paper. As early as 1945, MacDonald had asked state highway officials to submit plans for interstate routes. The highway engineers knew which cities were to be linked, although the exact routes into the cities had yet to be determined.[18]

Expressways and the Central City

During the 1940s, MacDonald and other BPR officials promoted the interstate highway system as an integral aspect of urban renewal planning for cities. In particular, MacDonald adopted the imagery promoted by Norman Bel Geddes, suggesting often that "the future of America lies on the roadways of to-morrow."[19] As an engineer, however, he was also much more practical and specific in linking new urban express highways with the rebuilding of the central cities. For instance, in his 1943 speech "Proposed Interregional Highway System as It Affects Cities" to the American Society of Civil Engineers, MacDonald laid out the idea that central business district survival depended on highway building and the elimination of "blighted areas contiguous to the very heart of the city." The interstate highway system, he asserted, "can provide unparalleled opportunity for rebuilding [cities] along functional lines, following rational master plans." In a similar speech at a U.S. Chamber of Commerce Conference on Urban Problems in 1947, MacDonald noted that the suburban drift of population provided opportunities to "reconvert" central-city land to more important public purposes, including urban highways. In 1950, in a discussion of "The Interstate System in Urban Areas" before the American Planning and Civic Association, the relentless MacDonald continued to emphasize the linkage between urban expressways and slum clearance, urban renewal, and new housing construction.[20]

Together with housing administrators in FWA, MacDonald submitted legislative proposals along these lines to President Harry S Truman. In 1949, however, Truman rejected the coordination of highway and housing programs, citing expense and difficulty of congressional passage. Not long after, BPR was transferred to the Department of Commerce. At that point, as Mark Gelfand noted in *A Nation of Cities: The Federal Government and Urban America, 1933–1965* (1975), the agency seemingly "lost its interest in the broad implications of the highway in the city and concentrated its attention exclusively on making travel by automobile and truck quicker and less expensive." By the early 1950s, then, federal agencies had abandoned the linkage between highways and housing and between urban expressways and urban renewal. Highway engineers with their narrowly technical concerns were left in control of BPR.[21]

However, there was no lagging of interest in the building of an interstate highway network. Numerous powerful components of the highway lobby—sometimes called "the road gang" or "the highwaymen"—were busily at work promoting the system. These interests included the automobile industry and the oil companies, the trucking industry and the Teamsters union, construction companies and unions, various automobile-related trade associations, urban politicians and state highway officials, and the like. More important, for a variety of reasons, President Eisenhower wanted the interstate highway program initiated. A presidential advisory committee on highways headed by General Lucius D. Clay urged in its 1955 report that such a program be given top priority by Congress. The pro-highway forces came together decisively in the mid-1950s and, with presidential as well as widespread public support, launched through Congress the Interstate and Defense Highway Act of 1956.[22]

The new highway law provided for the building of 41,000 miles of interstate highways, about 8,000 of them in urban areas, all to be completed by 1972. The cost was estimated at $27 billion (although by 1977, that figure had ballooned to $104 billion), and 90 percent of the cost was to be borne by the federal government and the rest by the states. To pay for the highway system, a companion bill established a Highway Trust Fund financed by new excise taxes on gasoline, diesel fuel, and tires, as well as a special tax on trucks and buses. It was an enormous and ambitious project, "the largest public works program ever undertaken in the United States," according to one study of urban transportation. It was also a program that would have significant, and not altogether positive, consequences for urban America.[23]

The 1956 legislation reflected on the federal level a narrowly conceived engineering position based on the idea of moving automobile and truck traffic efficiently from point to point. A 1957 symposium of urban experts reflected some of the early criticism of the interstate program:

At present the design and location of highway facilities are treated as strictly engineering problems in which the only objective considered is that of keeping vehicles in rapid motion. There is no responsibility for relating highway construction to plans for the future of the city. The location and design of highways are not consciously used as means of promoting other purposes than those of moving traffic.

In the 1940s, Thomas MacDonald and BPR sought to link metropolitan area highway construction with urban renewal and public housing. The Truman and Eisenhower administrations rejected such a linkage, even though a contradictory policy had been implemented in federal urban-renewal legislation, which required slum clearance projects to be integrated within comprehensive efforts at urban planning. Such comprehensive plans were not required for the interstates, nor was there any federal responsibility for aiding in the relocation of an anticipated ninety thousand people who would be displaced by highway construction each year. In effect, the federal government had abdicated its responsibility for relocation assistance, and housing reform was lost in the political shuffle.[24]

Saving the Central Business District

Other powerful interest groups, however, were quick to recognize the implications of interstate highway construction at the cities' core. The absence of any official interest in rebuilding inner-city housing for those people who were displaced meant that huge sections of central-city land could be cleared for other uses. ULI, founded in 1936 to serve the interests of downtown real estate owners and developers, had consistently pushed for central-city redevelopment. The great concern of the downtown realtors was that suburbanization, and especially the decentralization of retailing that accompanied the growth of suburban shopping centers, would ultimately sap the vitality of central-city economic activities. The automobile was largely to blame, experts contended, both because it facilitated suburban growth and clogged downtown traffic arteries. As the respected urban planner and architect Victor Gruen put it in the mid-1950s, "The rotting of the core has set in in most American cities, in some cases progressing to an alarming degree." In the decade following World War II, the ULI Central Business District Council focused on freeways as "the salvation of the central district, the core of every city."[25]

In a stream of pamphlets, newsletters, and technical bulletins, ULI sought to pave the way for central-city expressways. For James W. Rouse, a Baltimore real estate developer involved with ULI in the 1950s and later well-known as a builder of "new towns" and festival marketplaces, the pattern of inner-city decay threatened the future of the central business district. According to Rouse, the solution for downtown America was clear: "Major expressways must be ripped through to the central core" as an integral aspect of extensive redevelopment efforts. Another urban developer, James H. Scheuer, noted approvingly in a 1957 article for ULI that the interstate highway program's "inner belt expressways" would "inevitably slice through great areas of our nation's worst slums." In its monthly newsletter, *Urban Land,* ULI in 1956 urged urban communities to survey the "extent to which blighted areas may provide suitable highway routes." The Interstate Highway Act of 1956, ULI urban consultant James W. Follin wrote, provided "wide open opportunity" to eliminate blighted housing and recapture central-city land for redevelopment. Federal policy had rejected the linkage of highway building and urban renewal, but ULI clearly envisioned that the new urban expressways promised the salvation of the central business district.[26]

Representatives of other interest groups also expressed the same message. The automobile lobby, for instance, mirrored the views of

ULI, promising that expressways would aid in rebuilding urban America. Typically, in the 1956 pamphlet *What Freeways Mean to Your City,* the Automotive Safety Foundation assured readers that freeways were desirable, beneficial, and beautiful. They were good for the cities and their suburbs, they stimulated rising land values, and they prevented "the spread of blight and . . . slums." Forward-looking communities were "using the transportation potential of freeways to speed redevelopment of run-down sections along sound lines and to prevent deterioration of desirable sections." Similarly, in a 1962 article, the Highway Research Board contended that interstate highways were "eating out slums" and "reclaiming blighted areas." The inner-city freeway, in short, represented a "positive social good," especially if it was routed through "blighted" slum neighborhoods that might be reclaimed for more productive civic uses.[27]

The downtown developers, the automobile lobby, highway officials and experts, and planners and politicians at every level all shared the urban expressway dream. Echoing Thomas MacDonald, BPR Urban Road Division Chief Joseph Barnett as early as 1946 suggested that properly located urban expressways would help immeasurably in "the stabilization of trade and values in the principle or central business district." By 1954, City Manager L.P. Cookingham of Kansas City was declaring to urban colleagues that "no large city can hope for a real future" without expressways that cleared slums and preserved the central business district.[28] Unhampered by federal controls, the highway builders routed the new urban expressways in directions of their own choosing. Local agendas of the political and business elites often dictated such decisions. In most cities, the result was to drive the interstates through black and poor neighborhoods. As early as 1949, a federal housing official predicted that "the real masters of urban redevelopment will be the forces intent upon recapturing Negro living space for the 'right' people."[29]

Within a decade, this prophecy had been largely fulfilled, because urban expressway building usually meant black removal. Urban blacks were heavily concentrated in areas with the oldest and most dilapidated housing, where land acquisition costs were relatively low, and where organized political opposition was weakest. A "kill two birds with one stone" mentality prevailed almost everywhere. Cities sought to route interstate highways through slum neighborhoods, thus using federal highway money to reclaim downtown urban real estate. Inner-city slums could be cleared, blacks removed to more distant second-ghetto areas, the central business districts redeveloped, and transportation woes solved all at the same time—and mostly at federal expense.[30] In cities such as Miami, the interstate

highway program provided an opportunity to reshape the city spatially and to remove the black community entirely from potentially
valuable central-city land.

Interstate Planning in Florida

The pattern of expressway building in the Miami metropolitan area
fits easily into the national model previously outlined. Florida began
receiving federal aid for state highways in 1916, when congressional
legislation first initiated federal subsidies for roads. Road building
intensified during the 1920s, when increasing numbers of tourists
arrived in Florida by automobile. As early as 1927, Florida highway
officials had begun dreaming of an "Atlantic Coast Highway" that
would stretch from Maine to Florida and run through Jacksonville
and Miami—a vision ultimately fulfilled with the completion of I-95.
Even before the end of World War II, the Florida State Road Department was gearing up for the postwar road-building effort. For each of
the first three postwar years, $7 million in federal funds were ear-
marked for Florida on a "fifty-fifty matching basis." By 1945, state
highway engineers had also begun planning for the Florida portion of
the interstate highway system, initially established in the Federal
Highway Act of 1944. Florida was to have approximately 980 miles of
interstate highway, some 205 miles in urban areas, and the state's
highway engineers had begun surveying potential right-of-way, "especially those related to the urban routes."[31]

By the late 1940s, state road officials reported progress on the construction of an East Coast "interstate" highway between Jacksonville
and Miami, referred to in South Florida as the "super-duper" highway. In the Miami area, this original interstate highway was under
construction by 1947 (actually it was an existing state road that was
widened and repaved). This initially designated "interstate" highway
was a four-lane divided highway running through a sparsely settled
neighborhood on the western fringes of the Dade County and bypass-
ing downtown Miami. However, it was not the kind of high-speed,
limited-access expressway that people have come to identify with the
modern interstate system. State highway planners, though, already
were recommending inner-city expressways for Miami and other Florida cities as part of the interstate system. Such an expressway was
built in Jacksonville between 1947 and 1952, much of it clearing
away congested, inner-city "blighted" areas, whereas plans for Miami

remained on the drawing board. As the Florida State Road Department stated in April 1947 in its monthly magazine *Florida Highways,* "Studies have clearly shown that routes to and through the hearts of big cities are what are needed—not by-passes." Florida highway officials clearly shared the views of national road builders like Thomas MacDonald.[32]

The passage of the Interstate and Defense Highway Act of 1956 brought a new level of activity to the Florida State Road Department. Newly elected Florida Governor LeRoy Collins and state road board head Wilbur E. Jones had closely monitored the progress of federal highway legislation during 1955 and 1956, with an eye toward the implications for Florida. Jones had already prepared a long report for Governor Collins on "The Highway Problem," which laid out the economic benefits that Florida might expect from interstate highway building, especially in urban areas.[33] Consequently, Florida was well positioned to take quick advantage of massive federal funding for road building. Origin–destination studies of automobile traffic had already been conducted to determine tentative interstate routes, new highway engineers were hired, rights-of-way in urban areas were being acquired, and interstate offices were opened in Tampa, Jacksonville, Orlando, and Miami. Because of heavy automobile congestion in the cities, as well as rising land-acquisition costs, highway officials thought it important to begin first on the urban expressway portions of the 1,164-mile Florida interstate system. Miami was high on the list for federally funded expressways.[34]

The Miami Expressway Pattern

In Miami, planning was underway for building expressways into the urban core even before passage of the landmark 1956 federal highway legislation. Miami's downtown business leaders had been concerned about the future of the central city as early as the 1930s. By the early 1950s, city and county officials had begun drawing up plans for slum clearance in black neighborhoods. The Central Business District Council of the ULI had been to Miami to study the city's problems. The Florida State Road Department, in cooperation with city and county agencies, had conducted origin–destination studies of automobile traffic in the Miami area, and it had investigated expressways and central-city parking problems. As on the national level, the salvation of the central business district emerged as the expressed or implied goal in all of these studies.[35]

By the 1950s, the inner-city expressway had become the universally accepted solution to the problems of America's urban decay. The story was little different in Miami. A 1955 report on "trafficways" issued by the Miami Planning and Zoning Board provided the first comprehensive expressway plan for the rapidly growing tourist city. The report envisioned an extensive expressway system, with an elevated "downtown leg" that would serve the business district. In detailing the exact route into the central city, however, the trafficways plan seemed especially sensitive to neighborhood considerations. As noted in the report, "Locations have been chosen through or along the fringes of low value industrial and commercial areas rather than cutting through good residential districts, in order to preserve and help protect existing residential neighborhoods and promote an economically desirable use of land." Prepared by planning consultant Julian Tarrant, the trafficways plan contemplated "a system of fast, heavy-duty Expressways" that stretched north from the central business district along the right-of-way of the Florida Eastcoast Railroad tracks. At N.W. 14th Street, the route shifted northwest through the fringes of an industrial area and then north again along a route just east of N.W. 7th Avenue. A major intersection with an East–West expressway was planned at N.W. 23rd Street, but it too was located "in a semi-industrial area with considerable vacant land." Relatively little housing would have been lost to highway construction under this early plan, which would have routed the interstate around the eastern and northern edges of Overtown.[36]

The city's planning department prepared the 1955 Miami plan without consulting county or state officials. The Miami planners recognized that they were out of step with "the usual thinking of traffic engineers," asserting instead the primacy of "neighborhood preservation." However, the City of Miami had little control over expressway planning. Interstate highway location was generally the prerogative of the state highway departments. In Florida, the state road department usually consulted with local officials, especially politicians, but final route decisions rested in the hands of state highway engineers. The professional planners employed by the City of Miami obviously had some concerns about routing expressways through residential neighborhoods such as Overtown, but ultimately they were cut out of the final decision making on expressway locations. More influential, perhaps, were the downtown Miami businesspeople, realtors, and politicians who sought to expand the business district into Overtown. In late 1955, these business leaders formed the Miami First Committee to push an alternative expressway plan. With passage of the 1956 interstate highway act a few months later, state highway planners moved quickly to develop their own expressway plan for Miami.[37]

A new expressway proposal emerged in 1956, one that rejected essential downtown portions of the plan presented in 1955 by the Miami Planning and Zoning Board. The new highway plan was prepared by the nationally known engineering consulting firm of Wilbur Smith and Associates for the Florida State Road Department and the Dade County Commission. The plan entailed an urban expressway system of forty-one miles, including an inner beltway or loop around the central business district that was never built. The primary goal of moving traffic underlay the plan: "It is considered to be an ideal expressway system in that it serves practically every important traffic movement within the area." The new plan maintained the N.W. 7th Avenue route of the North–South Expressway (as I-95 was originally called) from northern Dade County south to about N.W. 17th Street. At that point, the expressway route veered in a southeasterly direction toward the Miami business district, slashing through the central part of Overtown along the way. Specifically, use of the Florida Eastcoast Railroad right-of-way was rejected to provide "ample room for the future expansion of the central business district in a westerly direction." The entire expressway system was to be elevated above street level, except in the sparsely built-up areas in northern and western Dade County. In addition, rather than a single East–West interchange located in an industrial area, the 1956 expressway plan proposed two major East–West, cloverleaf interchanges, both linked to new causeways to Miami Beach and new expressways to the West. Both interchanges were slated for residential areas, and one—the mammoth midtown interchange—eventually took out more than two dozen blocks at the heart of Overtown, including much of its main business district. Interestingly, the Wilbur Smith expressway plan remained completely silent on the matter of community dislocation.[38]

In contracting with Wilbur Smith and Associates to plan the Miami expressway system, Florida road officials had tapped one of the nation's leading experts on urban transportation planning. A professor of transportation and traffic engineering at Yale University, Wilbur S. Smith had founded his own consulting firm in New Haven, Connecticut, in 1952. By 1956, when states began gearing up for interstate construction, Smith's firm was well positioned to take advantage of the massive flow of federal dollars for highway planning and construction. Wilbur Smith shared the expressway vision of road builders such as Thomas MacDonald and Robert Moses. He saw the inner-city expressway, with its land clearance and urban renewal potential, as the savior of the central business district. He worked closely over the years with highway and automobile lobby groups such as the Automobile Manufacturers Association, the Highway Research Board, and the Portland Cement Association, and he consistently contended in his reports and other writings that cities had to adapt to and accommodate the automobile. As a big freeway advocate, Wilbur Smith also developed close ties to state highway officials represented in such groups as the American Association of State Highway Officials, as well as to federal highway officials in BPR (some of whom were later brought into Smith's firm). Smith's growing public reputation as a traffic expert by the mid-1950s first brought him to the attention of Wilbur Jones, head of the Florida State Road Department. Smith's Miami expressway plan was his first major freeway study following passage of the Interstate and Defense Highway Act of 1956. The two Wilburs—Smith and Jones—forged a close relationship during the Miami work, and the Florida State Road Department subsequently contracted with Wilbur Smith and Associates for expressway and interstate planning in Tampa, St. Petersburg, Orlando, Tallahassee, and other Florida cities. Wilbur Smith had much to do with expressway building in Florida and elsewhere, but he never expressed much interest in the housing and relocation problems of those residents who were displaced by urban expressways.[39]

By the end of 1956, the basic route of I-95 into Miami had been laid out by Wilbur Smith and his staff of engineers and technicians. Smith's expressway plan was quickly approved and adopted by the Florida State Road Department. Within one month, in December 1956, the Dade County Commission voted to approve the state plan. Soon, Miami's major newspapers and television stations endorsed the expressway plan, as did the Miami and Miami Beach city commissions and business groups such as the chamber of commerce. Several perfunctory public hearings were held, but despite the airing of citizen protests, the hearings had no influence in altering the Wilbur Smith expressway route. The state road department divided the expressway project into several segments, and acquisition of right-of-way and construction began almost immediately. An initial portion of the North–South Expressway in northern Dade County was opened in December 1960. Other portions of the expressway opened periodically over the next few years, the entire project being essentially completed by 1968.[40]

Public Response

Despite the massive dislocation of businesses and people anticipated as a result of expressway construction in Miami, opposition to the new interstate highway system was surprisingly mild and ineffective. At the first public hearing held on February 7, 1957, a substantial number of the five hundred or so people present indicated opposition to an elevated expressway. Former Miami Mayor Abe Aronovitz emerged as the most persistent spokesperson for this initial antiexpressway position. Aronovitz portrayed an elevated expressway as "a monstrosity straddling the City of Miami" that would destroy the city's beauty and charm, undermine downtown property values, create new slums, and enrage the citizenry. Aronovitz proposed instead that the North–South expressway be built in Biscayne Bay and parallel the shoreline. Other speakers at this hearing supported Aronovitz, whereas citizens at a subsequent hearing held in North Miami on September 27, 1957, generally complained that the expressway was taking their homes and businesses, and that an alternative route would be better. Highway officials considered Aronovitz an obstructionist who was "completely off base," but the opposition in North Miami, a middle-class white community, did provoke a reexamination of the route through that north Dade County area. Ultimately, however, Wilbur Smith and Wilbur Jones held firm. The highway builders asserted that professional and impartial engineering studies had identified the best expressway routes, and that public complaints were insufficient reason for deviating from those choices.[41]

A mild undercurrent of opposition to the Wilbur Smith expressway plan continued for several months. In February 1957, shortly after the expressway route had been finalized, a group of property owners broke into a Dade County Commission meeting and presented a petition with about three hundred signatures, protesting particularly about the downtown elevated portions of the expressway. The commission put off the protesters by asserting that the expressway decisions were irrevocable. In January 1958, the Miami Housing Authority sought to shift the expressway route slightly to protect a white public housing project from the bulldozer. This appeal was rejected by the state road department as too expensive because, as the *Miami Herald* stated, "it would put the route through highly developed commercial areas." Individual citizens, almost entirely from white neighborhoods, continued to write to the Florida road department, Governor Collins, even President Eisenhower, usually complaining about loss of property to the expressway. However, some of these citizens were quite perceptive about the ultimate effect of the expressway on Miami's residential patterns. In a letter to Wilbur Jones, for instance, one Miami woman not only dramatically envisioned the expressway as "a monstrosity which would arch like the back of a huge dinosaur over an area of the city," but predicted racial conflict as well. The expressway, Winifred Nelson wrote to state road chairman Jones, "would cause dissatisfaction and dissention between the races here, because it would necessarily displace many of the Negro race. They would have to move into the outer fringe of white sections, with the accompanying flaring-up of hatreds."[42]

There is no evidence that the road builders paid any attention to such citizen complaints, nor were they much concerned about the effect of the expressway on racial housing patterns. Actually, the elimination of black housing near the central business district was a generally accepted goal of Miami's downtown business leaders. As one local realtor informed the state road department in 1957, most of the downtown area affected by the expressway consisted of "slum type buildings housing negroes." Because "the city and the county have been stressing the need to have these removed," realtor J.N. Lummus suggested, the expressway presented an opportunity to achieve that goal. The Miami civic elite generally conceived of Overtown as "the City's principal problem," one that could be taken care of through highway building or other forms of urban renewal. At the time, few expressed much concern about the problem of black housing relocation.[43]

Surprisingly, in light of what eventually happened to Overtown, Miami's black community was also less than militant on the expressway route. The Wilbur Smith plan that routed the expressway directly through the black community did not generate any protests or demonstrations. Even the *Miami Times,* the city's black newspaper, grudgingly accepted the reality of the new expressway. The *Times* regretted the inevitable displacement of poor people from their homes, but editorialized in 1957 that "with the expansion and progress of a city, there is little you can do about it." A few years later, in urging a "yes" vote on a Dade County expressway bond issue, the *Times* again emphasized the theme of progress: "We are living in a progressive state. We cannot afford to take a backward step."[44]

The theme of progress pervaded public discussion of the Miami expressway system. Local realtors liked the expressway idea because, as one wrote Jones in 1957, it would "stimulate building in this downtown area, which is vital at this time." Similarly, in a letter to Florida Senator Spessard Holland in 1959, a Miami Beach real estate agent declared that nothing was "more important to the prosperity and well-being of the citizens of Florida than the interstate highway program."[45] The local business community lauded the potential effect of the new interstates, which would be "a priceless boon to Florida tourists and Florida's tourist industry." Florida highway officials relentlessly boosted the interstate program, emphasizing that "pleasant motoring is vital to the continued development of our state as a vacation land and an industrial and agricultural area." A 1961 article in *Better Roads,* the magazine of the national road-building lobby, painted a glowing vision of what Dade County might expect once the new highway system was completed: "Expressways and gigantic interchanges are bringing speed and comfort to Miami motoring, and less time spent in driving leaves more hours free for fun in Miami's famous sun."[46]

Local politicians also were enthusiastic about Miami's new expressway system. "We are very grateful in Miami for benefits that we expect I-95 to bring to our city and this area," one Miami city commissioner wrote to BPR Federal Highway Administrator Rex M. Whitton in 1965. When the pace of expressway building lagged, the politicians complained to legislators in Washington, D.C., about the negative consequences of construction delays.[47] Even the Greater Miami Urban League, which worked for better social and economic conditions among blacks, fell victim to the booster spirit on the expressway issue, as reflected in an official statement issued in 1957: "The Greater Miami Urban League feels that the proposed Miami Expressway is necessary for the continued progress of our city and commends the plan."[48]

The stand of the Miami Urban League seemed surprising, given that the expressway route ripped through the black community of Overtown and would soon destroy thousands of black housing units. Equally surprising was the moderately positive editorial position of the *Miami Times* on expressway building. However, Miami's blacks did not have much of an active political tradition yet, and South Florida was still part of the Deep South on issues of race relations. Several studies have noted that in the mid-1950s, black leaders in Miami tended toward an accommodationist position and, as a result, had "been able to establish a *modus vivendi* with municipal authorities" on many issues. Serious challenges to segregation did not come until 1959 and 1960, when the Congress of Racial Equality began sitting in at downtown lunch counters and standing in at Miami theaters. By 1960 activists, from the National Association for the Advancement of Colored People (NAACP) and the Urban League had integrated Dade County hotels, parks, beaches, swimming pools, and golf courses. However, between 1955 and 1957, when the expressway route was being established, Miami blacks were still more passive than active. At that point, the black community had not demonstrated much militancy or voting power, which made Overtown a relatively easy target for the highway builders and the downtown businessmen.[49]

The Expressway and Black Housing

Despite their apparent support of the expressways as necessary for municipal "progress," both the Greater Miami Urban League and the *Miami Times* urged official attention to the crucial issue of relocation housing. The expressway system, especially as it ran through Overtown, would uproot thousands of families. The Miami Slum Clearance Department initially reported in 1957 that fifty-seven hundred people would be dislodged in Overtown by highway construction. By 1959, the Dade County manager's office had increased that estimate to ten thousand people, with still other thousands to be displaced by slum clearance and urban renewal. By the early 1960s, a local housing reform association was estimating that at least three thousand black families would be uprooted from Overtown by the expressway, and possibly as many as twenty-three thousand individuals by all forms of urban redevelopment. The *Miami Herald* starkly posed the essential question as early as March 1957 in an article entitled, "What about the Negroes Uprooted by Expressway?" No agency was planning for relocation of the uprooted blacks, the *Miami Herald* asserted, and blacks were already moving into "former white areas along the fringes" of the ghetto. By the late 1950s, even before the expressway tore through Overtown, black housing density was on the rise and pressure was building for new housing areas for blacks. The problem, one knowledgeable University of Miami economist noted in 1958, was "where this Negro population can expand."[50]

The editor of the *Miami Times* had asked the same question a year earlier in March 1957: "The trouble is, where will these people go?" The Greater Miami Urban League was similarly worried about the housing problem of displaced blacks. J.E. Preston, president of the Miami Urban League, urged Governor Collins and Wilbur Jones of the state road department to begin planning for the social consequences of expressway construction in Miami. The Urban League, the *Miami Times,* and others who spoke for the black community urged a major program of relocation assistance, new public and private housing, and federal mortgage programs to help dislocated blacks resettle in other areas. Jones and Collins remained noncommittal, essentially maintaining the position that highway building and housing were two separate and distinct activities.[51]

Even though federal policy had purposely separated the two issues, urban expressway building was inevitably linked to the nation's inner-city housing problem. This was certainly true in Miami. By the 1930s, much of Overtown had been built up with the "shotgun" shacks that could be found in the black neighborhoods of most southern cities. During the next two decades, slumlords and private developers began removing and replacing these wooden structures with more profitable two- and three-story apartment houses, generally called "concrete monsters" in Miami. Density was high in Overtown, municipal services virtually unknown, and slum conditions rampant. Public housing began in the 1930s, but did not help much. The Miami Housing Authority (MHA) built three housing projects by the end of the decade, with a total of 1,515 housing units. One of these was Liberty Square, the black project that became the nucleus of Liberty City. The other two public housing projects were designated for whites. Despite a 31-percent increase in metropolitan Miami's black population during the 1940s, no new public housing projects were built until the 1950s.[52]

Housing reformers in Miami and elsewhere had been elated by passage of the federal Housing Act of 1949, with its programs for urban renewal and new public housing construction. That measure required local governments to provide relocation housing for people displaced by urban redevelopment. The federal Housing Act of 1954 went even further, requiring urban renewal to be carried out within the context of a comprehensive urban planning program. A successful local referendum in 1950 empowered MHA to build additional public housing, but only 762 new units went up by 1958. The City of Miami established a Department of Slum Clearance in 1952 to coordinate urban renewal and redevelopment, but little was accomplished during the decade.[53]

Part of the problem stemmed from fierce and highly organized opposition from wealthy slumlords, and from powerful business and real estate interests. A local Committee Against Socialized Housing, for instance, emerged in 1950 to fight public housing in Miami. The group had the backing of the city's chamber of commerce, the Miami Board of Realtors, several banks, and leading politicians, including the mayor.[54] By 1957, a Property Owners Development Association was actively lobbying against public housing and urban renewal, advocating instead "a private enterprise renewal program for central Miami." Still later, Miami slumlords organized a Free Enterprise

Association to fight public housing.[55] Reporting to BPR in 1957, one highway official noted that

> opposition to much needed urban redevelopment in Miami stems from a few real estate owners who own most of the property occupied by negroes. . . . These real estate owners bring up the bugaboo of federal interference with race integration overtones and justify their stand on the basis that the rundown neighborhoods could be improved by concerted effort of the property owners themselves.[56]

The Miami slumlords clearly were adamantly opposed to public housing and urban renewal.

However, housing reformers and city reporters for the Miami newspapers were persistent. Both the *Miami News* and the *Miami Herald* provided close coverage of housing issues throughout the 1950s, and both newspapers periodically published a series of investigative reports on housing, slums, and slumlords. In 1958, for example, the *Miami Herald* ran a series on slum housing, demonstrating the close personal and financial links between the director of Miami's slum clearance office and the city's slumlords.[57] As one Miami housing reformer, Elizabeth Virrick, put it in 1958, "The opposition to any change in the status quo here is unbelievable and is carried on by the very influential and wealthy and so-called respected people who own the extensive and profitable Negro slums." Not only did the slumlords have powerful friends in government, but as Virrick bitterly suggested, "Almost none of our officials [seems] to be interested in anything from which they cannot profit."[58]

In the era of McCarthyism, those who promoted public housing and urban renewal fought an uphill battle, particularly in the South. However, other problems undermined housing efforts in Miami, as well. Official obstructionism and bureaucratic infighting came to typify public housing and urban renewal efforts in the Miami metropolitan area. In the early 1950s, Miami city commissioners often failed to back up the Miami Housing Authority in its slum clearance efforts. Most city officials were actively opposed to public housing. The story was much the same at the county level, and Dade County zoning commissioners refused to rezone land for public housing. After Dade County's metropolitan government was created in 1957, new rivalries and conflicts developed among governmental units and agencies, hampering slum clearance and housing programs. Housing efforts in Dade County were set back several years by legal battles on the constitutionality of using eminent domain to acquire property for urban renewal and redevelopment. Occasionally, the state legislature failed to pass enacting legislation permitting Miami authorities to tap federal housing or relocation funds. When a large urban renewal project did get off the ground in Miami, one close observer noted that the state road department routed "the Expressway and an interchange running smack down the middle of it."[59]

Miami's urban expressway building, then, came at a time of considerable state and local opposition to federal housing assistance in Florida. Lines of political and bureaucratic authority were blurred, especially with the creation of Dade Metro in 1957. State politicians were still fighting the battle of federal interference. Even federal policy was confused and inconsistent, with urban renewal requiring relocation assistance whereas interstate highway construction did not. Under the circumstances, it is not surprising that few spoke out forcefully about the social consequences of I-95 in Miami.

Elizabeth Virrick, Slum Housing, and the Expressway

Among the few who did speak out on housing and redevelopment issues was Elizabeth Virrick, a housing reformer and activist in Miami. A resident of Miami since the mid-1920s, Virrick helped organize the Coconut Grove Citizens Committee for Slum Clearance in 1948 to improve black housing in Miami's Coconut Grove section. Virrick served through the 1950s and 1960s as the agency's executive director and chief source of energy and inspiration. She had battled the slumlords on public housing issues in the early 1950s, and she harassed the politicians relentlessly to do something about slums and housing. Virrick had acquired allies in the local press and a considerable degree of local influence by the mid-1950s.[60]

When the expressway plans became public in 1956 and 1957, Virrick immediately became alarmed that, as she wrote to Florida state road head Wilbur Jones, "the pathway of the new expressway will cause great hardship to the Negroes in the Central Negro area, both home owners and tenants, who will be displaced." She urged the creation of a relocation agency that would survey available housing in Miami and provide information and assistance to those displaced by highway building. Without such relocation assistance, Virrick argued, population densities in the Overtown area would rise rapidly, "aggravating the miserable slum conditions that already exist." Virrick did not get far with the state road department, because the business of that agency was highway building, not relocation housing. Jones commended Virrick's interest in the problem, but promised only to provide displaced families with sufficient notice "so that plans can be made well in advance to help them find new housing." The state road department provided an official thirty-day eviction notice to those in the path of the expressway.[61]

Throughout the expressway-building era, Elizabeth Virrick was a lonely but publicly respected voice speaking out on the necessity of linking highway construction with urban renewal and relocation housing. On behalf of her Coconut Grove committee, she constantly challenged elected officials, badgered staffers in city and county agencies, and cultivated the local press. She promoted her urban renewal goals for Miami with federal housing agencies, developed an enormous correspondence with housing reformers in other cities, and wrote articles for national housing journals on the Miami situation. By the 1960s, Virrick was serving on at least a dozen civic committees and advisory boards dealing with housing, planning, and community relations in the Miami area. She was a thorn in the side of the Miami real estate interests, some of whom were heavily invested in rental housing in Overtown and Liberty City. She used her press connections and her monthly *Ink Newsletter* to expose the machinations of the slumlords, whom she reported in 1962 as having "been very active in the region where the expressway is to go." During several referenda on public housing and urban renewal issues, Virrick debated slumlord representatives in public forums and on radio talk shows. Her persistence was legendary in Miami at the time, but results from her self-described "one-woman effort" were slow in coming.[62]

By 1964, when construction of the south leg of the expressway through Overtown and into the central business district was about to get under way, Virrick intensified her attack on "the helter-skelter spewing out of expressways without proper forethought and planning." In a series of hard-hitting columns in her monthly newsletters, renamed in 1964 *Ink: The Journal of Civic Affairs,* Virrick mounted an assault on the "Great Frankensteinian monsters"—the expressways that destroyed neighborhoods and parks, "disfigured" the city, and created new slums. She painted a harsh picture of the effects of expressway building in Miami:

With shocking ruthlessness, the expressways slash through our city without regard to the grim results of cutting through Lummus Park, part of Simpson Park, building an impenetrable wall that will cut the city in half, will separate many stores from the people who deal there, will uglify pleasant areas and make bad areas worse. We are told to take it or leave it. In our over-anxiety to move automobiles faster, we bow our heads to this dictatorship and take it.... Hasn't anyone heard of San Francisco where the road program was stopped and replanned because an alert citizenry demanded it?

Miami was suffering badly from "bulldozitis followed rapidly by asphaltitis." As Virrick phrased it with typical sarcasm, "The theme appears to be: never mind about anything, but Woodman, spare those twelve lanes for the automobile!" Obviously influenced by the national outcry against urban expressways that had emerged in the early 1960s, Virrick pleaded for "a fresh evaluation of the entire expressway system."[63]

But it was not to be. Elizabeth Virrick was the closest thing Miami had to an antihighway movement, but a one-woman crusade was not enough. The Miami expressway system was completed, at the cost of uprooting most of Miami's inner-city black community. Little was done at first in the way of providing decent housing for those in the path of the bulldozer. Things changed somewhat in the 1960s, as President John F. Kennedy's War on Poverty began cranking up and especially after President Lyndon B. Johnson's Great Society programs began to be implemented. New federal policy directives demanded greater attention to the social effects of expressway construction. The Federal Highway Act of 1962, for instance, required any federal highway building after 1965 to be coordinated with urban and metropolitan planning; such plans had to consider an expressway's "probable effect on the future development of the urban area." By the late 1960s, the U.S. Department of Transportation (DOT) had become extremely sensitive to the relocation issue, and DOT Secretary John A. Volpe had publicly acknowledged the need to link highway construction with prior acquisition of replacement housing.[64]

In Miami, a variety of federal programs attacked the problem of low-income housing. Some urban renewal projects were undertaken in Overtown, although they housed only a fraction of those displaced by the expressway. New "scattered site" public housing projects in other sections of metropolitan Miami absorbed some of those forced from Overtown. A Model Cities program in a neighborhood adjacent to Overtown provided new housing for others dislocated by redevelopment projects. The establishment of a new Metro-Dade County Department of Housing and Urban Development pulled together under professional leadership a variety of housing, relocation, and redevelopment functions. However, these efforts were all too late to save Overtown.[65]

Second Ghetto in Miami

Overtown was slated for destruction, but expressway building also initiated a vast racial restructuring of Miami's residential space. At the beginning of the expressway era in the 1950s, most of Miami's blacks resided in Overtown, but several smaller black residential districts were distributed throughout the metropolitan area. On the southern fringes of Miami, blacks had been living in a section of Coconut Grove since the 1880s and 1890s when black Bahamian immigrants began arriving in the area. The Liberty Square public housing project built in the 1930s became the nucleus of a new black community on the undeveloped northwestern periphery of Miami. A few miles away, the small black residential subdivision of Brownsville had grown from a settlement of a few hundred in the 1930s to a few thousand in the 1950s. Still farther north, a smaller number of blacks had settled in a section of Opa-locka, a white, working-class community of small and inexpensive homes. At the southern extremities of Dade County, fifteen to twenty miles from downtown Miami, small black communities had emerged in Homestead, Florida City, Goulds, Perrine, and Richmond Heights. Richmond Heights was a new, middle-class black subdivision of single-family homes built in the early 1950s; the other communities housed blacks mostly engaged in low-income agricultural labor in Dade County's extensive vegetable and citrus industries. Of sixty-five thousand blacks in Dade County in 1950, forty thousand lived in Overtown, with the remainder distributed among the smaller black communities.[66]

Until the 1950s, the expansion of black residential space was closely controlled by city and county government and by the local real estate industry. Recognizing the housing pressures created by rising population in Overtown, officials in 1945 permitted some black expansion in undeveloped areas of Liberty City and Coconut Grove, but fended off real estate developers who sought to enlarge the "negro settlement boundaries of Brownsville." County commission racial zoning was declared unconstitutional by the Florida Supreme Court in 1946, but other formal and informal mechanisms were used to maintain residential segregation and control the expansion of black areas. Despite the ruling, for instance, the Dade County attorney opined in December 1946 that the county could continue to "have an 'understanding' that the designated tracts are for negroes." In 1951, the Dade County Planning Board was still operating on the principle that "expansion of existing negro areas and the further designation of new areas for negro occupancy should be only on a 'controlled' basis."

Pursuing this goal, the planning board worked with private developers and builders in rezoning land for black housing in Opa-locka and Richmond Heights.[67]

The City of Miami was equally determined to control black housing expansion. Typically, in 1949 MHA, recognizing the need for "opening up additional areas for colored housing," sought state authority to build new public housing for blacks in distant areas outside the city limits. In 1951, city officials initiated condemnation proceedings to acquire a private black housing development for a police station and a sewer facility, thus creating a barrier between white and black neighborhoods. A year later, the Miami City Commission rezoned adjacent residential land as industrial, preventing the construction of a public housing project and enlarging the spatial barrier between the races. In addition, white neighborhood organizations, such as the Northwest Property Owners League, the Edison Center Civic Association, and the Opa-locka Civic Improvement Association, actively lobbied city and county governments and engaged in protest demonstrations as blacks began to push out of Overtown into nearby areas.[68]

Second-ghetto tensions flared in 1951, when the owners of the Knight Manor apartment complex, which was located in Edison Center on the eastern fringes of Liberty City and rented to whites, began renting to blacks. The Dade County Property Owners Association complained to Governor Fuller Warren that "by vacating white tenants and replacing them with colored tenants," the owners were disturbing the peace of "a long established white neighborhood." The group urged that the Dade County Commission open up more vacant land for black occupancy. A local Citizens Action League sprang up "to protect our Southern way of life." Others complained that "the negro area is to be extended into what has always been a white area." The Ku Klux Klan became active, reflecting the virulent brand of white hostility that often characterized the first stages of second-ghetto expansion. A series of dynamite bombings in late 1951 brought the Knight Manor conflict to a head, as militant whites sought to scare off their new black neighbors. Behind the scene, however, other forces were at work. The apartment owners were well-known Miami slumlords with investments in the black Coconut Grove area and in Brownsville, and one was a member of the Dade County Zoning Board. Edison Center whites believed, apparently with good reason, that the movement of blacks into Knight Manor was the opening wedge for designating the entire area for black residency, with the landowners and realtors profiting immensely.[69] As this incident and others suggest, the availability of black housing and the expansion of residential areas open to blacks was closely regulated and controlled.

Local government agencies and the real estate industry worked together closely in shaping housing and development policies.

In the decade following World War II, two significant changes in the black housing pattern in Miami began to emerge. First, the white property owners who controlled most of Overtown's housing initiated a private redevelopment program of sorts. To a certain extent, Overtown property owners sought to stave off pressure exerted after 1949 by local housing reformers such as Elizabeth Virrick for more low-cost public housing. However, the drive for bigger profits on rentals seemed to be the most powerful motivation for new building in the ghetto. Whatever the reason, by 1950, the slumlords were removing the tiny, wooden-frame shotgun shacks that predominated in Overtown. In their place, Overtown began sprouting 12- to 16-unit, 2- and 3-story apartment structures with U-shaped front courtyards. It was a profitable venture for the owners. The shotgun shacks generally were not destroyed but were moved to more remote parts of Dade County, where they were sold to big farmers to house migrant agricultural laborers. The "concrete monsters," as Virrick called the new apartments, doubled the number of housing units that could be squeezed onto the cleared land. The rent was higher for these "slums of the future," often double the seven-dollar weekly rents of the shotgun shacks. Between 1946 and 1950, at least 120 of these apartment structures were built in Overtown—approximately 1,600 apartment units. According to Luther Voltz, a *Miami Herald* reporter who covered the local housing and highway beat in the 1950s, the slumlords were earning an average 23-percent return annually on their investments in the "concrete monsters." Poorly planned and badly built, most of the apartments had only one bedroom, and few had much space for recreation or parking. Densities crept up and conditions quickly deteriorated as these Overtown apartments became new, more permanent slums.[70]

A second change in Miami's postwar black housing pattern was occurring simultaneously. A more sustained outward dispersal of black population from Overtown to the already established smaller black communities had begun to occur. A University of Miami study of black housing published in 1951 noted that "the most remarkable fact of postwar housing developments is the spreading of the Negro population over wider areas." In documenting the decentralization of Miami's black population, the study demonstrated the surge of house and apartment construction that was occurring in black communities throughout the metropolitan area. Between 1946 and 1950, some 6,795 housing units for blacks were constructed in Dade County, 5,165 or 76 percent of them in areas other than Overtown. Opa-locka led all black communities, with 1,807 new housing units during that 5-year period, almost all single-family or duplex homes, and almost all built by two white developers, Milton H. Davis and Julius Gaines. Apartment construction—"concrete monsters" again—was concentrated in Liberty City, Brownsville, and Coconut Grove. Much of this new private housing construction occurred in large-scale developments, such as the 1,000-unit Bunche Park project in Opa-locka or the 475 homes in the Richmond Heights subdivision.[71]

Several circumstances contributed to the beginnings of black population deconcentration in Miami. A decade and a half of depression and war after 1930 had slowed the residential housing market to a virtual standstill. A powerful suburban housing boom in the postwar era attempted to satisfy the long restrained demand for housing. Blacks in Miami demonstrated the same pent-up demands for satisfactory residential housing. Blacks in Overtown were densely crowded—150 people per residential acre compared with 12 people per residential acre for whites in Miami, according to an Urban League study in 1954. The inability to find suitable housing forced many familes to double up in Overtown apartments. The black population of the metropolitan area was growing rapidly—31.2 percent in the 1940s and 111 percent in the 1950s. The Miami area economy provided relatively good employment opportunities for black workers in tourism, the building trades, and other local industries, so many black families had the financial resources to purchase new homes. New housing and veterans legislation during these years gave blacks access to Federal Housing Administration and Veterans Administration mortgage money for the first time. It was only a matter of time before private builders and developers recognized the potential market for new housing among blacks in Dade County. As the Greater Miami Urban League noted in 1954, "Enlightened sources view the non-white population as a potential housing market which has not been fully explored." Once that idea penetrated the local real estate industry, home builders and subdivision developers found an eager market for new homes and apartments among blacks traditionally confined to Overtown.[72]

By the mid-1950s, then, some decentralization of blacks out of Overtown had already begun. Mostly, those moving out were settling in Brownsville, Liberty City, and Opa-locka. A corridor of black residential development was fanning out to the northwest of the central city. This development had been anticipated as early as the 1930s, when city officials and real estate developers tacitly agreed to designate the northwestern area of Miami for black expansion. The redlining of this entire area in real estate appraisals conducted locally for the Home Owners Loan Corporation reinforced the decision to permit black residential expansion there. Much of this section of metropolitan Miami was undeveloped or sparsely settled, leaving considerable room for growth of the second ghetto.[73]

Expressways and the Second Ghetto

Expressway building in the Miami metropolitan area beginning in the late 1950s triggered a dramatic increase in the growth of the second ghetto. Miami's black population was rising rapidly, Overtown was badly overcrowded, and the black community had unprecedented housing demands. Once the expressway route into downtown Miami became known, it was clear that housing would be destroyed rather than built in Overtown. Thousands of black families began searching for new housing in advance of the expressway. Not surprisingly, most looked to the corridor of black communities that had developed in the northwestern quadrant of the metropolitan area.

Moreover, the nature of black migration to the second ghetto changed dramatically in the late 1950s. In the past, black residential expansion was to areas specifically developed for blacks, and the process was carefully controlled. With the new pressures created by rising population and expressway building, as well as by the movement for civil rights and desegregation, the old rules no longer fully applied. Blacks began moving into white neighborhoods on the fringes of Brownsville and Liberty City. Residential turnover progressed rapidly once it started. In 1957, for example, a single black family moved into a neighborhood in the white residential zone separating Brownsville and Liberty City. White reaction was swift: a newly organized Seaboard White Citizens Council burned crosses on the black family's lawn. However, the actions of militant segregationists failed to deter blacks seeking new living space. Within the next three years, whites had abandoned that extensive midcity residential area completely. Formerly separate and indentifiable communities, Brownsville and Liberty City had merged, creating one large black community known today as Liberty City.[74]

The real estate industry was centrally involved in managing and directing the growth of the second ghetto. In 1958, Elizabeth Virrick attributed Miami's racial housing problems to, among other things, "the number of real estate people to the square inch." Sarcasm aside, Virrick was quite right, and Miami and South Florida generally had been a real estate agent's bonanza since early in the twentieth century.

The possibilities opened up by expressway building through Overtown were not lost on white property owners in Miami's black districts. White slumlords stood to suffer a temporary financial loss if their rental properties in Overtown were razed for highways and other redevelopment. However, clearing this downtown land for business or other public purposes ultimately would result in rapid increases in land value. Moreover, if the real estate interests and rental agents could control the development of new and more distant residential areas for Overtown's displaced blacks, steady profits from new rentals and sales could be expected.[75]

That some were thinking along these lines was reflected in a redevelopment and relocation plan reported in the *Miami Herald* in May 1961. Under the headline, "He'd Shift Negro District, Build a New 'Downtown,'" urban affairs writer Juanita Greene devoted a long article to the plans of Luther L. Brooks, head of the Bonded Collection Agency which managed mostly white-owned rental property in Miami's black neighborhoods. As Greene put it, Brooks' plan "would gradually erase the Central Negro District [Overtown] and make it part of a new downtown Miami." At the same time, "the 60,000 Negroes living downtown would move north to the 11-square mile Liberty City area." Actually, according to Miami city planners, Overtown had about 37,000 blacks in 1960—still an enormous number of people to uproot and relocate. It was an audacious move for Brooks to announce this plan publicly, but Greene reported that "it has attracted the interest of City of Miami and Metro planners, who are giving it more study."[76]

The idea of relocating blacks out of Overtown to more distant locations began in the 1930s. Brooks had been collecting rents for Miami slumlords for twenty-seven years, so he was fully cognizant of the long-term efforts to relocate blacks from the Overtown area. According to *Miami Herald* journalist Greene, by the early 1960s, the Bonded Collection Agency represented more than one thousand white and black landlords who owned some ten thousand rental units in black Miami. Managing a fleet of thirty-four radio-dispatched cars, Luther Brooks was the best-known white man in Overtown, as well as a power broker of sorts in white Miami. For decades, he had been the public spokesperson for the slumlords. He had led the real estate industry's fight against public housing and urban renewal. However, Brooks also came to recognize the potential of the second ghetto. As Juanita Greene wrote in a long *Miami Herald* article about him in 1963, Brooks "helped break the boundaries of the old Negro ghettos," moving black families "into border areas, then pushing the borders." In the absence of any official relocation efforts until the mid-1960s, the Bonded Collection Agency conducted an unofficial relocation program, providing the moving trucks as well as the relocation housing in second-ghetto areas. Thus, the 1961 Brooks plan for completely relocating Overtown's blacks reflected the thinking of Miami's slumlords. For years, the Overtown landlords had resisted the encroachments of the central business district. The potential of managing second-ghetto expansion, however, brought them into harmony with the thinking of the downtown businesspeople. The Brooks scheme coincided with plans for the Overtown area that had been proposed since the mid-1930s. The only thing new about the idea in 1961 was that interstate highway building in the inner-city now made its achievement possible.[77]

Blacks in Miami were not especially enthusiastic about the Luther Brooks plan to eliminate Overtown. The *Miami Times,* which generally had been supportive of the expressway in its editorials for several years, reported the Brooks removal plan without comment. However, other spokespeople in the black community were opposed. "For the last 20 years," one black preacher told the *Miami Herald,* "there has been talk of moving the downtown Negro area and the people here have been against it." Expressway building and urban renewal programs might now make the plan feasible, the Reverend John Culmer of St. Agnes Episcopal Church acknowledged, but the black neighborhoods would have to be consulted to avoid resentment and community opposition. Henry Arrington, a black attorney and a member of MHA, also spoke out against the Brooks proposal. Such a plan, Arrington argued, was to accept "the perpetuation of segregation" at a time when the black community was pushing for integration of housing.[78]

Arrington and other black leaders in Miami may have sought integrated housing, but that is not what was happening in Dade County in the 1950s and 1960s. The Brooks plan envisioned a reorganization of residential space on Miami's northwestern fringe, a process of racial change that was already occurring in an unplanned but nevertheless decisive way. Liberty City and Brownsville had already begun blending to form the nucleus of Miami's largest black community. Contiguous white residential areas, slated by the Brooks plan for black housing, were already changing. For instance, the Orchard Villa subdivision just south of Liberty City had turned from a primarily white community to a primarily black one in less than one year. In September 1958, the Orchard Villa Elementary School opened with 235 white pupils. In February 1959, the Dade County School Board decided to admit four black children to the school the next fall, touching off protest meetings, picketing, and rapid white flight from the area. When the Orchard Villa School closed for the summer in June, some 130 white children remained, and only eight showed up for the opening of school in September 1959. By 1961, the changing neighborhood pattern had pushed beyond Orchard Villa to Floral Park, another working-class white subdivision, where the same process of racial turnover was repeated.[79]

By the early 1960s, as expressway building increased, blacks also were moving in substantial numbers into incorporated municipalities such as Opa-locka and unincorporated communities such as Carol City, both white working-class neighborhoods in northwestern Dade County. North and west of Liberty City, Opa-locka lay in the path of expanding black population. Large-scale home construction for blacks in the Bunche Park section of Opa-locka in the 1950s set the stage for second-ghetto development in the 1960s and 1970s. Located to the north of Opa-locka, Carol City began in 1954 as a white residential development initially planned by the internationally known firm of Harland Bartholomew and Associates. Overbuilding in the 1950s and heavy mortgage foreclosures in the recession years of the late 1950s left Carol City a "ghost town of abandoned homes." Blacks began moving into the housing vacuum, and the neighborhood began to change from white to black residents. A University of Miami study of Carol City noted that by the early 1960s, "the emigration of white owners was so pervasive that vacancies existed in great quantities throughout the development." Throughout the period, according to Seymour Samet of the Dade County Community Relations Board, "block-busting realtors" were busily "at work selling homes to Negroes in previously all-white neighborhoods." By 1971, the *Miami Herald* was reporting that the "next ghetto is Carol City." Luther Brooks's plan was never officially implemented, but the process he outlined largely occurred anyway.[80]

Official policies, particularly those of Miami and Dade County planning and housing agencies, contributed to the shaping of the second ghetto. Black leaders were critical of MHA's housing and relocation policies. It was charged on numerous occasions that racial bias dictated MHA decisions to locate new public housing projects in existing black neighborhoods, or in areas clearly in transition from white to black. In a column in the *Miami Times* in August 1965, for instance, National Urban League director Whitney M. Young, Jr. accused Miami housing officials of "trying to place relocation housing in the path of ghetto expansion." One year later, state and local chapters of the NAACP charged MHA with "failing to follow available programs that could bring about integration as Negro ghettos are eliminated and of killing the possibility of integration by locating new public housing in already segregated areas."[81]

MHA officials denied any discriminatory intent, but later admitted that public housing in Miami was indeed segregated. At that point, MHA fell back on its policy of "free choice," by which eligible families could choose among available project locations. As MHA chairperson Martin Fine explained in October 1966, "Our system is designed to prevent segregation and we are not obliged under the act to force integration." A community relations board was established in the 1960s to ensure racial cooperation and, as the *Miami Times* put it, "to nip new Negro ghettos before they bud." But it was too late. In a 1969 study entitled *Psycho-Social Dynamics in Miami,* University of Miami sociologists described a pattern of "rapidly spreading black ghettos" in the northwestern section of Miami and Dade County. The shifting pattern of residential neighborhoods had a dynamic all its own, speeded by public policy decisions and the activities of real estate people, but essentially immune from forces pushing for racial integration.[82]

As in the past, the second ghetto was marked by high levels of residential segregation. Several sociological studies have demonstrated that of more than one hundred large American cities, Miami had the highest degree of residential segregation by race in 1940, 1950, and 1960. This was not a racial pattern that happened by accident, but one that reflected the controlled expansion of black residential areas through most of that period. By 1970, Miami's "index of residential segregation" had improved somewhat compared with other southern cities, but 92 percent of Miami blacks still lived in segregated neighborhoods. In 1980, after twenty-five years of civil rights activism in urban America, Miami still ranked near the top of a list of sixty metropolitan areas in the extent of black residential segregation. The recent study by sociologists Douglas S. Massey and Nancy A. Denton revealed that 77.8 percent of Miami area blacks lived in segregated communities in 1980. Although this statistic represented an improvement over earlier decades, it also suggested that the second ghetto with its pattern of racial segregation remains a pervasive fact of urban life in metropolitan Miami.[83]

In the decade following World War II, the pent-up and overcrowded population of Overtown had already begun to push out to new residential areas, especially Brownsville and Liberty City. The arrival and settlement of about eight hundred thousand Cuban exiles between 1959 and 1980 also shaped the Miami housing market, effectively limiting the housing choices of blacks displaced from Overtown by redevelopment activities.[84] However, it was the building of the Miami expressway system, along with accompanying urban renewal programs, that triggered the rapid development of a vast second ghetto in the northwestern section of the metropolitan area. Ten years of highway construction had enormous and irreversible consequences for Miami's urban and spatial development.

The Freeway and the City

Groundbreaking for the monster Miami midtown expressway interchange occurred in September 1966. The eight-lane, four-level interchange rose in some places as high as a seven-story building. The interchange also destroyed eighty-seven acres of housing and commercial property at the heart of Overtown, tearing as well through an already planned urban renewal development area. As the project began, a report for the *Miami Times* surveyed the scene: "A drive through the downtown Negro section gives one the idea that something like a king-size tornado had hit the place." No area of Overtown "seemed to have escaped the angered wrath of the bulldozers and wrecking cranes that have been busy at work demolishing homes, churches, apartment houses and business places." In Scott Greer's *Urban Renewal and American Cities* (1965), an urban renewal official in another city reported that the state highway department had just located a cloverleaf in the middle of an urban renewal area in a black neighborhood: "It was done carefully—like the story of Epaminondas (you remember?)—he was careful like his mother said. He put his foot exactly in the middle of that pie. Well, that's how the interchange sits in the urban renewal area." As this incident suggests, the Miami expressway story is not unique.[85]

Numerous other American cities suffered the social and human consequences of highway building in the interstate era. In Nashville, the Tennessee State Highway Department altered the original routing of Interstate-40, laying a wide ribbon of concrete directly through the center of the city's black business district.[86] Expressway building in Richmond, Virginia, tore through a stable black community north of the central city, dislocating families and businesses.[87] In 1956, blacks in St. Paul organized to fight against a proposed intercity freeway to Minneapolis (Interstate-94) that would cut directly through their neighborhood; the antifreeway movement was unsuccessful and the new urban interstate displaced one-seventh of St. Paul's black residents. As one critic put it, "Very few blacks lived in Minnesota, but the road builders found them."[88] In New Haven, Connecticut, the Oak Street Connector, an inner-city freeway linked to I-95, destroyed a blighted black housing area near the central business district, and at the same time cleared adjacent land for office buildings and high-income, high-rise housing.[89] In Columbus, Ohio, an inner-city express-way leveled an entire black community.[90] In Baltimore, Milwaukee, Indianapolis, and Cleveland, expressways plowed through black communities, destroying thousands of low-income housing units.[91] The interstate highway system provided an unparalleled opportunity to clear out inner-city blight and make room for central business district development.

In Florida, where Wilbur Smith and Associates were active in planning urban expressways, the story was similar. In Tampa, St. Petersburg, Jacksonville, and Orlando, interstate highways routinely ripped through, divided, and dislocated black communities, or permanently walled them off from white neighborhoods. In St. Petersburg alone, ten black churches were relocated away from the path of Interstate-275. In Tampa, interstates (I-4 and I-75) sliced through Latin sections of West Tampa and Ybor City, areas of transition where many blacks lived as well. In Orlando, I-4 provided a barrier separating blacks on the west side of town from the central business district and white communities on the east side. A Wilbur Smith plan for a downtown expressway running through Tallahassee was rejected at the last minute when the route of Interstate-10 was shifted several miles to the north of town.[92]

In other cities, the urban interstates served as racial barriers—"Chinese walls" dividing black neighborhoods from white. In Gary, Indiana, two East–West interstates (I-80 and I-94) merged as they plowed through town, and until recently, this so-called Tri-State Expressway effectively separated Gary's blacks on the North side of town from the whites on the South side. In Atlanta, according to historian Ronald H. Bayor, highways and roads were purposely planned and built "to sustain racial ghettos and control black migration." In particular, Interstate-20 in West Atlanta was designed as a racial barrier. In Memphis, the interstates hemmed in the black community in the northern sector of the city. In Los Angeles, according to Helen Leavitt in *Superhighway-Superhoax* (1970), the black ghetto district of Watts was "sealed off" from neighboring white communities by freeways.[93]

Black neighborhoods were not the only ones destroyed or sealed off by interstate highway building. In Wilmington, Delaware, I-95 slashed through the city's western side, demolishing a wide swath of housing in a white ethnic and working-class community. In St. Louis, Interstate-44 bisected an Italian ethnic enclave, dividing residents from one another and their churches and other communal institutions until a citizens movement forced the construction of an overpass. A whole range of ethnic neighborhoods gave way to expressways in Chicago as they headed South, Southwest, West, and Northwest out of the downtown "loop" area. In Boston, an inner-city expressway tore through and destroyed the Chinatown district and part of the city's Italian North End, dividing this ethnic community from the rest of the city. In the Providence, Rhode Island, central-city area, I-95 cut through a low-income, rooming house district where aged residents and small businesses were especially hard hit. In New York City, the Cross-Bronx Expressway (I-95) ripped through a massive "wall of apartment houses" that stretched for miles, gouging "a hugh trench" across a primarily working-class Jewish neighborhood. The Cross-Bronx Expressway fulfilled a two-decade-old dream of New York highway builder Robert Moses, but it also triggered the rapid decline of the South Bronx, currently a notorious urban wasteland of rubble and abandoned buildings. The story was much the same in dozens of cities around the nation.[94]

Like the black communities destroyed by expressways, white ethnic, working-class neighborhoods were vulnerable to the highway builders. These communities tended to be located near the urban core and their residents had few powerful political supporters. Land acquisition costs for interstate right-of-way were usually lower in these communities. Generally, city and highway officials perceived these areas as blighted neighborhoods of dense population and older or dilapidated housing—transitional neighborhoods that would soon be less white and more black. The potential for slum clearance and the physical redevelopment of such areas was often central to the thinking of local officials involved in planning urban expressway routes.

In a few cities, the urban expressway builders were halted by aroused community opposition before they could begin or, in some cases, before they could finish. In Boston and New York, for example, neighborhood groups and antihighway coalitions rose up to defeat some urban expressway projects. Citizen groups killed a planned inner-city freeway in Washington, D.C., that would have displaced more than thirty thousand people. Antifreeway forces in Phoenix turned back a proposed one hundred-foot high elevated expressway through the downtown area in a 1974 referendum. A partially completed six-lane elevated highway was halted abruptly in downtown Dallas, "a monument to the efforts of various citizen groups who successfully forestalled the disruption of a major urban neighborhood." When San Francisco banned all new expressway construction in 1959, plans for six new commuter expressways were shelved, including some that would have swept mercilessly through the city's famous Golden Gate Park. The doubled-decked and elevated Embarcadero Freeway was left incomplete and abandoned virtually in midair in the center of downtown San Francisco. Ben Kelley, a former public affairs director for the federal DOT, described the unfinished and forelorn Embarcadero as a "war memorial to freeway fighters."[95] The 1989 San Francisco earthquake finished what the original expressway opponents started thirty years earlier. Damaged beyond repair, the Embarcadero Freeway was slated for demolition by the San Francisco Board of Supervisors.

In New Orleans, enraged freeway opponents successfully fought off a senseless plan to build a four-story, eight-lane elevated expressway along the Mississippi River and through the edges of the city's historic French Quarter. The Riverfront and Elysian Fields Expressway actually had its origins in a 1946 plan proposed for New Orleans by the ubiquitous highway builder, Robert Moses. The planned expressway was part of an inner-city beltway of the type that Moses had favored in New York City and that BPR had incorporated in interstate highway planning. After several years of hot debate and controversy, historic preservationists succeeded in fighting off the Riverfront Expressway plan. In 1969, Secretary of Transportation John A. Volpe, a former highway builder himself in Massachusetts, caved in to vocal resistance and reluctantly terminated the I-10 loop through the Vieux Carré. About the same time, white uptown communities in New Orleans also beat back a plan for a new Mississippi River Bridge linked to I-10 at Napoleon Avenue, one of the city's beautiful, tree-lined residential boulevards.[96]

However, while white residents with vested interests were fending off the highway builders, nearby mid-city black communities were not nearly so successful. At the same time the French Quarter preservationists and the upscale whites of uptown New Orleans were holding mass meetings, dominating the opinion columns of the local newspapers, and pressuring their political leaders, the highway builders had leveled a wide swath along North Claiborne Avenue in central New Orleans for I-10. North Claiborne was the heart and center of an old and stable black creole community. It had a magnificent stand of old live oak trees dominating a broad "neutral ground" (the New Orleans term for the grassy boulevard strip separating lines of traffic). The open spaces of North Claiborne Avenue had served as an important community center, as a "hub of activity," and as a holiday gathering place for picnics and parades. It was a historic place of significance to the black residents of the neighborhood, providing a sense of identity and community. Unfortunately, in the late 1960s, the highway builders appeared on the scene, leveled the great old oaks, and rammed an elevated expressway through the neighborhood. It happened so quickly that few had time to organize or protest. Some of the same preservationists who fought the Riverfront Expressway were happy to suggest North Claiborne as an alternative. Stay off the riverfront, the *Vieux Carré Courier* urged in 1965, but Claiborne could "be developed to the limit, with at least two upper levels." Thus, New Orleans offers a complex case study of highway building, with the blacks ultimately victimized by the road builders with a little assist from local whites with power and influence. Currently, I-10 in New Orleans rolls through a devastated black community, a concrete jungle left in the shadows by a massive elevated highway.[97]

Citizen freeway revolts were successful in some places. By the early 1970s, a national antiexpressway movement of sorts had sprouted, as reflected in such groups as the Highway Action Coalition and the National Coalition on the Transportation Crisis.[98] In most cities, however, by the time enraged community opposition to expressway building emerged in the mid- to late 1960s, much of the damage had already been done to the physical landscape and the social fabric of urban America. FHA and state highway officials embarked on a public relations campaign in the 1960s, emphasizing the beneficial effect of expressways on urban life.[99] However, as landscape architects in Louisiana noted in 1971, "there is hardly a case where a freeway has enhanced a neighborhood through which it passes." Instead, one transportation specialist has suggested that "almost every major U.S. city bears the scars of communities split apart by the nearly impenetrable barrier of concrete."[100] Inner-city black and white ethnic neighborhoods were uprooted and destroyed. The residential changes set off by urban expressway building resulted in newer, second ghettos as blacks sought housing in transitional neighborhoods.

In 1970, Daniel P. Moynihan wrote that the interstate highway system was a "program of truly transcendent, continental consequence." Not only had it become the largest public works effort in history, but it was a program that would have "more influence on the shape and development of American cities," industrial location, economic activities, employment opportunities, and race relations than any other government initiative of the time.[101] Moynihan's judgment on the urban effect of the interstates was essentially correct. U.S. cities were physically reshaped by the broad bands of concrete and asphalt that snaked along riverfronts and through parks, neighborhoods, and business districts. Business and industrial locations came to depend on easy access to the expressway system, which tended to draw economic activities from the central city to the urban periphery.

In that sense, the dreams of those who sought to save the central business district were frustrated, because the urban expressways actually speeded the decentralization of population and economic activities. White urbanites pushed out the distant frontiers of suburbia, while relying on freeways for the commute to work. Inner-city black districts were torn apart or town down, as the bulldozer made its ubiquitous presence felt in urban America. By the tens of thousands, uprooted blacks sought new housing in the second ghettos of metropolitan areas. The expressways unleashed tremendous forces for change, resulting in a dramatic spatial and racial reordering of the American metropolis.

Overtown and Historic Memory

The expressway experience in Miami mirrored the national pattern. Few would deny the powerful and permanent effects of I-95 on the Miami metropolitan area. For the black community, the legacy is sad and bitter. Some forty thousand blacks made Overtown home before the expressway came, but fewer than ten thousand currently remain in an urban wasteland dominated by the expressway. The "concrete monsters" of the 1950s still dot the landscape, sharing space with rubble-strewn vacant lots, boarded-up stores, welfare hotels, and abandoned buildings. The homeless congregate in makeshift living quarters under elevated portions of the expressway, where real homes once stood. A once thriving community, full of economic and cultural vitality, is gone—a victim of the automobile and the highway builders, and of the politicians and planners and realtors and businesspeople who pushed for or profited from the new expressway. Central business district functions have gradually expanded into the former confines of Overtown—city, county, and state government office buildings, a police station, transit facilities, parking lots, a modern basketball arena, new middle-class condominiums, even trendy shops and upscale townhouses in one eastern fringe area. Miami civic leaders traditionally argued that the nearness of Overtown was to blame "for stifling the economic growth of the central business district." The building of I-95 mostly took care of that problem, and the idea of pushing the business district into what remains of Overtown is fully alive in the 1990s.[102]

Expressway building through Overtown also left a legacy of mistrust and suspicion among Miami's black leaders and housing reformers.

The story of what happened to Overtown has become part of the political folklore of black Miami. Black politicians and civic leaders regularly remind the white establishment of what they did to Overtown. Listen to Athalie Range, Miami's first black city commissioner, who spoke at a planning conference in 1971:

The Greater Miami area is a classic example of the transportation planners' disregard of the inner-city populace. After conducting not one single public hearing in the Central District of the City of Miami, 5,000 housing units were destroyed between 1960 and 1969 in the all-black downtown area of Miami to make room for the North–South Expressway. . . . The result is that new slums were immediately created by demolition of 5,000 housing units of low-cost housing in one area.

"Overtown still bears the scars of the highway," a black city planner in Miami noted in 1981. Dorothy Fields, director of the Black Archives in Miami, asserted that the destruction of Overtown was done "by design"; the expressway "divided Colored Town and destroyed the community." Opa-locka mayor Robert Ingram, born in Overtown, remembered in 1982 that "the expressway ran right down the middle [of Overtown]. It split the community and displaced people." The Reverend Bryan Walsh, director of the Catholic Services Bureau in Miami and a long-time activist in community relations, said in a 1981 interview, "I believe that I-95 represents a sociological disaster for Miami. Many of the problems faced by the city today are traceable to I-95 and not to the refugee influx. . . . What is clear is that the planners had little understanding or concern for the human problems involved."[103]

Long after I-95 ripped through the black community, the painful memory still lingers. When the Park-West redevelopment scheme got underway in June 1986, the *Miami Times* ran an editorial entitled "Doing It to Overtown Again." T. Willard Fair, director of the Greater Miami Urban League, angrily recalled in 1986 that "urban renewal and the coming of the expressway helped to destroy the community." As one *Miami Herald* reporter put it, "A whole generation of wary black leaders suspect the latest redevelopment plans are the final land grab in a long history of official deceit." "Overtown had a history," black attorney Jesse McCrary noted recently, but government and business acting together destroyed the community: "They took a little at a time. First they cut the finger off, and then they cut the hand off, and then they cut the arm off, and pretty soon Overtown is dead." The traumatic events of the expressway-building era have remained vividly etched in the historic memory of black Miami.[104]

The destruction of Overtown and the creation of the second ghetto, moreover, are events that have cast a long shadow in Miami's recent history. Devastating race riots in 1968, 1980, 1982, and 1989 have revealed the extent of black anger and frustration. A succession of postriot studies has singled out housing as one of the most pervasive and serious grievances among Miami's blacks. The highway builders gave little thought to the social and human consequences of uprooting families and destroying communities. Housing policies were specifically severed from highway building until the mid-1960s. As a result, historian Carol E. Hoffecker has written, "The interstates were just one more federal bulldozer tearing at the remaining fabric of sagging urban interiors." In Miami and dozens of other cities, official housing policies remained festering sores that were ripped open during the ghetto riots of the 1960s.[105]

The interstate highway system, then, has had a major effect on urban America, especially the inner cities. State highway engineers who designed and built the system were primarily interested in expressways that moved automobile traffic quickly and efficiently. However, they also were sympathetic to the interests of downtown businesspeople who sought to redevelop inner-city blight and save the central business districts. In the 1940s and 1950s, when the interstate routes were initially planned, few contested the idea of tearing down the slums and forcing inner-city blacks to more distant areas. Once federal and state highway officials determined that the interstates should push through the central cities, the die was cast. Cheaper land acquisition costs in low-income neighborhoods simply confirmed that these areas were best for urban expressways. Inner-city residents most directly affected by expressways usually had the least political clout. That the interests of powerful, central city business and political groups meshed with those of the highway officials and road builders helped speed the process of route location and expressway construction. As urban historian John F. Bauman noted in a study of Philadelphia, "After World War II, the economic concerns of downtown businessmen dovetailed with the reform agenda of housers, planners, and organized labor," all of whom supported urban redevelopment schemes.[106]

The players were slightly different in Miami, but the conjunction of interest groups on the expressway issue was quite similar. The slumlords of Overtown, usually opposed to the chamber of commerce variety of businesspeople, eventually fell into line on the Overtown route of I-95 once they realized they could profit from black residential dispersal. Even some black leaders and organizations got co-opted at the beginning, if only temporarily. Not surprisingly, those with power and money called the shots. Everyone, or almost everyone, profited— suburban residents who drove to central-city jobs, business interests seeking more downtown space to expand, and the slumlords and real estate people who managed the growth of the second ghetto. The black community of Overtown, however, did not prosper in the reorganization of urban space stimulated by expressway building.

Clearly, federal urban policy in the years after World War II had an enormously powerful and shaping role. Shortly after the passage of the landmark 1956 interstate highway legislation, noted urbanologist Lewis Mumford remarked, "When the American people, through their Congress, voted a little while ago for a twenty-six billion dollar highway program, the most charitable thing to assume about this action is that they hadn't the faintest notion of what they were doing."[107] In the narrowest sense, Mumford may have been right, but there were many highway officials, policy makers, downtown businesspeople, and special interest groups who knew exactly what they were doing. In the case of the interstate highway program, the federal government provided most of the funding, but important decisions about location were left to state road departments working in conjunction with local officials. The federal government, in short, provided vast financial resources for urban redevelopment but left key decision making to the state and local levels, where special interests often dictated policy. Without the constraints of citizen participation until the mid-1960s, and without the necessity for providing replacement housing, the highway builders ran roughshod over the urban landscape. Federal interstate highway policy clearly intensified the racial transformation of residential space in the modern American city. In Miami and elsewhere, highways and housing, race and space, have been integrally linked in the shaping of urban public policy.

NOTES

1. Mark I. Gelfand, *A Nation of Cities: The Federal Government and Urban America, 1933–1965* (New York: Oxford University Press, 1975), 222.

2. National Commission on Urban Problems, *Building the American City* (Washington, D.C.: U.S. Government Printing Office, 1969), 81; U.S. House of Representatives, Committee on Public Works, *Study of Compensation and Assistance for Persons Affected by Real Property Acquisition in Federal and Federally Assisted Programs* (Washington, D.C.: U.S. Government Printing Office, 1965), 24, 26, 105; Michael Sumichrast and Norman Farquhar, *Demolition and Other Factors in Housing Replacement Demand* (Washington, D.C.:

National Association of Home Builders, 1967), 47–48, 76; Alan A. Altshuler, *The City Planning Process: A Political Analysis* (Ithaca, N.Y.: Cornell University Press, 1965), 339; Chester Hartman, "The Politics of Housing: Displaced Persons," *Transaction: Social Science and Modern Society* 9 (July/August 1972), 53–65.

3. National Commission on Urban Problems, *Building the American City,* 91.

4. William H. Claire, "Urban Renewal and Transportation," *Traffic Quarterly* 13 (July 1959), 417. For the linkage between expressways and redevelopment, see also Peter Hall, *Cities of Tomorrow: An Intellectual History of Urban Planning and Design in the Twentieth Century* (Oxford, England: Basil Blackwell, 1988), 291–292; Thomas H. MacDonald, "The Case for Urban Expressways," *American City* 62 (June 1947), 92–93; Robert Moses, "Slums and City Planning," *Atlantic Monthly* 175 (January 1945), 63–68; James W. Follin, "Coordination of Urban Renewal with the Urban Highway Program Offers Major Economies in Cost and Time," *Urban Land* 15 (December 1956), 3–6; James W. Rouse, "Transportation and the Future of Our Cities," *Urban Land* 22 (July–August 1963), 7–10.

5. Arnold R. Hirsch, *Making the Second Ghetto: Race and Housing in Chicago, 1940–1960* (Cambridge, England: Cambridge University Press, 1983), especially 1–39.

6. Raymond A. Mohl, "Trouble in Paradise: Race and Housing in Miami during the New Deal Era," *Prologue: Journal of the National Archives* 19 (Spring 1987), 7–21; Paul S. George and Thomas K. Peterson, "Liberty Square, 1933–1937: The Origins and Evolution of a Public Housing Project," *Tequesta: The Journal of the Historical Association of Southern Florida* 49 (1988), 53–68.

7. Minutes of the Dade County Planning Board, 27 August 1936, George E. Merrick Papers, box 2, Historical Association of Southern Florida, Miami, typescript; Dade County Planning Council, "Negro Resettlement Plan," 1937, National Urban League Papers, Part I, Series VI, box 56, Library of Congress, mimeographed; George E. Merrick, *Planning the Greater Miami for Tomorrow* (Miami: Miami Realty Board, 1937), 11; *Miami Herald,* 5 April 1945; R. C. Gardner, "To the Taxpayers and Citizens of the City of Miami," February 1949, Fuller Warren Papers, Box 21, Florida State Archives, Tallahassee, typescript.

8. Warren M. Banner, *An Appraisal of Progress, 1943–1953* (Miami: National Urban League, 1953), 20–25, 33; *Miami Herald,* 1 November 1946, 29 May 1947, 2 December 1952.

9. Charles Abrams, *Forbidden Neighbors: A Study of Prejudice in Housing* (New York: Harper, 1955), 120–136; Stetson Kennedy, *The Klan Unmasked* (Boca Raton: Florida Atlantic University Press, 1990), 219–231; Teresa Lenox, "The Carver Village Controversy," *Tequesta: The Journal of the Historical Association of Southern Florida* 50 (1990), 39–51; Harold M. Rose, "Metropolitan Miami's Changing Negro Population, 1950–1960," *Economic Geography* 40 (July 1964), 221–238.

10. Clay McShane, "Transforming the Use of Urban Space: A Look at the Revolution in Street Pavements, 1880–1924," *Journal of Urban History* 5 (May 1979), 279–307; Thomas H. MacDonald, "Twenty Years of Road Building Progress in the United States," *Florida Highways* 2 (February 1925), 10–13, 20; Charles L. Dearing, *American Highway Policy* (Washington, D.C.: The Brookings Institution, 1941), 219–265; Bruce E. Seely, *Building the American Highway System: Engineers as Policy Makers* (Philadelphia: Temple University Press, 1987), 11–145; James J. Flink, *The Automobile Age* (Cambridge, Mass.: MIT Press, 1988), 170–171; Public Works Administration, *America Builds: The Record of PWA* (Washington, D.C.: U.S. Government Printing Office, 1939), 184.

11. Robert A. Caro, *The Power Broker: Robert Moses and the Fall of New York* (New York: Knopf, 1974), 328–346, 386–389, 515–573; Robert Moses, "The Comprehensive Parkway System of the New York Metropolitan Region," *Civil Engineering* 9 (March 1939), 160–162; Seely, *Building the American Highway System,* 151–153, 155. For Moses, see also Joann P. Krieg, ed., *Robert Moses: Single-Minded Genius* (Interlaken, N.Y.: Heart of the Lakes Publishing, 1989).

12. David Brodsly, *L.A. Freeway: An Appreciative Essay* (Berkeley and Los Angeles: University of California Press, 1982), 111–112. For early highway development in Los Angeles, see also Scott L. Bottles, *Los Angeles and the Automobile: The Making of the Modern City* (Berkeley and Los Angeles: University of California Press, 1987).

13. For the acceptance of the automobile by planners, see Mark S. Foster, *From Streetcar to Superhighway: American City Planners and Urban Transportation, 1900–1940* (Philadelphia: Temple University Press, 1981); Paul Barrett, *The Automobile and Urban Transit: The Formation of Public Policy in Chicago, 1900–1930* (Philadelphia: Temple University Press, 1983); Howard L. Preston, *Automobile Age Atlanta: The Making of a Southern Metropolis, 1900–1935* (Athens: University of Georgia Press, 1979); Blaine A. Brownell, "Urban Planning, the Planning Profession, and the Motor Vehicle in Early Twentieth-Century America," in *Shaping an Urban World,* ed. Gordon E. Cherry (New York: St. Martin's, 1980), 59–77.

14. David J. St. Clair, *The Motorization of American Cities* (New York: Praeger, 1986), 120–148.

15. Foster, *From Streetcar to Superhighway,* 153; Norman Bel Geddes, *Magic Motorways* (New York: Random House, 1940).

16. Gerald Silk, *Automobile and Culture* (New York: Harry N. Abrams, 1984), 198–299; Larry Zim, Mel Lerner, and Herbert Rolfes, *The World of Tomorrow: The 1939 World's Fair* ((New York: Harper and Row, 1988), 116–121.

17. W. Stull Holt, *The Bureau of Public Roads: Its History, Activities and Organization* (Baltimore: Johns Hopkins University Press, 1923); Seely, *Building the American Highway System,* 137–191; Gelfand, *A Nation of Cities,* 222–224. For MacDonald, see Federal Highway Administration, *America's Highways, 1776–1976: A History of the Federal-Aid Program*

(Washington, D.C.: U.S. Government Printing Office, 1976), 176–179. For the 1939 administrative reorganization, see Richard Polenberg, "The New Deal and Administrative Reform," in *Research in the Administration of Public Policy,* ed. Frank B. Evans and Harold T. Pinkett (Washington, D.C.: Howard University Press, 1975), 104.

18.   Gelfand, *A Nation of Cities,* 244; Seely, *Building the American Highway System,* 187–191; Mark H. Rose, *Interstate: Express Highway Politics, 1941–1956* (Lawrence: Regents Press of Kansas, 1979), 60.

19.   Thomas H. MacDonald, "Paving America," *State Government* 18 (May 1945), 80.

20.   Thomas H. MacDonald, "Proposed Interregional Highway System as It Affects Cities," 21 January 1943, Thomas H. MacDonald Papers, U.S. Department of Transportation Library, Washington, D.C., mimeographed; Thomas H. MacDonald, "The Federal Aid Highway Program and Its Relation to Cities," 11 September 1947, Thomas H. MacDonald Papers, U.S. Department of Transportation Library, Washington, D.C., mimeographed; Thomas H. MacDonald, "The Interstate System in Urban Areas," 16 May 1950, Thomas H. MacDonald Papers, U.S. Department of Transportation Library, Washington, D.C., mimeographed. During this period, MacDonald wrote and spoke widely about the highway and the city. See, for example, Thomas H. MacDonald, "The Urban Traffic Problem, *Annual Meeting of the Councillors of the American Automobile Association* (Washington, D.C.: American Automobile Association, 1939), 100–106; Thomas H. MacDonald, "The City's Place in Post-War Highway Planning," *American City* 58 (February 1943), 42–44; Thomas H. MacDonald, "The Case for Urban Expressways," *American City* 62 (June 1947), 92–93; Thomas H. MacDonald, "Improved Methods of Transport and Their Significance," *Scientific Monthly* 66 (January 1948), 57–61; Thomas H. MacDonald, "Future of Highways," *U.S. News and World Report,* 29 (December 1950), pp. 30–33.

21.   Rose, *Interstate,* 61–62; Gelfand, *A Nation of Cities,* 226.

22.   "Clay Committee Submits Huge Highway Program," *National Municipal Review* 44 (March 1955), 156–158; Stephen E. Ambrose, *Eisenhower: The President* (New York: Simon and Schuster, 1984), 250–251, 301, 326; Charles C. Alexander, *Holding the Line: The Eisenhower Era, 1952–1961* (Bloomington: Indiana University Press, 1975), 41–42. The most extensive study of the 1956 highway legislation is Rose, *Interstate,* 69–94, but see also Federal Highway Administration, *America's Highways, 1776–1976,* 466–485; Richard O. Davies, *The Age of Asphalt: The Automobile, the Freeway, and the Condition of Metropolitan America* (Philadelphia: J.B. Lippincott, 1975), 16–27; Gary T. Schwartz, "Urban Freeways and the Interstate System," *Southern California Law Review* 49 (March 1976), 406–513; Edward Weiner, *Urban Transportation Planning in the United States: An Historical Overview* (New York: Praeger, 1987), 8–16. For the "road gang," see John Burby, *The Great American Motion Sickness: Or Why You Can't Get There from Here* (Boston: Little, Brown, 1971), 295–319, and Helen Leavitt, *Superhighway—Superhoax* (Garden City, N.Y.: Doubleday, 1970), 111–155.

23. John R. Meyer and José A. Gómez-Ibañez, *Autos, Transit, and Cities* (Cambridge, Mass.: Harvard University Press, 1981), 7; William V. Shannon, "The Untrustworthy Highway Fund," *New York Times Magazine,* 15 (October 1972), 31, 120–132.

24. Wilfred Owen, *Cities in the Motor Age* (New York: Viking, 1959), 31–33.

25. Victor Gruen, "The City in the Automobile Age," *Perspectives* 16 (Summer 1956), 48; Hal Burton, *The City Fights Back* (New York: Citadel, 1954), 78. See also Arthur M. Weimer, *Investors and Downtown Real Estate.* Technical Bulletin no. 39 (Washington, D.C.: Urban Land Institute, 1960), 12–16; Marc A. Weiss, "The Origins and Legacy of Urban Renewal," in *Urban and Regional Planning in an Age of Austerity* ed. Pierre Clavel et al. (New York: Pergamon, 1980), 53–80.

26. James W. Rouse, "Will Downtown Face Up to Its Future?" *Urban Land* 16 (February 1957), 4; James H. Scheuer, "Highways and People: The Housing Impact of the Highway Program," in *The New Highways: Challenge to the Metropolitan Region,* Technical Bulletin no. 31 (Washington, D.C.: Urban Land Institute, 1957); James W. Follin, "Coordination of Urban Renewal with the Urban Highway Program Offers Major Economies in Cost and Time," *Urban Land* 15 (December 1956), 3, 5.

27. Automotive Safety Foundation, *What Freeways Mean to Your City* (Washington, D.C.: Automotive Safety Foundation, 1956), 32; Floyd I. Thiel, "Social Effects of Modern Highway Transportation," *Highway Research Board Bulletin* No. 327 (1962), 6–7; Schwartz, "Urban Freeways and the Interstate System," 484–485.

28. Joseph Barnett, "Express Highway Planning in Metropolitan Areas," *Transactions of the American Society of Civil Engineers* 112 (1947); 650; L. P. Cookingham, "Expressways and the Central Business District," *American Planning and Civic Annual* (1954) 140–146. For similar views, see "Build Expressways Through Slum Areas," *American City* 66 (November 1951), 125; John Clarkeson, "Urban Expressway Location," *Traffic Quarterly* 7 (April 1953), 252–260; Harry W. Lochner, "The Integration of Expressways With Other Urban Elements," *Traffic Quarterly* 7 (July 1953), 346–352.

29. George B. Nesbitt, "Relocating Negroes from Urban Slum Clearance Sites," *Land Economics* 25 (August 1949), 285; George B. Nesbitt, "Break Up the Black Ghetto?" *The Crisis* 56 (February 1949), 48–52.

30. An extensive literature substantiates these generalizations. For a sampling, see Jon C. Teaford, *The Rough Road to Urban Renaissance: Urban Revitalization in America, 1940–1985* (Baltimore: Johns Hopkins University Press, 1990); Bernard J. Frieden and Lynne B. Sagalyn, *Downtown, Inc.: How America Rebuilds Cities* (Cambridge, Mass.: MIT Press, 1989), 15–37; Joe R. Feagin, *The Urban Real Estate Game: Playing Monopoly with Real Money* (Englewood Cliffs, N.J.: Prentice-Hall, 1983), 103–121; A. Q. Mowbray, *Road to Ruin* (Philadelphia: Lippincott, 1969); Anthony Downs, *Urban Prospects and Problems* (Chicago: Rand McNally, 1970), 218–219; Lawrence M. Friedman, *Government and Slum Housing: A Century of Frustration* (Chicago:

Rand McNally, 1968), 147–172; Edward Higbee, *The Squeeze: Cities without Space* (New York: William Morrow, 1960), 216–218.

31. "Federal Aid Roads in Florida," *Florida Highways* 1 (July 1924), 12–13; E. W. James, "Federal Aid Highway System and Its Relation to Florida," *Florida Highways* 2 (April 1925), 1–3, 20; Roland M. Harper, "Some Statistics of Automobile Traffic into Florida," *Florida Highways* 2 (July 1925), 1–2; "Skirting Another Ocean," *Florida Highways* 4 (January 1927), 4; J. E. Dovell, *The State Road Department of Florida* (Gainesville: Public Administration Clearing Service, University of Florida, 1955), 4–15; State of Florida, *Fifteenth Biennial Report of the State Road Department of the State of Florida, 1943–1944* (Tallahassee: State of Florida, 1945), 10–12, 25, 33.

32. "Interstate Highways in Florida," *Florida Highways* 15 (April 1947), 11; "Jax-Miami Turnpike Looms," *Florida Highways* 19 (October 1951), 28; State of Florida, *Sixteenth Biennial Report of the State Road Department of the State of Florida, 1945–1946* (Tallahassee: State of Florida, 1947), 25; State of Florida, *Seventeenth Biennial Report of the State Road Department of the State of Florida, 1947–1948* (Tallahassee: State of Florida, 1949), 13, 27; W. M. Parker, "Planning Jacksonville's $34,000,000 Interstate System," *Florida Highways* 15 (October 1947), 9–17; "Jacksonville Prepares for Opening of First Expressway Unit," *Florida Highways* 20 (November 1952), 9–10; Miami Planning and Zoning Board, *The Miami Long Range Plan: Report on Tentative Plan for Trafficways* (Miami: City of Miami, 1955), 11.

33. Wilbur E. Jones to LeRoy Collins, 12 April 1955, 26 May 1955, 14 November 1955, 6 January 1956, 4 June 1956, 22 June 1956, LeRoy Collins Papers, box 36, Florida State Archives, Tallahassee; George Smathers to LeRoy Collins, 7 June 1956, ibid.; Spessard L. Holland to LeRoy Collins, 16 June 1956, ibid.; Wilbur E. Jones, "The Highway Problem," 1955, ibid., typescript.

34. Florida State Road Department, *The Interstate System in Florida* (Tallahassee: State of Florida, 1957); State of Florida, *Twenty-Second Biennial Report of the State Road Department, 1957–1958* (Tallahassee: State of Florida, 1959), 9–11, 18; William B. Killian to Spessard Holland and others, 30 June 1960, Florida Department of Transportation Records, Central Files, microfilm reel 1768, Florida Department of Transportation, Tallahassee (hereafter cited as Florida DOT Records). The only history of Florida highways is Baynard Kendrick, *Florida Trails to Turnpikes, 1914–1964* (Gainesville: University of Florida Press, 1964), but it has little to say about interstate highways, preferring instead to emphasize state legislation of 1949 banning cows, hogs, goats, and mules from state highways as one of the chief achievements of the postwar years.

35. Jesse Walter Dees, *Urban Sociology and the Emerging Atomic Megalopolis* (Ann Arbor, Mich.: Ann Arbor Publishers, 1950), 381–388; Mac Smith, "Miami Can Save Its Downtown Section, Expert Says," *Miami Daily News,* 3 May 1956; Bert Collier, "What's the Future for Downtown?" *Miami Herald Sunday Magazine,* 11 August 1956; Lawrence Thompson, "Will Traffic Survey Join Others in Dusty Files?" *Miami Herald,* 21 November 1956; Burton, *The*

City Fights Back, 12, 314; Max S. Wehrly, "Downtown Miami," *American Planning and Civic Annual* (1951), 144–150; City of Miami, *Proposed Capital Improvement Budget: Report of the Long Term Capital Improvement Budget Committee* (Miami: City of Miami, 1950); Miami Planning and Zoning Board, *The Miami Long Range Plan: Proposed Generalized Land Use Plan* (Miami: City of Miami, 1955), 13–19; Miami Planning and Zoning Board, *The Miami Central Business District: Some Facts and Conclusions* (Miami: City of Miami, 1956); Bernard Fremerman, "Downtown Versus Suburban Shopping in Miami, Florida: A Study of Consumer Motivation," 1957, Special Collections Library, Florida State University, Tallahassee, typescript.

   36.   Miami Planning and Zoning Board, *The Miami Long Range Plan*, 2, 5, 6, 10, 13–15, 20.

   37.   Miami Planning and Zoning Board, *The Miami Long Range Plan*, 5; John A. Montgomery, *History of Wilbur Smith and Associates, 1952–1984* (Columbia, S.C.: Wilbur Smith and Associates, 1985), 26.

   38.   Wilbur Smith and Associates, *A Major Highway Plan for Metropolitan Dade County, Florida, Prepared for State Road Department of Florida and Dade County Commission* (New Haven, Conn.: Wilbur Smith and Associates, 1956), unpaginated frontmatter, 33–44; *Miami Herald*, 21 November 1956. See also Metro-Dade County Traffic and Transportation Department, *A Study of Traffic and Transportation in Metropolitan Dade County, 1958* (Miami: Metro-Dade County, 1959), 5–6, 16, 23, and Metro-Dade County Public Works Department, *Your New Expressway* (Miami: Metro-Dade County 1964), for a folio of maps and plans showing the route of the North–South Expressway through Overtown and into the central businesss district. In the early 1960s, a few adjustments were incorporated into the 1956 expressway plan, generally to accommodate downtown businesspeople who were concerned about ramp locations and the height of the expressway bridge over the Miami River. However, the basic expressway route directly through Overtown remained unchanged. See Miami Planning and Zoning Board, *A Comprehensive Analysis of Miami's Neighborhoods. Phase II: Report of the Miami Comprehensive Plan* (Miami: City of Miami, 1961), 54–58; Wilbur Smith and Associates, *Alternates for Expressways: Downtown Miami, Dade County, Florida* (New Haven, Conn.: Wilbur Smith and Associates, 1962); A. C. Church, "A Chronology on the Miami Expressway from Date of the Original Wilbur Smith Report until the Present," 10 December 1963, Florida DOT Records, Central Files, reel 1770, typescript.

   39.   Montgomery, *History of Wilbur Smith and Associates*, 25–27; Rufus Jarman, "Traffic Is a Monster," *Saturday Evening Post*, 28 January 1956, 41, 81–82; Theodore M. Matson, Wilbur S. Smith, and Frederick W. Hurd, *Traffic Engineering* (New York: McGraw-Hill, 1955), 605–607; Wilbur S. Smith, "Traffic and Transportation in Urban Renewal," *Civil Engineering* 30 (October 1960), 45–47; Wilbur Smith and Associates, *Future Highways and Urban Growth* (New Haven, Conn.: Wilbur Smith and Associates, 1961); Wilbur Smith and Associates, *Parking in the City Center* (New Haven, Conn.: Wilbur Smith and Associates, 1965); Wilbur Smith and Associates, *Transportation* *and Parking for Tomorrow's Cities* (New Haven, Conn.: Wilbur Smith and Associates, 1966).

40. "CC Urges Expressway Plan Adoption," *The Metropolitan Miamian* (March 1957), p. 1; City of Miami, *A Report on Downtown Miami, Florida* (Miami: City of Miami, 1959) 19–27; "Expressways Are Changing Face of Miami and Dade County," *Better Roads* 31 (December 1961), 20–22; "How Go Our X-ways?" *The Miamian,* 56 (November 1963); *Miami Herald,* 13 February 1957; "Metro Triggered Huge Expressways," *Metro Bulletin,* 28 July 1961, p. 3; "Transcript of Public Hearing on North–South Expressway," Miami, 7 February 1957, Florida DOT Records, Central Files, reel 1761, typescript; "Transcript of Public Hearing on North–South Expressway," North Miami, 27 September 1957, ibid., typescript; State of Florida, *Twenty-Third Biennial Report of the State Road Department, 1959–1960* (Tallahassee: State of Florida, 1961), 10–11; State of Florida, *Twenty-Fourth Biennial Report of the State Road Department, 1961–1962* (Tallahassee: State of Florida, 1963), 15–16; Florida State Road Department, *26th Biennial Report, 1965–1966* (Tallahassee: State of Florida, 1967), 10; Metro-Dade County, *Six-Year Capital Improvements Program, 1962–1968* (Miami: Metro-Dade County, 1962), 13–15.

41. "Transcript of Hearing," 7 February 1957, Florida DOT Records, Central Files, reel 1761; "Transcript of Hearing," 27 September 1957, ibid.; Abe Aronovitz to State Road Department 6 February 1957, ibid.; Aronovitz to Bertram D. Talley, 28 March 1957, Records of the U.S. Department of Transportation, record group 30, box 70, U.S. National Archives, Suitland, Maryland (hereafter cited as U.S. DOT Records); Aronovitz to LeRoy Collins, 27 March 1957, Collins Papers, box 126; Wilbur E. Jones to LeRoy Collins, 23 April 1957, Collins Papers, Box 126; Wilbur S. Smith to Wilbur E. Jones, 18 April 1957, Florida DOT Records, Central Files, reel 1761; Wilbur Smith and Associates, *Alternate Expressway Location, North Miami, Florida* (New Haven, Conn.: Wilbur Smith and Associates, 1958).

42. *Miami Herald,* 13 February 1957, 30 January 1958; J. T. Knight to State Road Department, 28 January 1958, U.S. DOT Records, RG 30, box 71; Wilbur Jones to J. T. Knight, 29 January 1958, U.S. DOT Records, RG 30, Box 71; Winifred Nelson to Wilbur Jones, 13 March 1957, Florida DOT Records, Central Files, reel 1761.

43. J. N. Lummus, Jr. to Gordon R. Elwell, 12 February 1957, Florida DOT Records, Central Files, reel 1761; Gordon R. Elwell to Wilbur E. Jones, 12 February 1957, ibid; City of Miami, *Fourth Annual Six-Year Capital Improvement Report, 1959–1960* (Miami: Department of Engineering, City of Miami, 1959), 115.

44. *Miami Times,* 2 March 1957, 30 April 1960.

45. Van C. Kussrow to Wilbur E. Jones, 21 February 1957, Florida DOT Records, Central Files, reel 1761; Stanton D. Sanson to Spessard L. Holland, 5 August 1959, ibid., reel 1767.

46. "New Links for Florida's Interstate Road Net," *Florida Business and Opportunity* (December 1960), 17; "Expressways Are Changing Face of Miami," 21–22.

47. Sidney M. Aronovitz to Rex M. Whitton, 13 August 1965, U.S. DOT Records, record group 398, box 360, U.S. National Archives, Washington, D.C.; Chuck Hall to Alan Boyd, 14 November 1967, box 310, ibid. Hall was Dade County mayor, and Boyd was U.S. Secretary of Transportation.

48. Greater Miami Urban League, "Statement on Expressway and Housing," 1957, National Urban League Papers, Part I, Series I, box 107, mimeographed transcript. Copies of this statement also can be found in Florida DOT Records, Central Files, reel 1761, and in Collins Papers, box 126.

49. Edward Sofen, *The Miami Metropolitan Experiment,* rev. ed. (Garden City, N.Y.: Doubleday, Inc., 1966), 11–12; Edward C. Banfield, *Big City Politics* (New York: Random House, 1965), 104; Philip Meyer et al., *Miami Negroes: A Study in Depth* (Miami: The Miami Herald, 1968), 4, 26–33; Natalie Motise Davis, "Blacks in Miami and Detroit: Communities in Contrast" (Ph.D. diss., University of North Carolina, 1976), 79. For the civil rights movement in Miami, see Raymond A. Mohl, "The Pattern of Race Relations in Miami Since 1940," in *The Black Heritage of Florida,* ed. David Colburn and Jane Landers (Gainesville: University Press of Florida, 1993), forthcoming.

50. *Miami Times,* 16 March 1957; Paul C. Watt, "Relocation of Persons Displaced by Highway Construction," Administrative Report, 13 February 1959, Metro-Dade County Manager's Office, Elizabeth Virrick Papers, Historical Association of Southern Florida, Miami, mimeographed (hereafter cited as Virrick Papers). Also Coconut Grove Citizens Committee for Slum Clearance, *Ink Newsletter* 14 (October 1962), unpaginated, Coconut Grove Citizens Committee for Slum Clearance, *Ink Newsletter* 15 (April–May 1963), unpaginated, both in Virrick Papers; Meyer et al., *Miami Negroes,* 23; "What about the Negroes Uprooted by Expressway?" *Miami Herald,* 4 March 1957; Reinhold P. Wolff, "Population Trends," in *Metropolitan Dade County, Florida, Planning Conference, June 30–July 2, 1958* (Miami: Metro-Dade County, 1958), 19.

51. *Miami Times,* 16 March 1957; J. E. Preston to LeRoy Collins, 26 April 1957, Collins Papers, box 126; Preston to Wilbur E. Jones, 26 April 1957, Florida DOT Records, Central Files, reel 1761; Greater Miami Urban League, "Statement on Expressway and Housing." In 1971, the Dade County Community Relations Board reported that eighteen thousand residents had been dislocated from Overtown since 1965—approximately half the entire community. *Miami News,* 10 September 1971.

52. Paul S. George, "Colored Town: Miami's Black Community, 1896–1930," *Florida Historical Quarterly* 56 (April 1978), 432–447; *Miami Herald,* 15 May 1950; *Better Housing: [First] Report of the Housing Authority of the City of Miami* (Miami: City of Miami, 1940); Haley Sofge, "Public Housing in Miami," *Florida Planning and Development* 19 (March 1968), 1–4.

53. Elizabeth Virrick, interviews with Raymond A. Mohl, 8 October and 11 October 1986; *Miami Herald,* 2 March, 4 June, 25 June 1950, 17 November 1951; Minutes, Miami City Commission, 5 September 1951, Miami City Hall, microfilm edition; Sofge, "Public Housing in Miami," 1–4. For federal housing legislation, see Richard O. Davies, *Housing Reform during the Truman Admin-*

istration (Columbia: University of Missouri Press, 1966); Leonard Freedman, *Public Housing: The Politics of Poverty* (New York: Holt, Rinehart and Winston, 1969); R. Allen Hays, *The Federal Government and Urban Housing: Ideology and Change in Public Policy* (Albany: State University of New York Press, 1985), 79–106; Friedman, *Government and Slum Housing*, 94–172; and Gelfand, *A Nation of Cities*, 105–156.

54. *Miami News*, 3 March, 4 March 1950; *Miami Herald*, 17 April, 18 April, 25 June, 26 June 1950, 9 December 1952; Harry Simonhoff, "Low Rent Housing and Negro Segregation," *Jewish Floridian*, 31 March 1950, 2.

55. *Miami Herald*, 17 December 1957, 7 August 1967; [Miami] Property Owners Development Association, Newsletter (August 1957), unpaginated, copy in National Urban League Papers, Part I, Series III, box 18.

56. Joseph Barnett to F. C. Turner, 23 December 1957, U.S. DOT Records, RG 30, box 70.

57. *Miami Herald*, 17 March, 18 March, 19 March, 20 March, 21 March 1958.

58. Elizabeth Virrick to Arthur Field, 14 March 1958, Virrick Papers; Elizabeth Virrick to Marion Massen, 31 August 1958, Virrick Papers.

59. Undated clippings, circa 1950, Elizabeth Virrick Scrapbooks, Virrick papers; Elizabeth Virrick to W. C. Herrell, 14 March 1957, Virrick Papers; Elizabeth Virrick to George Hollahan, 26 March 1957, Virrick Papers; Elizabeth Virrick to Norman L. Anderson, 11 April 1958, Virrick Papers; Elizabeth Virrick to Dorothy Montgomery, 23 April 1958, Virrick Papers; Elizabeth Virrick to Alvin A. Mermin, 31 August 1958, Virrick Papers; Coconut Grove Citizens Committee for Slum Clearance, *Ink Newsletter,* 16 (March 1964), unpaginated, Virrick Papers; Dade County Conference on Civic Affairs, *Ink: The Journal of Civic Affairs* 16 (December 1964), unpaginated, Virrick Papers; Elizabeth Virrick, "The Separate Department for Housing Law Enforcement—What Happened to it in Miami," *Journal of Housing* 11 (June 1954), 193–194, 214; Aileen Lotz, "The Birth of 'Little Hud,' " *Florida Planning and Development* 19 (January 1968), 1–3, 6.

60. Elizabeth Virrick, "Civic Cooperation in Miami," in *Grass Roots Private Welfare,* ed. Alfred de Grazia (New York: New York University Press, 1957), 64–68; Elizabeth Virrick, "Pardon Me, Miami, Your Slums Are Showing," *Florida Home* 3 (June 1953), 6–7, 38; Elizabeth Virrick, "People vs. Slums," *Florida Home* 3 (July 1953), 6–7; Martin Millspaugh and Gurney Breckenfeld, *The Human Side of Urban Renewal* (Baltimore: Fight-Blight, 1958), 121–155; Elizabeth Virrick, interviews with Raymond A. Mohl, 8 October, 11 October, 25 October 1986, 31 January 1987, 28 March 1987.

61. Elizabeth Virrick to Wilbur Jones, 9 May 1957, Virrick Papers; Wilbur Jones to Elizabeth Virrick, 3 July 1957, Virrick Papers; *Miami Herald,* 9 December 1965.

62. Coconut Grove Citizens Committee for Slum Clearance, *Ink Newsletter* 14 (March 1962), unpaginated, Virrick Papers; Elizabeth Virrick to Alvin A. Mermin, 31 August 1958, Virrick Papers. Information about Virrick's multifaceted activities has been gleaned from her personal correspondence, manuscripts, agency and organization files, scrapbooks, and newspaper clipping files. Before her death in 1990, Ms. Virrick graciously permitted the author complete access to these materials. This collection has since been archived at the Historical Association of Southern Florida, Miami.

63. Elizabeth Virrick, "Expressways: Boon or Blight?" *Ink Newsletter* 16 (April 1964), unpaginated, Virrick Papers; Elizabeth Virrick, "Expressways," *Ink: The Journal of Civil Affairs* 16 (November 1964), unpaginated, Virrick Papers; Elizabeth Virrick, "Is This Planning?" *Ink: The Journal of Civic Affairs* 17 (January 1966), unpaginated, Virrick Papers.

64. Weiner, *Urban Transportation Planning in the United States,* 19–20; Kenneth R. Geiser, *Urban Transportation Decision Making: Political Processes of Urban Freeway Controversies* (Cambridge, Mass.: Urban Systems Laboratory, MIT, 1970), 20; U.S. Department of Transportation, *First Annual Report, Fiscal Year 1967* (Washington, D.C.: U.S. Government Printing Office, 1968), 71.

65. Miami Housing Authority, *Relocation Housing Report* (Miami: Miami Housing Authority, 1964); Elizabeth Virrick, "Model Cities," *Ink: The Journal of Civic Affairs* 18 (December 1966–January 1967), unpaginated, Virrick Papers; Elizabeth Virrick, "Public Housing in Brownsville," *Ink: The Journal of Civic Affairs* 18 (February 1967), unpaginated, Virrick Papers; Elizabeth Virrick, "Slums Suddenly Discovered in Dade County," *Ink: The Journal of Civic Affairs* 18 (May 1967), unpaginated, Virrick Papers; Aileen Lotz, "The Birth of 'Little Hud,'" *Florida Planning and Development,* 19 (January 1968), 1–3, 6 and (February 1968), 1–3, 12; Metro-Dade County Planning Department, *Multiple Use Opportunities for Midtown Miami: East–West Expressway—Interstate 395 Midtown Interchange to Biscayne Bay* (Miami: Metro-Dade County, 1971), 10–11, 15–17.

66. Raymond A. Mohl, "The Settlement of Blacks in South Florida," in *South Florida: The Winds of Change,* ed. Thomas D. Boswell (Miami: Association of American Geographers, 1991), 112–139; Miami Planning Board, *Dwelling Conditions in the Two Principal Blighted Areas: Miami, Florida* (Miami: City of Miami, 1949); Reinhold P. Wolff and David K. Gillogly, *Negro Housing in the Miami Area: Effects of the Postwar Building Boom* (Coral Gables, Fla.: Bureau of Business and Economic Research, University of Miami, 1951); Elizabeth Virrick, "New Housing for Negroes in Dade County," in *Studies in Housing and Minority Groups,* ed. Nathan Glazer and Davis McEntire (Berkeley and Los Angeles: University of California Press, 1960), 135–143.

67. *Miami Herald,* 4 April 1945, 1 November, 28 November, 4 December 1946; Banner, *An Appraisal of Progress,* 20–24.

68. J. T. Knight to Dorothy McMaster, 30 September 1949, Warren Papers, Box 21; Banner, *An Appraisal of Progress,* 33; *Miami Herald,* 4 April 1945, 25 October 1949; Minutes, Miami City Commission, 5 December 1951.

69. Ira D. Hawthorne to Fuller Warren, 28 August 1951, 25 September 1951, Warren Papers, box 22; Hawthorne to Miami City Commission and Dade County Commission, 10 September 1951, Warren Papers, box 22; Lorine S. Reder to Fuller Warren, 8 August 1951, Warren Papers, box 21; M. L.

Hammack to Fuller Warren, telegram, 16 August 1951, Warren Papers, box 21; "$850,000 Housing Project Revealed," *Miami News,* 23 March 1947, clipping in Agnew Welsh Scrapbooks, Miami-Dade Public Library; Millspaugh and Breckenfeld, *The Human Side of Urban Renewal,* 135–137; Abrams, *Forbidden Neighbors,* 120–136; Kennedy, *The Klan Unmasked,* 219–233; Joe Alex Morris, "The Truth about the Florida Race Troubles," *Saturday Evening Post,* 21 June 1952, 24–25, 50, 55–58; Lenox, "The Carver Village Controversy," 39–51.

70. *Miami Herald,* 15 May 1950, 11–18 December 1955, 25 March 1957, 1 November, 2 November, 3 November, 5 November, 6 November 1959; Wolff and Gillogly, *Negro Housing in the Miami Area,* 8, 11, 21; Luther Voltz, "Rebuilding of Slums Underway," undated *Miami Herald* clipping, circa 1950, Elizabeth Virrick Scrapbooks, Virrick Papers; Millspaugh and Breckenfeld, *The Human Side of Urban Renewal,* 146; Rose, "Metropolitan Miami's Changing Negro Population," 224.

71. Wolff and Gillogly, *Negro Housing in the Miami Area,* 4–6, 8, 21; *Miami Herald,* 5 February, 16 April 1950, clippings, Welsh Scrapbooks; *Miami News,* 14 May 1950, ibid.; Teresa Lenox, "Opa-locka: From Dream to Ghetto" (graduate seminar paper, Florida Atlantic University, 1988).

72. Kenneth T. Jackson, *Crabgrass Frontier: The Suburbanization of the United States* (New York: Oxford University Press, 1985), 231–245; Wolff and Gillogly, *Negro Housing in the Miami Area,* 8–9, 11; H. Daniel Lang, *Food, Clothing and Shelter: An Analysis of the Housing Market of the Negro Group in Dade County* (Miami: Greater Miami Urban League, 1954), 35.

73. Mohl, "Trouble in Paradise," 14–20; Reinhold Wolff, *Greater Miami Population and Housing Survey: Real Estate Division* (Coral Gables, Fla.: University of Miami, 1949), unpaginated; Metro-Dade County, *Population and Housing, April 1958: Metropolitan Dade County, Florida* (Miami: Metro-Dade County, 1958), 7.

74. *Miami Herald,* 4 March 1957, 9 March 1957; *Miami News,* 1 March 1962; Rose, "Metropolitan Miami's Changing Negro Population," 225–226.

75. Elizabeth Virrick to Dorothy Montgomery, 23 April 1958, Virrick Papers.

76. Juanita Greene, "He'd Shift Negro District, Build a New 'Downtown,' " *Miami Herald,* 28 May 1961; Miami Planning and Zoning Board, *A Comprehensive Analysis of Miami's Neighborhoods,* 31; James W. Morrison, *The Negro in Greater Miami* (Miami: Greater Miami Urban League, 1962), 8.

77. *Miami News,* 2 March 1962; *Miami Herald,* 14 April 1963; *Miami Times,* 2 December 1966; Millspaugh and Breckenfeld, *The Human Side of Urban Renewal,* 145.

78. *Miami Herald,* 28 May 1961; *Miami Times,* 3 June 1961.

79. Dade County Schools, "Orchard Villa Survey," 13 November 1958, Dade County Public School Collection, Historical Association of Southern Florida; *New York Times,* 16 August 1959; *Miami Herald,* 29 May, 30 May 1961.

80. Greater Miami Urban League, "Facts About Miami's Negro Population," 1964, National Urban League Papers, Part II, Series I, box 72, mimeograph; Lenox, "Opa-locka"; C. E. Wright, "Carol City—A Complete One-Man-Built Florida Town—to House, Serve 40,000," *Municipal South* 2 (March 1955), 20–22; Clyde C. Wooten, *Psycho-Social Dynamics in Miami* (Coral Gables, Fla.: Center for Advanced International Studies, University of Miami, 1969), 531–554; *Miami Times,* 7 March 1964 (for Samet comment); *Miami Herald,* 2 April 1971.

81. *Miami Times,* 20 August 1965, 23 September 1966.

82. *Miami Times,* 21 October, 4 November 1966; Haley Sofge to Theodore R. Gibson, 1 December 1966, Virrick Papers; Wooten, *Psycho-Social Dynamics in Miami,* 349; Metro-Dade County Planning Department, *Mobility Patterns in Metropolitan Dade County, 1964–1969* (Miami: Metro-Dade County Planning Department, 1970), 98–100.

83. Donald O. Cowgill, "Trends in Residential Segregation of Non-Whites in American Cities, 1940–1950," *American Sociological Review* 21 (February 1956), 43–47; Karl E. Taeuber and Alma F. Taeuber, *Negroes in Cities: Residential Segregation and Neighborhood Change* (Chicago: Aldine, 1965), 39–41; Annemette Sorenson et al., "Indexes of Racial Residential Segregation for 109 Cities in the United States, 1940–1970," *Sociological Focus* 8 (1975), 125–142; Douglas S. Massey and Nancy A. Denton, "Trends in the Residential Segregation of Blacks, Hispanics, and Asians: 1970–1980," *American Sociological Review* 52 (December 1987), 802–825; *Miami Herald,* 30 December 1987.

84. Morton D. Winsberg, "Housing Segregation of a Predominantly Middle Class Population: Residential Patterns Developed by the Cuban Immigration into Miami, 1950–74," *American Journal of Economics and Sociology* 38 (October 1979), 403–418; Morton D. Winsberg, "Ethnic Competition for Residential Space in Miami, Florida, 1970–1980," *American Journal of Economics and Sociology* 42 (July 1983), 305–314; Raymond A. Mohl, "On the Edge: Blacks and Hispanics in Metropolitan Miami since 1959," *Florida Historical Quarterly* 69 (July 1990), 37–56.

85. *Miami Times,* 18 February, 23 September 1966; Scott Greer, *Urban Renewal and American Cities: The Dilemma of Democratic Intervention* (Indianapolis, Ind.: Bobbs-Merrill, 1965), 68.

86. Ben Kelley, *The Pavers and the Paved* (New York: Donald W. Brown, 1971), 97–107; Lisa Hirsch, "Roads," *City* 2 (September–October 1968), 27–30; David Hodge, "Social Impacts of Urban Transportation Decisions: Equity Issues," in *The Geography of Urban Transportation,* ed. Susan Hanson (New York: Guilford, 1986), 302–303.

87. Christopher Silver, *Twentieth-Century Richmond: Planning, Politics, and Race* (Knoxville: University of Tennessee Press, 1984), 183–197.

88. Altshuler, *The City Planning Process,* 17–83; Frieden and Sagalyn, *Downtown, Inc.,* 28–29; F. James Davis, "The Effects of Freeway Displacement on Racial Housing Segregation in a Northern City," *Phylon* 26 (Fall 1965), 209–215; Evelyn Fairbanks, *The Days of Rondo* (St. Paul: Minnesota Historical Society Press, 1990), a memoir of St. Paul's black community before its destruction by expressway building.

89. Allan R. Talbot, *The Mayor's Game: Richard Lee of New Haven and the Politics of Change* (New York: Praeger, 1970), 111, 113–114, 117; Smith, "Traffic and Transportation in Urban Renewal," 45–47.

90. Mark H. Rose and Bruce E. Seely, "Getting the Interstate Built: Road Engineers and the Implementation of Public Policy, 1955–1985," *Journal of Policy History* 2 (1990), 37.

91. Anthony Downs, "Community Reaction to a New Transportation Corridor and the Effects of Relocation on the Community," *Relocation: Social and Economic Aspects,* Special Report no. 110 (Washington, D.C.: Highway Research Board, 1970), 25–27; Patricia A. House, "Relocation of Families Displaced by Expressway Development: Milwaukee Case Study," *Land Economics* 46 (February 1970), 75–78; Richard J. Whelan, "The American Highway: Do We Know Where We're Going," *Saturday Evening Post,* 1 December 1968, 22–27, 54–64; David J. Van Tassel and John J. Grabowski, eds., *The Encyclopedia of Cleveland History* (Bloomington: Indiana University Press, 1987), 1–11. For a summary of research on relocation and its consequences, see Chester Hartman, "The Housing of Relocated Families," *Journal of the American Institute of Planners* 30 (November 1964), 266–286.

92. For Tampa, see Gary R. Mormino and George E. Pozzetta, *The Immigrant World of Ybor City: Italians and their Latin Neighbors in Tampa, 1885–1985* (Urbana: University of Illinois Press, 1987), 306–307. The St. Petersburg expressway pattern is outlined in Samuel Davis, "Interstate-275 and the Black Community of St. Petersburg" (seminar paper, University of South Florida, n.d.). For Orlando, see Richard E. Foglesong, "Baiting the Mousetrap: Driving I-4 Through Orlando" (paper delivered at the 89th Annual Meeting of the Florida Historical Society, Orlando, Florida, 10 May 1991). For Tallahassee, see Wilbur Smith and Associates, "Supplemental Report, Interstate Route Location, Tallahassee, Florida," report, March 1959, U.S. DOT Records, RG 30, box 70, mimeographed; W. C. Peterson to George M. Williams, 5 May 1959, U.S. DOT Records, RG 30, box 70.

93. The Gary statement is based on the author's personal experience, having lived in Gary from 1967 to 1970. For Atlanta, see Ronald H. Bayor, "Roads to Racial Segregation: Atlanta in the Twentieth Century," *Journal of Urban History* 15 (November 1988), 3–21. For Memphis, see Robin Flowerdew, "Spatial Patterns of Residential Segregation in a Southern City," *Journal of American Studies* 13 (April 1979), 93–107. For Los Angeles, see Leavitt, *Superhighway—Superhoax,* 5.

94. For Wilmington, see Carol E. Hoffecker, *Corporate Capital: Wilmington in the Twentieth Century* (Philadelphia: Temple University Press, 1983), 135–157. For St. Louis, see Gary Ross Mormino, *Immigrants on the Hill: Italian-Americans in St. Louis, 1882–1982* (Urbana: University of Illinois Press, 1986), 240–243. For Chicago, see Glen E. Holt and Dominic A. Pacyga, *Chicago: A Historical Guide to the Neighborhoods. The Loop and the South Side* (Chicago: Chicago Historical Society, 1979), 10, 197, 117, 119. For Boston, see Kenneth R. Geiser, *Urban Transportation Decision Making,* 258–264. For Providence, see Sidney Goldstein and Basil G. Zimmer, *Residential*

Displacement and Resettlement of the Aged (Providence: Rhode Island Division on Aging, 1960); Basil G. Zimmer, *Rebuilding Cities: The Effects of Displacement and Relocation on Small Business* (Chicago: Quadrangle Books, 1964). For the Cross-Bronx Expressway and its effect on the community, see Caro, *The Power Broker*, 839–394; Marshall Berman, *All That Is Solid Melts into Air: The Experience of Modernity* (New York: Simon and Schuster, 1982), 290–312; and Jill Jonnes, *We're Still Here: The Rise, Fall, and Resurrection of the South Bronx* (Boston: Atlantic Monthly Press, 1986), 117–126.

95. For antihighway movements in Boston and New York, see Alan Lupo et al., *Rites of Way: The Politics of Transportation in Boston and the U.S. City* (Boston: Little, Brown, 1971); Allan K. Sloan, *Citizen Participation in Transportation Planning: The Boston Experience* (Cambridge, Mass.: Ballinger, 1974); Ralph Gakenheimer, *Transportation Planning as Response to Controversy: The Boston Case* (Cambridge, Mass.: MIT Press, 1976); Geiser, *Urban Transportation Decision Making*, 248–330; Richard J. Whalen, *A City Destroying Itself: An Angry View of New York* (New York: William Morrow, 1965), 31–33; Ada Louise Huxtable, *Will They Ever Finish Bruckner Boulevard? A Primer on Urbicide* (New York: Collier Books, 1972), 18–24. For Washington, D.C., see Howard Gillette, Jr., "A National Workshop for Urban Policy: The Metropolitanization of Washington, 1946–1968," *The Public Historian* 7 (Winter 1985), 7–27. For Phoenix, Dallas, and San Francisco, see, respectively, Davies, *The Age of Asphalt*, 34–35; Delbert A. Taebel and James V. Cornehls, *The Political Economy of Urban Transportation* (Port Washington, N.Y.: Kennikat, 1977), 135; Phil Patton, *Open Road: A Celebration of the American Highway* (New York: Simon and Schuster, 1986), 104; Bruce B. Brugmann et al., *The Ultimate Highrise: San Francisco's Mad Rush Toward the Sky* (San Francisco: San Francisco Bay Guardian Books, 1971), 23; Kelley, *The Pavers and the Paved*, 95.

96. Robert Moses, *Working for the People: Promise and Performance in Public Service* (New York: Harper, 1956), 67–68; Robert Moses, *Public Works: A Dangerous Trade* (New York: McGraw-Hill, 1970), 772–776; John W. Lawrence, *Study of the Proposed Riverfront and Elysian Fields Expressway and an Alternate Proposal* (New Orleans: Tulane University School of Architecture, 1965); Ed Palmer, "The Riverfront Wrangle," *New Orleans* 1 (October 1966), 13–16; Priscilla Dunhill, "An Expressway Named Destruction," *Architectural Forum* 126 (March 1967), 54–59; Thomas N. Whitehead, "Urban Planning: Historical Preservation of the Vieux Carré," *Louisiana Studies* 9 (Summer 1970), 73–87; Richard O. Baumbach, Jr., and William E. Borah, *The Second Battle of New Orleans: A History of the Vieux Carré Riverfront-Expressway Controversy* (University: University of Alabama Press, 1981). For the Napoleon Avenue Bridge controversy, see Mississippi River Bridge Authority, *A Summary: Mississippi River Crossing Studies, 1965–1970* (New Orleans: Mississippi River Bridge Authority, 1970), and the extensive files of the Uptown Civic Association, Marta B. Lamar Papers, University of New Orleans. Both issues were extensively covered in the chief organ of the preservationists, the *Vieux Carré Courier,* between 1967 and 1970.

97. *Vieux Carré Courier,* 22 January 1965; Jason Berry, "Claiborne Carnival Comeback," *Gambit,* 13 February 1982, 15–16; Claiborne Avenue Design Team, *I-10 Multi-Use Study* (New Orleans: Claiborne Avenue Design Team, 1976).

98. See files of reports, brochures, news clippings, mimeographs, and newsletters such as *The Concrete Opposition* (Highway Action Coalition), Marta B. Lamar Papers, University of New Orleans. For the highway revolt generally, see "The Revolt Against Big City Expressways," *U.S. News and World Report,* 1 January 1962, 48–51; Priscilla Dunhill, "When Highways and Cities Collide," *City* 1 (July 1967), 48–54; "The War Over Urban Expressways," *Business Week,* 11 March 1967, 4–5; Jack Linville, "Troubled Urban Interstates," *Nation's Cities* 8 (December 1970), 8–11; Juan Cameron, "How the Interstate Changed the Face of the Nation," *Fortune* 84 (July 1971), 78–81, 124–125.

99. For the positive economic, social, and aesthetic effects of expressways, see Bureau of Public Roads, *Highways and Economic and Social Changes* (Washington, D.C.: U.S. Government Printing Office, 1964); Federal Highway Administration, *The Freeway in the City: Principles of Planning and Design* (Washington, D.C.: U.S. Government Printing Office, 1968); James T. Jenkins, Jr., "The Interstate System," *American Road Builder* 41 (September 1964), 9–24; Donald Appleyard et al., *The View from the Road* (Cambridge, Mass.: MIT Press, 1964); Christopher Tunnard and Boris Pushkarev, *Man-Made America: Chaos or Control?* (New Haven, Conn.: Yale University Press, 1963), 157–276; Hays B. Gamble and Thomas B. Davinroy, *Beneficial Effects Associated with Freeway Construction: Environmental, Social, and Economic,* National Cooperative Highway Research Program Report no. 193 (Washington, D.C.: Transportation Research Board, 1978). See also Michael Chernoff, "The Effects of Superhighways in Urban Areas," *Urban Affairs Quarterly* 16 (March 1981), 317–336. The following is a pathetic example of FHA's effort to justify inner-city expressways: "The budding basketball star of tomorrow," an FHA official asserted, "could be a kid who learned how to dribble, pass, and shoot because an Interstate Highway came through his neighborhood. And this same youth, who wiled away hours of his life wondering what to do next, can now cavort on a basketball court laid out under a structurally modern viaduct." Quoted in Robert Goodman, *After the Planners* (New York: Simon and Schuster, 1971), 81.

100. *The Freeway and Baton Rouge* (Baton Rouge: Department of Landscape Architecture, Louisiana State University, 1971), 5; Hodge, "Social Impacts of Urban Transportation Decisions," 303.

101. Daniel P. Moynihan, "Policy vs. Program in the '70's," *The Public Interest* 20 (Summer 1970), 94.

102. Rose, "Metropolitan Miami's Changing Negro Population," 224; Robert M. Press, "Miami's Overtown: Blacks Fight Inequality to Revive Community," *Christian Science Monitor,* 20 March 1984, 5; *Miami Herald,* 30 November, 28 December 1981, 5 January 1982, 29 November, 2 December 1983, 19 May, 26 June, 12 August 1984, 10 August, 7 September 1986; *Miami Times,* 16 December 1982, 5 June 1986; *Miami News* 6 October 1983, 1 May 1984, 28 April 1987.

103. Athalie Range, "Citizen Participation in the Metropolitan Transportation Planning Process," in *Metropolitan Transportation Planning Seminars:*

Miami, Florida, January 7–8, 1971, report prepared for the U.S. Department of Transportation (Washington, D.C.: U.S. Department of Transportation, 1971), 39; *Miami Times,* 16 December 1982; *Miami Herald,* 31 December 1982; Rev. Bryan Walsh, interview with Jennifer Braaten, 23 December 1981.
104. *Miami Times,* 20 March, 5 June 1986; *Miami Herald,* 29 November 1983; Henry Hampton and Steve Fayer, *Voices of Freedom: An Oral History of the Civil Rights Movement from the 1950s through the 1980s* (New York: Bantam Books, 1990), 649.
105. National Commission on the Causes and Prevention of Violence, *Miami Report: The Report of the Miami Study Team on Civil Disturbances in Miami, Florida, during the Week of August 5, 1968* (Washington, D.C.: U.S. Government Printing Office, 1969); U.S. Commission on Civil Rights, *Confronting Racial Isolation in Miami* (Washington, D.C.: U.S. Government Printing Office, 1982); Bruce Porter and Marvin Dunn, *Crossing the Bounds: The Miami Riot of 1980* (Lexington, Mass.: D.C. Heath, 1984); Hoffecker, *Corporate Capital,* 141.
106. John F. Bauman, *Public Housing, Race, and Renewal: Urban Planning in Philadelphia, 1920–1974* (Philadelphia: Temple University Press, 1987), 79.
107. Lewis Mumford, *The Highway and the City* (New York: Mentor Books, 1964), 244.

5

DAVID R. GOLDFIELD

Black Political Power and Public Policy in the Urban South

"Yᴇʟʟᴏᴡ Jɪᴍ" was a resourceful slave. Between 1847 and 1853, Yellow Jim earned nearly nineteen hundred dollars for his master, James Rudd. However, if you asked Rudd what Yellow Jim did in Louisville to receive such a handsome sum, his response would be vague. In truth, Rudd probably did not care to know the secret of Yellow Jim's success as long as his slave dutifully remitted a fair return. A terse notation on Yellow Jim in Rudd's ledger indicates that Rudd should have been more involved in the slave's activities: "Dec. 11, 1853. Ranaway."[1]

There were many Yellow Jims in the antebellum urban South, a fact that was maddening to those who worried about the effect of urban life on slavery. Yellow Jim was able to expand the narrow margins of his life by hiring out his own time, selecting a place to live, frequenting shops that sold liquor, attending church, mingling with whites and fellow blacks, slave and free, and even learning to read and write. His very name bespoke the ambiguous lines of race in the Old South. Yet, almost all of his activities were, at one time or another, illegal, not only in Louisville, but in most other antebellum southern cities.

Yellow Jim's ambiguous status reflected both the tensions within white society on how to regulate urban blacks and the persistence of blacks to test the limits of their bondage. The crucial role of black labor in the antebellum urban South drove a wedge into white society. Slave and free black males worked in the tobacco factories of Richmond; drove the drays from the wharves of Charleston, Mobile, and New Orleans; paved the roads; shod the horses; and cut the hair of whites in Louisville and Savannah. Black women performed domestic services, including caring for children, laundering, marketing, and housekeeping. Restricting the mobility and choice of labor meant limiting access by employers, which, in turn, adversely affected economic development. Occasionally, especially during the turbulent 1850s, crackdowns occurred and local authorities increased police patrols and closed shops, churches, and schools. However, generally, the value of black labor overcame the misgivings of white decision makers, and cities invariably lapsed back into customary patterns.

Such indulgence angered working-class whites in particular: it fudged racial boundaries and threatened their livelihood. Although regulations barred blacks from the professions, they were free to take artisanal trades that competed directly with whites. City councils, concerned about the growing political clout of working-class whites, often responded positively to their antiblack petitions. Enforcement was another matter. There, the interests of the slaveholders prevailed. To restrict and remove slaves from the workplace damaged the investment of the slaveholder. As the example of Yellow Jim indicated, slaves could earn respectable sums for their masters. The proliferation of regulation and the weakness of enforcement reflected these opposing interests in white urban society.

The efforts of urban blacks themselves played a role in the distinction between legislation and enforcement. The free black population, existing precariously between slavery and freedom, had managed to carve a place in urban society. Free Negro barber William Johnson of Natchez, Mississippi, and Charleston tailor James M. Johnson had amassed more property and capital than many whites in their respective communities. Free blacks had formed churches, mutual-aid societies, and social clubs. They also had maintained close ties with the white elite. Their gentle entreaties to influential white patrons often spared their class from harsh legislation. The fascinating correspondence of James M. Johnson reveals these delicate and crucial relations in Charleston, especially in the years immediately preceding the Civil War, when the city's white workers mounted strong campaigns to expel free blacks. Combined with the paternal bonds that existed between some masters and their urban-based slaves, these relationships implied that blacks had at least some influence among the white power structure.[2]

Racial Policies during Segregation
and before Voting Rights

The relative protection from adverse policies that urban blacks experienced in the antebellum era vanished after the Civil War. The abolition of slavery removed a major obstacle to white solidarity. The urban South still needed dependable black labor, but protecting investments was no longer a reason to prefer or indulge black workers. Urban leaders forged white solidarity to secure their economic and political dominance in the new era. White supremacy was the carrot offered to whites for surrendering their political autonomy; black rule and race war were the alternatives. Urban policies restricted black geographic and occupational mobility, segregated blacks in public facilities and schools, and excluded them from urban services. Although urban blacks persisted in challenging these conditions, often at great personal peril, their economic and political fortunes suffered serious setbacks through the early decades of the twentieth century.

The flurry of adverse legislation directed at urban blacks during the decades after the Civil War reflected the growing concentration of blacks in southern cities. The percentage of blacks in the urban South declined steadily in the late antebellum period. After the war, however, blacks flooded into southern cities seeking friends, family, and work. The memoirs of Frederick Douglass and other former slaves make it clear that before the Civil War, slaves considered work in the city a significant upgrade in their status.[3] However, slaves, of course, could not make that decision—to leave the farm for the city. People freed from slavery could, and did.

When blacks arrived in southern cities after the Civil War, they found existing black-run institutions to help them with the transition to urban life. Many plantation slaves were already familar with some aspects of city living, either through relatives or through occasional excursions to sell produce. Also, southern cities were hardly metropolises, so adjustments were not difficult and blacks from rural areas eagerly joined churches, filled schools, and entered the local economy and political culture.

By the early 1870s, and especially after the depression of 1873, the fortunes of urban blacks began to decline, though not without a struggle. The reassertion of conservative white power across the South was especially noticeable in the cities where intimidation, violence, and exclusion marked race relations for the rest of the nineteenth century, culminating in the lynching spree of the 1890s.

The policies emanating from these changed circumstances are well known. Segregation was a means to redefine race relations after slavery. Although some historians have noted that segregation actually was an improvement over the exclusion urban blacks experienced in the antebellum era, the effective result of racial separation was exclusion—exclusion from jobs, from a decent education, from numerous public facilities, from public services, from politics, and from the courts.[4] The system not only separated, but humiliated as well, identifying black facilities as inferior and establishing a complex etiquette that explicitly reinforced that inferiority.

Another consequence of readjusted race relations was the limiting of urban economic opportunities. The definition of "nigger work"— menial tasks relegated to blacks—narrowed. By the early decades of the twentieth century, whites were moving into such occupations as barber, tailor, waiter, dockworker and construction worker. The urban educational system reinforced the menial labor futures of black boys and girls. The curriculum at inferior black schools stressed vocational subjects, and blacks were discouraged from attending secondary schools. Most cities lacked a black public high school during the first decades of the twentieth century. As the urban South industrialized and mechanized after 1900, whites excluded blacks from the new industries and technologies. A postbellum Yellow Jim would not have had to turn over his earnings to his master, but he would have had fewer employment options.

The removal of blacks from the political arena was another consequence of racial policies. In southern cities, the removal was never total. In the 1940s, roughly one out of five southern blacks was registered to vote, 85 percent of whom lived in cities.[5] In cities such as Mayor Edward H. Crump's Memphis or Mayor William B. Hartsfield's Atlanta, blacks voted in significant numbers, although their votes were captive of white political organizations that occasionally doled out some patronage. The consequences of political impotence were evident to casual visitors to southern cities before the 1950s (and later in some smaller communities). Paved roads typically ended at the borders of black neighborhoods. The neighborhoods themselves were poorly drained, rarely serviced, and fitted with dilapidated housing. Black schools were often makeshift, ramshackle, and overcrowded. If the visitor entered a downtown store, a government office, or a bank, he or she would not see any black faces, save those performing janitorial work. Furthermore, if the visitor entered the leading club, or attended church, he or she would not see black members in either place. In the informal world of southern decision making, these institutions were important conduits to power. Blacks, inconsequential players in the public arena, were invisible in the private city, as well.

Southern urban blacks were not uncomplaining victims of these racial policies. Building on antebellum traditions, black neighborhoods became communities. Black churches offered more than spiritual sustenance: they provided leadership, fellowship, recreational and educational facilities, and a variety of social service functions. Black culture and history often were bootlegged into black schools. Businesses owned and operated by blacks opened to serve a clientele ignored or insulted by downtown merchants. Life insurance companies and clothiers owned and operated by blacks and black barbers, attorneys, physicians, and restauranteurs expanded the traditional teacher–preacher middle class while providing essential services for the black community. Scarcely a southern city existed without a fashionable black business thoroughfare—Sweet Auburn in Atlanta, for example.

Black neighborhoods were especially successful in shielding children from the harsh and humiliating aspects of a segregated society. Black leaders such as Charleston native Harvey Gantt and Supreme Court Justice Thurgood Marshall, who grew up in segregated Baltimore, recall their sheltered childhood as a time when they were virtually oblivious to the realities of southern race relations.[6]

Blacks also launched protests against their inferior status. They boycotted streetcars early in the century, they joined white workers in labor actions, and they applied for membership in local National Association for the Advancement of Colored People (NAACP) chapters during the 1920s and 1930s. Most of these activities were unsuccessful and fraught with danger. Still, they reflect that race relations in the urban South during the first third of the twentieth century were not set in stone. Victories were small but significant, and perhaps included the funding of a black high school, the appointment of a black health official, the expansion of black voter registration, the capitalization of "Negro" by the local newspaper, the use of "Mr." or "Mrs.," and the growing numbers of whites at home and in Washington who were willing to speak out, however timidly, for a moderation of race relations.

Inspired by the New Deal and spurred by the opportunities of World War II, southern urban blacks launched major campaigns on two fronts in the two decades after 1945. First, urban blacks sought to expand voting rights. Yellow Jim had some freedom because he had some economic leverage; his postbellum offspring lost much of that leverage. Economic hardship and declining political fortunes increased the vulnerability of urban blacks to adverse economic and social policies. The prospect of challenging these policies looked dim unless southern urban blacks could break white solidarity and one-party rule. Fighting for political rights seemed the most promising strategy from the perspective of the 1940s: without political pressure to open up employment, housing, and education, the economic status of urban blacks would remain low. The U.S. Supreme Court decision in *Smith* v. *Allwright* (1944) to abolish the white primary was an important step in securing political rights. In response, chapters of the Negro Voters' League sprung up in cities across the region to register blacks and to take advantage of the ruling. During the 1940s and early 1950s, black registration in New Orleans, for example, jumped from 400 to 28,000.[7] Political advances inspired other actions.

The attack on segregation became a second front in the strategy of urban blacks to secure their civil, economic, and social rights. With the assistance and leadership of NAACP, urban blacks filed court cases challenging the constitutionality of segregation, especially in education. They attempted, at least in the upper South (Virginia, Kentucky, North Carolina, and Tennessee) in 1947, to integrate public waiting rooms. More direct action was too dangerous at this time. Urban blacks eventually sought to improve their economic status by eliminating segregation and exclusion in employment and lending practices.

During the 1940s, it seemed as if voting rights would become the major focus of southern urban blacks. The *Smith* v. *Allwright* decision had galvanized urban blacks; a new breed of white political leader emerged in southern cities who was more interested in economic development than in race-baiting (William Berry Hartsfield in Atlanta and deLesseps S. Morrison in New Orleans were only two of the more prominent examples);[8] and postwar migrations had swelled the numbers of blacks in the urban South to the point where they could influence policy. However, the civil rights initiatives of the Harry S Truman administration and the effective use of race- and red-baiting by the old guard southern politicians froze the southern political spring and helped divert black efforts elsewhere. The 1954 *Brown* v. *Board of Education* decision, the Montgomery bus boycott, and the electrifying sit-in demonstrations beginning in 1960 further reordered priorities.[9] Still, black leaders recognized that the ballot was essential to changing racial policies in the urban South, even after segregation had fallen. It was not yet clear how the ability to eat at a lunch counter, sit in the orchestra of a movie theater, or try on a pair of shoes would appreciably improve the situation of rank-and-file blacks. The successful demonstrations leading to desegregated public facilities imparted a sense of mission, identity, and power to southern urban blacks. The psychological gains were real and important. However, more substantive victories would prove elusive without the right to vote.

Although southern black leaders could agree on little else after 1965, there was a consensus that the ballot would work as a magic elixir on the southern body politic. Martin Luther King predicted on the eve of the Selma demonstrations in 1965, "If Negroes could vote . . . there would be no more oppressive poverty." A year later, Stokely Carmichael was more practical but no less enthusiastic about the potential of voting rights. He reasoned that "if a black man is elected tax assessor, he can collect and channel funds for the building of better roads and schools serving black people—thus advancing the move from political power into the economic arena.[10]

In the quarter century since Martin Luther King and Stokely Carmichael hailed the ballot, the political landscape of the urban South has changed dramatically. Only a handful of black elected officials existed in southern towns and cities in 1965. Two decades later, there were 3,500 local black elected officials in the South and 2,100 local black elected officials in the rest of the nation. Although more than 70 percent of these leaders served communities of fewer than 5,000 people, black politicians had made notable gains as big-city mayors by the mid-1980s, holding office in cities such as Charlotte, Atlanta, New Orleans, Little Rock, and Birmingham.[11] Yellow Jim had affected urban policy through his initiative and his economic value to whites; his progeny now had political leverage. Would beneficial public policies and economic opportunity follow?

Black Political Power and Urban Services

Poor or absent urban services in black neighborhoods historically have reflected white supremacy and black political impotence in southern cities. Since the Voting Rights Act of 1965, black elected officials have had a significant effect on the provision of services to black neighborhoods. Surveys of communities with black elected officials have indicated that paved streets and recreational facilities were direct consequences of black officeholding.[12] Part of the service improvement reflected changes in federal policies and the abilities of black elected officials to take advantage of those changes. The application of these policies not only addressed service shortcomings but sought to rectify the historic isolation and official neglect of these neighborhoods.

During the 1920s, southern cities institutionalized the segregation of black neighborhoods through zoning and planning policies. As a

1929 Houston City Planning Commission report noted, "Because of long established racial prejudices, it is best for both races that living areas be segregated."[13] In subsequent years, cities adopted strategies designed to confine blacks to certain areas and eliminate slum housing in districts adjacent to vulnerable white neighborhoods. Federal policies after World War II complemented southern urban strategies.

Federal urban renewal enabled southern urban leaders to accomplish two objectives. First, they demolished unsightly dwellings occupied mainly by blacks near the city center. Second, in place of these structures, cities erected hotels, office buildings, civic centers, or highways. Aside from destroying existing black neighborhoods, such policies created a major housing crisis for blacks. In Atlanta between 1957 and 1967, urban renewal accomplished the demolition of 21,000 housing units occupied primarily by blacks; during this time, the city constructed only 5,000 public housing units. City officials reserved renewal land for a stadium, a civic center, and acres of parking lots.[14]

By the late 1960s, federal urban policy retreated from renewal and stressed conservation. The Lyndon B. Johnson administration designed the Model Cities program to create self-sufficient neighborhoods and residents. Atlanta was the first city in the nation to receive a Model Cities grant. The target neighborhood included a population of 45,000 people, indicating that the program allowed cities to define *neighborhood* loosely. The city used the funds to provide shuttle bus service, a day-care program, the construction of an educational complex, and the resurfacing of streets.[15] In Tampa, city officials expended nearly twelve million dollars in Model Cities money between 1970 and 1975, mostly in black neighborhoods. The tally of accomplishments was impressive: more than two thousand homes renovated; the construction of a multipurpose service center; street paving, refurbishing of playgrounds, a new park and picnic grounds complex; and a 1,648-unit moderate-income housing project.[16]

The shift in federal urban policy coincided with the growing power of black neighborhoods at city hall. Neighborhood politics became a key factor in upgrading low-income neighborhoods during the 1970s and in the electoral campaigns of Maynard Jackson in Atlanta, Henry L. Marsh III in Richmond, and Clarence Lightner in Raleigh. The neighborhood preservation movement also figured in the mayoral elections in San Antonio, Houston, and New Orleans in the late 1970s.[17]

However, the legacies of discrimination and federal policies and the limits of southern urban politics transcended the abilities of black elected officials and their white allies to make significant service improvements in black neighborhoods, especially in those areas at the lower end of the economic scale. The first problem was financial. Black urban neighborhoods were so badly serviced before the 1960s that to bring streets, housing, parks, police, fire, and health services to the quality of white areas would break the budgets of most southern cities. Atlanta mayor Ivan Allen, Jr., posed the problem for himself and his successors in the mid-1960s:

For one hundred years, metropolitan and city centers of the Southeast almost totally ignored anywhere from 25 to 40% of the population. . . . There were no building regulations. There was no code enforcement. There was no planning. There was no effort to provide any form of housing . . . , garbage was not picked up regularly, the streets were not paved. . . . Today in a rapidly expanding market, as millions more people move into urban centers, we find a great need of running fast in both directions. Not only are we endeavoring to provide extended and better services for all the people who live in the city, but also we are trying to take up the slack of what has been the slums of the deteriorated areas of each city.[18]

Federal programs picked up some of the financial slack, but Congress spread Model Cities funds over 150 cities, thinning out the program's budget. The demise of Model Cities during the Nixon administration and the substitution of Community Development Block Grants further vitiated service assistance to black neighborhoods. Congress intended the block grant program "principally [to] benefit people of low and moderate income."[19] In practice, most of the money went to assist not the poorest neighborhoods, but marginal areas where local politicians could boast quick results. In Memphis, for example, a local advisory panel designated most of the grants for black neighborhoods, but only those black neighborhoods of moderate income with a relatively high proportion of homeowners.[20] Also, some city administrations used the block grants to fund long-term capital improvements such as sewers and roads throughout the city.

The withdrawal of the Ronald W. Reagan administration from urban programs was less traumatic in southern cities than elsewhere because the percentage of federal funds rarely exceeded 10 percent of local budgets. Southern cities and states, therefore, were better able to fill the funding gap, as opposed to places such as St. Louis and Detroit, where upward of 25 percent of those cities' budgets depended on federal funding.[21] However, as the block grant program suggested, the problem was less financial than one of setting priorities.

Black Political Power and
Economic Opportunity

Turning to the issue of economic opportunity for southern urban blacks, the results were similarly mixed. One of the most successful economic policies instituted by southern urban administrations after 1965, and especially in the 1970s and 1980s, has been affirmative action. Under the direction of Richmond's black mayor, Roy West, and his allies on the city council, for example, the city instituted an aggressive affirmative action program that required public contractors to set aside 30 percent of their subcontracts for minority firms. Before 1983, when the city initiated the policy, 0.67 percent of Richmond's contracts went to minority-owned businesses. By 1986, that figure had jumped to nearly 40 percent. Black-run administrations also have expanded black participation in the city bureaucracy. During Maynard Jackson's first term as mayor of Atlanta (1973–1977), the percentage of professional and administrative positions in city government held by blacks jumped from 19 percent to 42 percent.[22]

Generally, white economic leaders have gone along with affirmative action policies. Former Atlanta Mayor Andrew Young offered two reasons for this consensus: (1) expanded consumer demand and (2) insurance against civil disturbances. As he explained in 1985, "We've given out 230 contracts worth $130 million to blacks in the last three years. That circulates to beauty parlors, barber shops, gets young people off the street. That's why we don't have black people jumping up and down . . . like black folks in Jamaica or Miami."[23]

The minority set-aside programs and the presence of blacks in the city bureaucracy also may have opened doors for blacks in the private sector. The performance and visibility of white-collar blacks in public-sector positions set examples and loosened reservations among some private employers. Also, as black populations increased in several southern cities and as their political power grew, white employers found economic advantages in hiring blacks. As one white executive noted, "It is simply good business" to hire blacks.[24] Some communities have taken pride in the visibility of blacks in professional positions. In Jackson, Mississippi, for example, by the mid-1970s, it was routine for whites to see black reporters and announcers on local television stations, black managers in downtown stores, and black bank employees. One white Jackson official boasted that his city was "the most integrated place in America."[25]

One result of these changes in public- and private-sector employment has been the expansion of the urban black middle class. As

Leslie Dunbar of the Southern Regional Council wrote in 1980, the "irreversible achievement of the civil rights movement . . . is that the black middle class has greatly expanded." Political scientists Earl Black and Merle Black estimated that by 1980, nearly 30 percent of southern black workers were employed in middle-class occupations, more than 40 percent in metropolitan areas, compared with 4 percent in 1940. The best indirect evidence was the continued in-migration: between 1975 and 1985, more than 850,000 blacks moved south, compared with slightly more than 500,000 who left. These in-migrants tended to be younger and better educated as a group than earlier black in-migrants—nearly two out of three held at least a high-school diploma (compared with a 45-percent rate among blacks already living in the South).[26] Metropolitan areas in the South Atlantic states have been the major recipients of black middle-class migration. Cities such as Atlanta, Charlotte, Richmond, and the Raleigh–Durham–Chapel Hill area with expanding service economies have been attractive to white-collar blacks. These interregional movements have resulted in an increase in the percentage of blacks in the South for the first time in the twentieth century—from 53 percent in 1980 to 56 percent in 1988.[27]

Although the black middle class has expanded, there has not been a corresponding decline in black poverty in the urban South. The number of blacks below the poverty line increased during the 1980s, and the income and employment disparities between whites and blacks were as great as ever. In Houston, the average black family earned roughly 60 percent of what their white counterparts earned, and the black unemployment rate was three times that for whites. In Atlanta, the "black mecca," approximately the same disparities prevailed in income and unemployment. In Birmingham, blacks earned just 58 percent of what whites earned and were more than four and a half times as likely as whites to be below the poverty line.[28]

Employed blacks were concentrated in the most menial occupations, even in public sector work where white-collar blacks had made significant advances. In Birmingham, for example, 45 percent of the city's black employees worked in maintenance positions compared with 14 percent of whites, and 16 percent of blacks worked in managerial and professional occupations compared with 30 percent of whites.[29] Job-growth statistics in Atlanta belied Mayor Andrew Young's trickle-down theory. Between 1960 and 1988, whites enjoyed a 90-percent job gain; for blacks, the increase was 5 percent.[30]

Although proponents of the Sunbelt South talked wistfully of avoiding the fate of hard-pressed northern cities, the extent of black poverty in the urban South indicated that southern cities shared unhappy circumstances with their counterparts elsewhere. During the 1980s, the overwhelmingly black downtown residential core of Atlanta was the second poorest neighborhood in the nation. Despite Sunbelt hyperbole, some southern cities ranked at the bottom of the so-called hardship rating, a measure documenting the degree of unemployment, limited education, crowded housing, and poverty in a particular city. Based on these indices, New Orleans, Miami, and Birmingham ranked below Cleveland or Detroit.[31]

Despite the advance of urban black political power and the growing numbers of black elected officials since 1965, the economic status of the majority of the black urban population has not changed. At least three factors account for this situation. First, the changing nature of the national economy has drastically reduced the demand for remunerative semiskilled occupations. Second, the social and spatial configurations of the modern metropolis lower the visibility of the poor populations. Third, the policy priorities and administrative objectives of modern local government limit redistributionist responses to the problem of the black underclass.

Service-oriented Economy and Urban Policy

Urban blacks had been involved only on the margins of southern industry before 1960. In response to federal legislation, new industrial opportunities in textiles and steel opened to blacks during the 1960s. The irony was that these industries were already in decline and poised to lay off tens of thousands of workers over the next two decades. The economy of the South, and of the nation, was changing to a service orientation. Cities no longer hosted industries, but became the location of so-called knowledge functions: higher education; legal, financial, and accounting services; insurance; data processing; government; and corporate administration. These functions generated high-skilled, high-paid positions, beyond the reach of most black urban residents.

However, there was another tier of employment in the service economy. During the 1960s, the majority of service jobs were minimum wage, or scarcely above the minimum wage, with limited futures. These were the jobs flipping hamburgers, cleaning high-rise office buildings and hotels, and washing cars. In addition, many of the low-tier openings were in the burgeoning suburbs of metropolitan areas and, therefore, were inaccessible to inner-city blacks. Middle-class population and economic base were leaving southern cities, as they had left cities elsewhere. Between 1960 and 1975, for example, Atlanta experienced an absolute loss of 2,000 jobs because the city's share of metropolitan employment fell from 20 percent to 12 percent. In 1960, central Atlanta contained 90 percent of the metropolitan area's office space. By 1980, that proportion had declined to 42 percent because nearly 100 industrial parks ringed the city.[32] Blacks were unlikely to move to suburban jurisdictions. There were transportation problems, housing discrimination, and housing prices beyond the reach of most low-income blacks because suburbs zoned residential land to effectively eliminate or reduce the likelihood of low-income or multifamily dwellings. The future composition of the service economy is unlikely to improve the prospects of the black underclass. Better than 80 percent of the service jobs that will be created in the 1990s are in the lower tier.[33]

Multicentered Metropolis and Urban Policy

As the disjunction between jobs and residence has implied, the social and spatial configuration of the southern metropolis has militated against the black underclass. Through most of the twentieth century, the metropolitan area has consisted of city and suburb. Since 1970, however, there has been a concentration on settlement, economic base, and even culture and entertainment of the metropolitan periphery. These out-towns are often parts of what the *New York Times* in 1978 called a "multicentered urban chain" held together by ribbons of highway.[34] They have attained a sufficient residential density to support even major league sports franchises, such as the Texas Rangers in Irving, Texas, between Dallas and Fort Worth. Though most southern metropolitan areas are not as large as the Dallas–Fort Worth metroplex, the sprawling, automobile-dependent metropolises of the 1990s suit the spatial traditions of the South well.

In racial terms, the multicentered metropolis stretches distances between blacks and whites, middle-class and poor. Commuting patterns in southern metropolitan areas are more often cross suburban than suburb to city. Even commutes to the central city frequently are along elevated freeways separated from the decay below. Hermetically sealed office buildings and underground garages further shield the middle class from urban problems. If the problem cannot be seen, it may not exist.

However, the class divisions implied by contemporary metropolitan spatial arrangements may be more serious than the racial separation. For the first time in southern history, the urban black middle class is becoming detached from the rest of the black population. Fair housing laws, greater affluence, and the absense of exclusionary traditions in the new out-towns have accelerated middle-class black suburbanization. Blacks in Atlanta's suburbs, for example, increased by 200 percent between 1970 and 1980.[35]

Intellectual isolation has accompanied physical separation among different black social groups. Black Charlotte attorney Mel Watt noted that the attitude of many successful young black urban professionals seems to be: "I have made it and I don't owe anybody from the past or future anything." The "me" generation is color blind. Eddie Williams, a southern black who currently heads the Joint Center for Political Studies in Washington, D.C., urged blacks to "move from an era of moral persuasion with its non-negotiable demands, to an era of politics, where everything is negotiable."[36]

In the era of white supremacy, all blacks had shared segregation and the demeaning etiquette of southern race relations; the virtual demise of those constraints broke the bond of suffering uniting all blacks, whatever their socioeconomic differences, as well as some of the institutions that bound them to each other, such as black businesses and black schools. Although there had always been divisions within the black community, most could agree on breaking down the barriers of racial inferiority. Now that agreement can only occur on an intellectual rather than an experiential level, both the intellectual and experiential gaps between the two groups are widening. As black sociologist William Julius Wilson predicted in 1978, "There are clear indications that the economic gap between the black underclass . . . and the higher-income blacks will very likely widen and solidify."[37]

The policy implications of social and spatial stratification are that black underclass issues are less likely to receive high priorities at city hall, regardless of the race of the mayor and city council. Black voters are no longer content with having a black face in city hall; they are restless as reflected by the Rev. Hosea Williams' challenge to Maynard Jackson in Atlanta's 1989 mayoral race. Black elected officials, for their part, complain that black voters do not understand the limits of the political process. A black council member in Riviera Beach, Florida, complained recently that "Black expectations are high when a black is elected. They want us to change the world in one day, and when we don't do this they brand us as 'Uncle Toms.' "[38] Atlanta's

Andrew Young was more philosophical about the pressure: "For ten years we went around yelling 'Freedom Now'—and a lot of people translated that into having a black congressman, meaning we're going to have all of our freedom now, so on Monday morning they come to city hall and say, 'Where is it?' "[39]

Political Culture and Urban Policy

The nature of the southern political process in the 1990s and the changes in urban administration reinforce the other difficulties in framing social policies. The reality of southern urban politics is that although blacks currently may control or have a major influence over electoral politics in most southern cities, whites still control the urban economy. Atlanta political scientist Mack Jones put the matter simply: "The economy is controlled by white interests . . . and black elected officials need the support of these same white elements in order to maintain existing services."[40] During his first term as mayor of Atlanta, Maynard Jackson discovered that confronting the white economic establishment severely limited his ability to govern—to build support for affirmative action programs and to target development that would benefit blacks. As federal funds diminished, the role of local banks and other major businesses increased.

Cultivating white economic leaders is necessary for black candidates as well as black elected officials. Blacks in the antebellum urban South often advanced their fortunes by connecting with a prominent white. The modern version of this relationship is the Manhattan coalition. Atlanta's mayor during the 1940s and 1950s, William B. Hartsfield, perfected this alliance of blacks and wealthy whites. Both groups were frightened by the growing numbers of working-class whites who proved susceptible to race-baiting candidates. The white elites were concerned about the city's image—"too busy to hate," as Hartsfield coined it—and blacks worried that their modest gains could be jeopardized by racist officeholders.[41]

As black political power grew after the Voting Rights Act of 1965, the Manhattan coalition spread through most of the urban South. New Orleans's first black mayor, Dutch Morial, won his initial term by combining a sizable black vote with the support of "business-oriented" whites.[42] In the 1980s, Charlotte Mayor Harvey Gantt and Birmingham Mayor Richard Arrington put together similar coalitions to gain victory.

The well-to-do whites are less important to black candidates for their votes than they are for their campaign financing, political expertise, and access to the media. This should not imply that once in office, black elected officials do the bidding of downtown elites. However, it means that economic development, especially the development of downtown, enjoys a high priority at city hall. Perhaps the best contemporary example is Andrew Young, who was mayor of Atlanta from 1981 to 1989. In July 1988, Atlanta Chamber of Commerce President Gerald Bartels assessed Mayor Young's contribution to the city's economic development. "The mayor is our clean-up hitter," Bartels noted. "He is such an eloquent speaker, and he has an outstanding grasp of worldwide economics." Young took office in 1981, and Bartels acknowledged that "it's been a love affair ever since."[43] Young was particularly effective in luring foreign, especially Asian and Middle Eastern, firms into Atlanta. Between 1983 and 1988, nearly two hundred foreign companies established operations in the city. The mayor also convinced the black community to go along with a regressive sales tax to fund infrastructure.[44]

Implicit in the equation between black political power and white economic power is the notion that politics in the 1990s is often a question of resources. If politics is a question of resources, then black politicians have few of those resources, and their black constituents even fewer. The media, campaign financing, economic leadership, and political campaign consultants and experts (from pollsters to advertising personnel) are dominated by whites. This does not mean they are hostile or indifferent to black interests. It may mean, however, that they are less sensitive to and less aware of the needs of poor black urban residents.

Aside from resources, the increasing competitiveness of the Republican party at the local and state levels furthers policy options. White Democratic candidates must walk an electoral tightrope: their major constituencies are blacks and working-class whites, two groups with little in common. Depending on the size of the black electorate in the state or county, Democratic candidates also must appeal to the crucial and ever-growing middle-class white electorate. That electorate, more often than not, is concentrated in a state's metropolitan areas. Black candidates, running in jurisdictions where the black electorate is less than 60 percent, also must appeal for some white votes and retain white economic support once elected. As state legislatures use 1990 census figures to redistrict, they are creating more majority-black districts. The benefits of increasing the number of blacks in the state legislature, however, may be undermined by further isolating black voters. Democratic leaders will ignore such districts, assuming a victory, and Republicans will concede them to concentrate on winning new majority-white districts. These factors combine to favor policies that ensure low taxes, promote economic development, and provide modest social services. Although other policy priorities such as education and the environment have broken through, even at the expense of raising taxes, these issues often are framed in terms of economic benefits.[45]

Future political trends in the urban South do not augur well for social policy. First, local politics have become increasingly pluralistic with the addition of new ethnic groups such as Asians and Latin Americans. An estimated one hundred thousand Salvadorans currently live in Houston, for example, most of them unregistered, but who will be eligible to vote within the next five years.[46] In Atlanta, there are sizable blocs of Vietnamese, Koreans, Cambodians, and Laotians whom blacks, Jews, and other groups are seeking out to forge political coalitions. More than seventy-five thousand Hispanics resided in the Atlanta metropolitan area in 1987. As early as the 1970s, the Atlanta Community Relations Commission translated all city documents into Spanish. In recent years, there have been efforts to increase the hiring of Hispanic police officers and, in 1986, Andrew Young pledged to "see that Hispanics get a fair share of the [city] contracts."[47] Young also established the mayor's task force on Hispanics. During the 1970s, the total foreign-born population in the South rose 120 percent, compared with an increase of 46.4 percent nationally.[48] The point is that the much-publicized ethnic cauldron of Miami politics is no longer a regional anomaly. If pluralistic politics in the urban South plays out as it has elsewhere, policies directed to a particular race will unlikely receive much support.

Another adverse future trend for urban social policy is the growing awareness of the need for regional cooperation. The idea of metropolitan government boomed in the 1960s and took root in a few areas of the South such as Miami, Jacksonville, and Nashville. Elsewhere, though, racial and tax issues limited cooperation. Since then, there has been a de facto, or creeping, metropolitanism with the establishment of special districts and authorities to deal with issues such as airport management, mosquito control, and pollution. Metropolitan regions recently have discovered the economic advantages of cooperation. The Denver region formed the "Metro Denver Network" in 1987, a regionwide information system for business recruitment. Currently, Charlotte, Atlanta, and Columbia, South Carolina, are beginning to market themselves in regional terms. Social issues must play a subsidiary role in such efforts, given the growing racial disparities between central city and suburb in the South.[49] Staunch opposition to annexation in suburban Richmond, to the extension of the Metropolitan Atlanta Rapid Transit Authority rail system to suburban Atlanta, and the general unwillingness of suburban school districts to merge with city schools almost everywhere in the metropolitan South mean that those who want to achieve metropolitan cooperation will not discuss any issues that will raise the racial concerns of suburban counties and localities.

We are, as political scientist John J. Harrigan has noted, in the "postreform era" of urban policy.[50] The federal government has pulled back sharply from the massive grant programs of the 1960s and 1970s. Southern state and local governments are more concerned with public–private partnerships, major building projects, and maintaining current tax advantages. Perhaps local government in the South, traditionally not strong—especially compared with county and state governments—is receding in power and effectiveness. The fragmentation of authority among boards, authorities, special districts, citizen groups, city managers, and council members has eroded executive authority. The result is usually that no one government body has exclusive authority over a major problem.

Changes in metropolitan administration are reflected in the transformation of urban administration over the past decade. Mayors and council members are "managers," even when a city manager is present. James Peterson of the Council for Urban Economic Development noted this transition: "The old mayor [divided] up the pie by special-interest groups and [by] going to the state and local government for help. The new mayor is the manager." The management metaphor stresses financial responsibility, reliance on computers, and "work management systems" borrowed from private industry. The result is a streamlined administration, with fewer, better-paid workers, higher technology, and marketing and service innovations.[51]

In keeping with the objective of efficiency, some local governments have begun to privatize their services. If elected black and white officials pay less attention to the most needy neighborhoods, what can one say about private franchises? It is not far-fetched to depict a southern city of the twenty-first century where public services are no longer public. Already in some communities, police functions have become privatized. In 1988, neighborhoods in Fort Lauderdale, Florida, began to barricade streets and hire private security guards to check entering motorists. In the meantime, the unfortunate residents of poor neighborhoods, virtually unprotected by public or private security, are the victims of escalating violence.

This is not to say that urban policy has abandoned the black underclass. Middle-class black leaders stress that a broader class agenda is more likely to achieve a policy consensus than narrower racial concerns. These leaders are supportive of affirmative action policies and economic development initiatives. Black elected officials argue that such strategies eventually redound to the benefit of low-income blacks. Andrew Young's administration increased minority contracts to 35 percent of the total. These funds, Young explained, "bubble up to feed the hungry, clothe the naked, and heal the sick." However, one of Young's black adversaries in Atlanta, the Rev. Hosea Williams, questioned the mayor's trickle-down theory, that is, "how the mayor [planned] to cure Atlanta's black inner-city problems, second only to those of Newark on the poverty charts."[52]

Young and his colleagues responded by arguing that a prosperous city would more likely be an equitable city. Curtis B. Gans, director of the black-oriented Committee for the Study of the American Electorate, summarized this thinking in 1985: "Blacks ... must have an economic-class agenda rather than a black agenda." He admitted that "ending racism does not result in significant change for the ... black underclass." The trick is to devise "programs that speak to the unique problems of the long-term poor" of both races.[53] It is difficult, however, to see how broadening the social policy agenda will ease its acceptance among political leaders of any race, or shake the belief that economic development is itself the best social policy. The assumption is that the white middle-class will be more likely to go along with social policy as long as the word "black" is not attached to it. The objection, though, is less to the racial association than to the policy itself.

Recent Policy Initiatives

Recent policy initiatives have focused on self-help or what was called ghetto enrichment during the late 1960s. These initiatives have sought to upgrade not only the physical environment, but families and individuals trapped in these communities. Black middle-class leaders are increasingly willing to discuss aspects of life among the black poor that were taboo before the mid-1980s. Mary Pringle, a black educator from Virginia, has claimed that racism is no longer a valid defense for black poverty. Even if it were, the example of recent immigrants from Southeast Asia indicates that culture—in this case, "their traditional background values, their collective achievement orientation, their patience and diligence"—has deflected the effect of racial animosity. Pringle believes that the black poor need "new myths" that depict them as "destined for success rather than doomed to failure."[54]

Some believe that one obstacle to the creation of "new myths" is the dependence of the black underclass on government programs. This notion not coincidentally follows the erosion of federal urban policy and the growing limitations on social policy options of local government. The alternative is self-help. Robert L. Woodson, head of the National Center for Neighborhood Enterprise and chair of the Council for a Black Economic Agenda, has become one of the leading advocates of the self-help approach. He has urged blacks to quit "waiting for a government Moses to save them. . . . If black America is to achieve its rightful place in American society, it will not be by virtue of what white America grants to black Americans but because of what black Americans do for themselves." Specifically, Woodson has suggested black enterprise for poor black districts; the use of traditional institutions such as churches to purchase and develop land, upgrade housing, and lease properties; and the formation of tenant groups in public housing to manage these units as is already the case in several southern cities. One resident–manager group in New Orleans boasted fewer than thirty evictions between 1978 and 1985.[55]

Many of these efforts come under the heading of "empowerment." However, when profiling most poor black neighborhoods of the urban South, that heading does not come immediately to mind. Many of these neighborhoods have been victims of urban renewal, discriminatory zoning, and historically skewed service budgets. It is one thing to make urban social policy, but quite another to "unmake" generations of policies that have had severe social effects. The people in these neighborhoods are often young, undereducated, and plagued by problems ranging from poor nutrition to high crime. The policy problems of these areas are so diverse and overwhelming that they require diverse policy approaches and overwhelming resources. The same public–private partnership that characterizes economic development policies needs to be applied to the black underclass. That is already occurring in some communities in the form of low-interest loans, fair-share job programs, head-start programs, day-care facilities, nutrition education, and housing repair and construction initiatives. The policy solutions are out there if only the numerous obstacles to implementation can be overcome.

Recall the brief story of Yellow Jim, the slave who apparently defied many of the policy proscriptions of his society. Yellow Jim eventually committed the ultimate defiance by running away. White urban residents in the Old South were unwilling to practice the racial policies they preached. Cities are basically economic engines unless they are artificially propped for governmental or military exigencies. Antebellum urban southerners bowed both to the economic realities of urban life and to the close connections—perhaps an antebellum Manhattan coalition—between white master and black slave.

Currently in the urban South, the black underclass is, in some respects, more constricted than Yellow Jim. To where can blacks run away? Also, political coalitions and social relations are much more fragmented and ephemeral in the contemporary South than they were in the antebellum era. Economic development policy may be one of the few cohesive instruments left in the political arena. Here is the element of continuity with the earlier era—urban policy still revolves primarily around economic issues. Perhaps it is as black Atlanta politician Michael Lomax asserted in 1988, "We'll see these problems [of the black underclass] addressed when the business community understands the total cost."[56] Then maybe we can answer positively the question posed by Lewis Mumford a half-century ago: "Does a city exist to promote the life of its citizens? Or do the citizens exist in order to increase the size, importance, and the commercial turnover of the city?"[57]

NOTES

1. Richard C. Wade, *Slavery in the Cities: The South 1820–1860* (New York: Oxford University Press), 53.

2. For the annotated version of James M. Johnson's correspondence, see Michael P. Johnson and James L. Roark, eds., *No Chariot Let Down: Charleston's Free People of Color on the Eve of the Civil War* (Chapel Hill: University of North Carolina Press, 1984).

3. See, for example, Frederick Douglass, *My Bondage and My Freedom* (New York: Harpers, 1855), 318, 328.

4. Howard N. Rabinowitz, *Race Relations in the Urban South, 1865–1890* (New York: Oxford University Press, 1978).

5. David R. Goldfield, *Black, White, and Southern: Race Relations and Southern Culture, 1940 to the Present* (Baton Rouge: Louisiana State University Press), 47.

6. Ibid, 92.

7. *Smith v. Allwright*, 321 U.S. 649 (1944); figures from Arnold R. Hirsch and Joseph Logsdon, "Simply a Matter of Black and White: The Transformation of Race and Politics in Twentieth-Century New Orleans," in *Creole New*

Orleans: Race and Americanization, ed. Arnold R. Hirsch and Joseph Logsdon (Baton Rouge: Louisiana State University Press, 1992), 293.

8. See Harold H. Martin, *William Berry Hartsfield: Mayor of Atlanta* (Athens: University of Georgia Press, 1978), and Edward F. Haas, *DeLesseps S. Morrison and the Image of Reform: New Orleans Politics, 1946–1961* (Baton Rouge: Louisiana State University Press, 1977).

9. *Brown* v. *Board of Education of Topeka,* 347 U.S. 483 (1954).

10. Both quotes from David R. Goldfield, *Black, White, and Southern,* 193, 206.

11. Figures from David R. Goldfield and Blaine A. Brownell, *Urban America: A History,* 2d ed. (Boston: Houghton Mifflin, 1990), 431.

12. See especially James W. Button, *Blacks and Social Change: Impact of the Civil Rights Movement in Southern Communities* (Princeton, N.J.: Princeton University Press, 1989).

13. Quoted in Robert D. Bullard, "Blacks in Heavenly Houston," in *In Search of the New South: The Black Urban Experience in the 1970s and 1980s,* ed. Robert D. Bullard (Tuscaloosa: University of Alabama Press, 1989), 20.

14. Robert D. Bullard and E. Kiki Thomas, "Atlanta: Mecca of the Southeast," in *In Search of the New South: The Black Urban Experience in the 1970s and 1980s,* ed. Robert D. Bullard (Tuscaloosa: University of Alabama Press, 1989), 79–80, 84.

15. Goldfield and Brownell, *Urban America,* 366.

16. Robert A. Catlin, "Blacks in Tampa," in *In Search of the New South: The Black Urban Experience in the 1970s and 1980s,* ed. Robert D. Bullard (Tuscaloosa: University of Alabama Press, 1989), 151, 154.

17. See Richard M. Bernard and Bradley R. Rice, eds., *Sunbelt Cities: Politics and Growth Since World War II* (Austin: University of Texas Press, 1983).

18. Quoted in Goldfield, *Black, White, and Southern,* 192–193.

19. Quoted in Goldfield and Brownell, *Urban America,* 389.

20. Christopher Silver, "The Changing Face of Neighborhoods in Memphis and Richmond, 1940–1985," in *Shades of the Sunbelt: Essays in Ethnicity, Race, and the Urban South,* ed. Randall M. Miller and George E. Pozzetta (Westport, Conn.: Greenwood, 1988), 120–121.

21. Figures from Goldfield and Brownell, *Urban America,* 434.

22. Ibid., 432–433.

23. Quoted in Goldfield, *Black, White, and Southern,* 229.

24. Quoted in Button, *Blacks and Social Change,* 196.

25. Quoted in Goldfield, *Black, White, and Southern,* 209.

26. Quote and figures from ibid., 244; Earl Black and Merle Black, *Politics and Society in the South* (Cambridge, Mass.: Harvard University Press, 1987), 53.

27. "Black Migration Shifts," *Washington Post,* 10 January 1990.

28. Figures from Bullard, "Heavenly Houston," 24; Bullard and Thomas, "Atlanta: Mecca," 89, 93; Ernest Porterfield, "Birmingham: A Magic City," in *In Search of the New South: The Black Urban Experience in the 1970s and 1980s,* ed. Robert D. Bullard (Tuscaloosa: University of Alabama Press, 1989), 135–136.

29.　Porterfield, "Birmingham," 136.

30.　Neal Peirce, "Atlanta Booming But Still Deeply Divided," *Charlotte Observer,* 16 July 1988.

31.　Robert D. Bullard, "Introduction: Lure of the New South," in *In Search of the New South: The Black Urban Experience in the 1970s and 1980s,* ed. Robert D. Bullard (Tuscaloosa: University of Alabama Press, 1989), 9.

32.　Figures from David R. Goldfield, *Promised Land: The South since 1945* (Arlington Heights, Ill.: Harlan Davidson, 1987), 155–156.

33.　Goldfield and Brownell, *Urban America,* 426.

34.　"New Metropolitan Areas," *New York Times,* 14 November 1978.

35.　Bullard and Thomas, "Atlanta: Mecca," 78. Some of this increase undoubtedly resulted from the inclusion of historically black rural or small-town communities that date from the post–Civil War era.

36.　Quotes from Goldfield, *Black, White, and Southern,* 254.

37.　Quoted in ibid., 221.

38.　Quoted in Button, *Blacks and Social Change,* 229.

39.　Quoted in Goldfield, *Black, White, and Southern,* 191.

40.　Quoted in Bullard and Thomas, "Atlanta: Mecca," 94.

41.　See Virginia H. Hein, "The Image of 'A City Too Busy to Hate': Atlanta in the 1960s," *Phylon* 33 (May 1972), 205–221.

42.　Beverly Hendrix Wright, "New Orleans," in *In Search of the New South: The Black Urban Experience in the 1970s and 1980s,* ed. Robert D. Bullard (Tuscaloosa: University of Alabama Press, 1989), 58.

43.　Quotes from "Atlanta: A Tale of 2 Cities," *Charlotte Observer,* 10 July 1988.

44.　See Art Harris, "Atlanta, Georgia: Too Busy to Hate," *Esquire* 103 (June 1985), 129.

45.　For a complete discussion of blacks in southern politics, see Merle Black and Earl Black, *Politics and Society in the South* (Cambridge, Mass.: Harvard University Press, 1987).

46.　Louis Dubose, "Invisible City," *Southern Exposure* 16 (Winter 1988), 24–26.

47.　Figures and quote from Ronald H. Bayor, "Models of Ethnic and Racial Politics in the Urban Sunbelt South," in *Searching for the Sunbelt: Historical Perspectives on a Region,* ed. Raymond A. Mohl (Knoxville: University of Tennessee Press, 1990), 109.

48.　Elliot R. Barkan, "New Origins, New Homeland, New Region: American Immigration and the Emergence of the Sunbelt, 1955–1985," in *Searching for the Sunbelt: Historical Perspectives on a Region,* ed. Raymond A. Mohl (Knoxville: University of Tennessee Press, 1990), 144.

49.　Goldfield and Brownell, *Urban America,* 442–443.

50.　John J. Harrigan, *Political Change in the Metropolis* (Boston: Little, Brown, 1985), 341.

51.   All quotes from Neal Peirce, " 'New' Mayors Slash Staff, Act Like Corporate Boss," *Washington Post,* 4 May 1985.

52.   Both quotes from Goldfield, *Black, White, and Southern,* 245, 246.

53.   Quoted in William Raspberry, "The Dilemma of Black Politics," *Washington Post,* 9 January 1985.

54.   Quoted in William Raspberry, "Why Blacks Need a New Myth," *Washington Post,* 19 July 1985.

55.   Robert L. Woodson, "Self-Help Is the Answer for Poor Blacks," *Washington Post,* 12 May 1985.

56.   Quoted in "Atlanta: A Tale of Two Cities," *Charlotte Observer,* 10 July 1988.

57.   Quoted in Daniel Schaffer, *Garden Cities for America: The Radburn Experience* (Philadelphia: Temple University Press, 1982), 62.

6

CARL ABBOTT

Through Flight to Tokyo: Sunbelt Cities and the New World Economy, 1960–1990

Wʜᴀᴛ was the defining characteristic of a "hot" city for the American 1980s?

Was it the birth of Silicon Valley–clones like the Silicon Desert of Phoenix, the Silicon Forest of Portland, or the Silicon Mountain of Colorado Springs?

Was it construction of a new downtown stadium in the manner of Seattle and Minneapolis?

Was it the election of a Hispanic mayor as in Miami, San Antonio, and Denver?

Was it leadership in the popular arts like Nashville, Austin, and Los Angeles?

No . . . the true mark of a city "on the make" was the inauguration of a through flight to Tokyo.

People are accustomed to the range of imagery drawn from the world of transportation. When Walt Whitman bid his soul to embark on a "passage to India," he certainly did not want to end up on a "slow boat to China." Most people would prefer life on "Easy Street" to "Skid Row." Members of the jet set pursue fast-track careers to secure a niche in "Main Line" society.

As we look toward the twenty-first century, it may be time to add the "through flight to Tokyo" as an updated metaphor for the recent dynamics of the American economy. In particular, the past half century has brought profound changes to the economic base of the reputed Sunbelt, turning the historically subordinate cities and states of the South and West into centers for economic growth. A generation ago, historian C. Vann Woodward summarized the changes in process in the postwar South as the "bulldozer revolution." The next step is to examine the additional effects of a "jumbo jet revolution" on the larger Sunbelt in past decades of the twentieth century.[1]

Although the choice of Tokyo as the symbolic destination may betray some West Coast provincialism, through flights to Japan were available at the start of the 1990s not only from Anchorage, Honolulu, Los Angeles, San Francisco, Portland, and Seattle, but also from Minneapolis, Chicago, New York, Atlanta, and Dallas. The meaning stays the same even if the metaphor includes direct flights to Rome and Rio de Janiero. Air connections to major world cities symbolize two types of economic change that have reshuffled the fortunes and prospects of American cities and regions. The first is the globalization of American society and economy. The second is the emergence of an information-based economy in which the movement of individuals and information has assumed equal importance with the movement of raw materials and manufactured goods.

The effects of the globalized information economy have been uneven across nations, regions, and cities. The theoretical literature identifies two contradictory principles that may be shaping the spatial distribution of new activities. The "world city" hypothesis suggests that specialized domestic transactions and international services concentrate in a few comprehensive metropolises that organize national or even multinational economies. New information industries and producer services such as business consulting and advertising supposedly cluster in the same way as the long-established financial sector.[2] Other writers see an opposite tendency in which administrative and information activities are free to locate in a variety of communities. As footloose activities with few locational constraints, they are open to the attractions of amenities and place.[3]

From Western Europe to North America to East Asia, this spatial uncertainty has invited attempts to design urban development policies that capitalize on the increasing importance of international exchange and information.[4] Although such development efforts are obviously relevant to economic restructuring of the American Northeast, a logical focus for U.S. analysis is the American Sunbelt that arcs from the South Atlantic coast to the Pacific Ocean. To the degree that the leading trends have opened new economic opportunities, the effects should be most evident and sweeping in regions traditionally oriented toward the production of natural resources and manufacturing for domestic markets. The trends may have helped to confirm the prominence of New York, but they also have helped Los Angeles and Washington, D.C., to evolve into international cities.[5] Other Sunbelt cities also have achieved growth through economic diversification. Indeed, international and informational opportunities have helped many of the Sunbelt's major cities break out of a one-dimensional relationship with a previously dominant national core and emerge as centers of change in their own right.

The goal of this chapter is to introduce a comparative framework for detailed case studies of the interactions of leadership, policy, and previous economic base in the American urban response to the new world economy.[6] After sketching the overall policy context for the new economic trends, it follows with two types of comparative analysis of the responses among Sunbelt cities. The chapter describes the extent to which the twenty-eight largest southern and western metropolitan areas have followed the two trends. In turn, the classification raises the question of the reasons for variations within the broad patterns. The economic career of each city involves a unique interaction among resource endowment, industrial base, community goals, civic leadership, public policy, and strategic decisions. The chapter also explores the range of possibilities with brief narratives of selected cases. An "Atlanta model" (information sector roles lead, world roles follow) and a "Miami model" (international roles lead, information functions follow) defines the extremes. Other cities have followed intermediate development paths. For example, the emergence of Los Angeles as a world city followed a middle route of broadly diversified growth benefiting from both trends.

New Economies and Old Policies

The trends toward a globalized and information-based economy have been at work over the past thirty years, interacting to reshape the direction of American growth. However, each trend has devoloped within a different policy environment. The growth of international connections for American cities has come within a context of explicit national policy, because international relations is directly a federal responsibility. Local business and civic leaders have reacted to new opportunities within a framework of policies intended to manage national needs within world political and economic systems. The information economy, in contrast, has largely developed through private sector initiatives in the use of changing mechanisms of communication and control. In the absence of substantial national policy, localities have looked for openings within the world corporate system.

The new global reach that Americans have observed over the past generation has been a "re-internationalization" of the United States. From the early nineteenth century until 1914, the nation depended heavily on foreign capital, foreign trade, and immigration. Between 1914 and the 1950s, however, two rounds of continental warfare and postwar reconstruction kept most European capital at home. Legislation in 1921 and 1924 curtailed immigration to the United States. Foreign trade as a percentage of American gross national product (GNP) fell from an early twentieth century range of 10 percent to 15 percent to 6 percent to 7 percent by the 1950s.[7]

A direct aim of postwar American policy was to reestablish the international presence of the United States in support of national economic and political goals. Metropolitan effects have been inadvertant consequences. Reforms of American immigration law in 1965, for example, were motivated by national concerns about humanitarian and economic needs and the symbolic role of United States in the world system. As the total of legally admitted immigrants grew from 2,515,000 between 1951 and 1960 to 3,322,000 between 1961 and 1970, 4,493,000 between 1971 and 1980, and approximately 6,000,000 between 1981 and 1990, there have been striking consequences for southern and western cities. Most of the newcomers by the 1980s were Asians (47 percent) and Latin Americans (37 percent), whose natural ports of entry and frequent points of settlement are the cities of the South and West. In 1987, the Sunbelt accounted for seven of the ten metropolitan areas listed most frequently as the place of intended residence for these new Americans.[8]

The 1970s also were pivotal for American overseas commerce. National security policy and economic policy after World War II called for the revival of the European and Japanese economies and the expansion of trade through reciprocal tariff reductions. Imports and exports of merchandise as a proportion of American GNP edged from 6.8 percent to 8.2 percent between 1960 and 1970, before shooting to 17.0 percent in 1980 and falling slightly to 14.6 percent in 1987. Other industrial nations as a group are still twice as dependent on foreign trade as the United States. The U.S. economy, however, has not been so heavily oriented to the outside world since the boom years from 1915 to 1917, when American farmers, manufacturers, and shipbuilders kept Britain and France in action on the Western Front. These full effects have been felt at the same time that Middle Eastern and Latin American resources and East Asian manufactures have increased in importance to the American economy. The growth of overseas trade thus has been accompanied by an unplanned shift to Gulf and Pacific ports.[9]

New participants and customers for American service industries paralleled the growing importance of merchandise trade. The number of U.S. offices operated by foreign banks climbed from 50 in 1970 to 579 in 1980 and nearly 800 by 1985 (accounting for 13 percent of all U.S. deposits).[10] The American tourist industry does an increasing business with travelers from abroad. Investors from Canada, Japan, and Europe have found U.S. real estate and businesses to be increasingly attractive investments, especially for balances accumulated through trade surpluses. The book value of direct foreign investment in U.S. enterprise doubled in the 1950s and again in the 1960s but jumped by six times during the 1970s and tripled again between 1980 and 1987.[11]

Local economic development strategies since the mid-1970s have recognized this changing international context. Nearly every major city currently sends trade delegations on international tours. Economic development organizations in major cities publish multi-language brochures and sponsor seminars on doing business with Brazilians and Koreans. State governments maintain trade offices on both edges of the Eurasian continent. Booster diplomacy has been supplemented by more concrete efforts to support international ambitions—foreign trade zones, $20 million international trade and marketing centers, $200 million plans to upgrade marine terminals, and $2 billion investments in new airports.

If the international economy reflects national policy choices, the evolution of the world's information economy can best be understood as a private-sector response to new communication technologies that increase efficiency and productivity. In this sense, the information economy stretches back to the organizational revolution of the late nineteenth and early twentieth centuries. Growth of big business and big government coincided with the development of the telegraph, telephone, railroad, and typewriter, which allowed the physical separation of control from production. The size of organizations and the specialization of information-consuming activities continued to increase with electronic data storage and communication.[12] Information workers grew from 30 percent of all workers in the advanced economies of Western Europe and North America at midcentury to 50 percent by 1990.[13] Transactional cities identified by geographers and economists in the late 1970s and early 1980s, became the sorting points within information flows. They concentrated political and economic decision makers and the occupations and industries that centered on the generation, processing, distribution, and recombination of information.[14]

Much of the information economy currently is global in scale. Transactional cities have the potential to interact directly in world networks as well as national networks, as evidenced by the international dimension of investment, tourism, and financial markets. Passengers on the through flight to Tokyo are likely to include homebound tourists, plant managers, and students from new U.S. campuses of Japanese universities; they also are likely to include American journalists, state trade delegates, professors on Fulbright scholarships, and entrepreneurs hoping to crack Asian markets. The growing separation of corporate decision making and physical production across national borders since the 1970s and the rise of hard-copy telecommunications such as telex and fax have helped to separate the information economy from national policy. In some views, multinational corporations transcend political states in the independence of their decision making as well as their spatial reach.[15] One result is thousands of new factories and assembly plants scattered from Matamoros, Mexico, to Shanghai, China. Another is the downtown skyscraper district cloned from New York to Hong Kong, Houston, Singapore, and San Francisco.

The new information economy has been analyzed extensively as a technological and market phenomenon, but it has been largely ignored in economic development planning.[16] Individual cities have found it difficult to define an entry point that allows them to influence market decisions.[17] The idea of constructing "teleports," as in New York and San Antonio, for example, is an effort to define a contemporary equivalent of nineteenth-century canals and railroads. The acknowledged importance of labor-force quality is difficult to translate into programs with quick payoffs for elected officials. Most cities and states are left to recycle the weakest part of traditional development programs, pursuing specific information processing or producing facilities exactly as they have pursued individual manufacturing facilities.

Joining the New Economy

For many years, Washington D.C., was proudly known as the "nation's city." Boosters in the 1970s, however, began to declare that their "new international city" was a "world center for research and information." Houston in 1982 proclaimed itself "a world class city," "an international city with a dazzling future," a city whose "global consciousness" attracts "world attention." In 1986, Andrew Young commented that it was an easy step from the United Nations to Atlanta's city hall, because "Atlanta and the Southeast are probably among the best areas in the world from which to generate a view of the present economic situation.[18]

In each case, the language of civic promotion combined awareness of both the informational trends and the international trends. The recognition is explicit in the quotes from the Washington Board of Trade and implicit in the Houston and Atlanta statements. "Consciousness" and "attention" are reciprocals in a two-way information exchange. A view from North Georgia implies a processing of information across national boundaries.

To move beyond updated boosterism to measure the relative effects of the two trends on specific cities, however, raises the classic dilemma of apples and oranges. Each trend is the product of several incommensurable components. How, for example, does one compare the effects of Mexican shoppers in San Diego, Filipino immigrants to San Jose, Korean automobile shipments through Portland, and Japanese ownership of Los Angeles banks? Moreover, it is unclear that any single indicator, such as employment by occupation or industry, can adequately express and compare both trends simultaneously.

A first approximation is to use a simple additive ranking and point system to construct two composite scores for each city. Relative rankings in the information economy are based on four categories that measure the following: (1) white-collar employment (zero to three points); (2) employment in finance, insurance, real estate, and corporate administration (zero to two points); (3) major corporate headquarters (zero to two points); and (4) role as a federal administrative center (zero to two points)[19] Rankings as international cities are defined by the six categories: (1) foreign-born population (zero to two points); (2) foreign trade (zero to two points); (3) role as an international information center (zero to one point); (4) foreign banking connections (zero to two points); (5) foreign investment (zero to one point); and (6) importance of foreign markets for local businesses (zero to one point).[20]

The method assigns point totals for each factor at the beginning of the 1960s (to a possible maximum of nine) and measures change to the 1980s. Cities could gain additional points either by percentage increases greater than those for all U.S. metropolitan areas (i.e., foreign born or employment); by an increased share of a national total (i.e., corporate headquarters or foreign trade); or by substantial absolute increases (i.e., various federal and international roles).

The result is two conceptual dimensions for measuring the degree of change in the twenty-eight largest southern and western metropolitan areas (see Table 6.1). It certainly is possible to challenge any specific point assignment or position, especially in relation to international roles about which subjective judgment enters. The positions are suggestive rather than definitive. However, the overall pattern of distinctions among the various cities has common sense plausibility.

Participation in the information economy changed (see Table 6.2).

TABLE 6.1
Largest Metropolitan Areas in South and West, by Rank Nationally, 1986

Area	Rank
Los Angeles–Anaheim–Riverside–Oxnard	2
San Francisco–Oakland–San Jose	4
Dallas–Fort Worth	8
Houston–Galveston	9
Washington, D.C.	10
Miami–Fort Lauderdale	11
Atlanta	13
Seattle–Tacoma	17
San Diego	19
Tampa–St. Petersburg	20
Phoenix	21
Denver–Boulder	22
Portland–Vancouver	26
New Orleans	27
Norfolk–Newport News	28
Sacramento	30
San Antonio	31
Charlotte	35
Salt Lake City	37
Oklahoma City	38
Memphis	41
Nashville	43
Birmingham	44
Greenboro–Winston–Salem	45
Orlando	46
Jacksonville	47
Honolulu	49
Richmond	50

SOURCE: U.S. Bureau of the Census, *Statistical Abstract of the United States 1988* (Washington: U.S. Department of Commerce, 1988), 28–30

NOTE: The twenty-eight cases are the southern and western metropolitan areas included in the fifty largest U.S. metropolitan areas as of 1986, ranked in descending order from the largest areas. Populations for this top fifty ranged upward from 800,000. Consolidated metropolitan areas were used for greater Los Angeles, San Francisco–Oakland–San Jose, Dallas–Fort Worth, Houston–Galveston, Miami–Fort Lauderdale, Seattle–Tacoma, Denver–Boulder, Portland–Vancouver.

TABLE 6.2
Changes in Relative Importance of Information Sector, Sunbelt Metropolitan Areas since 1960

City	Point total	
	1960s	1980s
San Francisco	8	10
Washington, D.C.	6	10
Dallas	6	9
Los Angeles	5	8
Atlanta	4	8
Seattle	4	6
Denver	4	6
Richmond	4	6
Salt Lake City	4	4
San Diego	3	4
Sacramento	3	4
Oklahoma City	3	4
Jacksonville	3	4
Nashville	3	3
Phoenix	2	5
Houston	2	5
Honolulu	2	4
Orlando	2	3
Portland	2	3
New Orleans	2	2
San Antonio	2	2
Charlotte	2	2
Greensboro	2	2
Miami	1	4
Tampa	1	4
Birmingham	1	2
Norfolk	1	1
Memphis	0	1

NOTE: See note 19 for derivation of index numbers.

In 1960, San Francisco was the most important transactional center for the Sunbelt states, followed by Washington, D.C., and Dallas, by Los Angeles, and by a set of regional centers such as Atlanta, Seattle, Denver, Richmond, and Salt Lake City. By the 1980s, Washington, D.C., had caught up with San Francisco, Atlanta had matched Los

TABLE 6.3
Changes in Relative Importance of International Connections,
Sunbelt Metropolitan Areas since 1960

City	Point total	
	1960s	1980s
San Francisco	6	9
Los Angeles	4	10
Houston	3.5	5
Miami	3	9
New Orleans	3	4
Honolulu	2	6.5
Seattle	2	5.5
San Antonio	1.5	2
Washington	1	6
San Diego	1	4
Phoenix	1	2
Portland	1	2
Norfolk	1	2
Sacramento	1	2
Salt Lake City	1	1
Tampa	1	1
Dallas	0.5	4.5
Charlotte	0.5	1
Atlanta	0	4
Jacksonville	0	2
Orlando	0	1.5
Denver	0	0
Oklahoma City	0	0
Memphis	0	0
Birmingham	0	0
Nashville	0	0
Greensboro	0	0
Richmond	0	0

NOTE: See note 20 for derivation of index numbers.

Angeles, and Phoenix and Houston had moved past Oklahoma City
and Nashville. The biggest changes were in Washington D.C., and
Atlanta, whereas seven cities did not show any change.

Similar changes in global connectivity occurred (see Table 6.3).
Here too, San Francisco entered the 1960s as the most clearly interna-

TABLE 6.4
Extent of Change in Information Functions and International Connections, 1960–1980

Change in index points: International roles	Change in index points: Information functions				
	0	+1.0	+2.0	+3.0	+4.0
0	Salt Lake Nashville Greensboro	Memphis Birmingham Oklahoma City	Richmond Denver	Tampa	
+0.5	San Antonio Charlotte				
+1.0	New Orleans Norfolk	Portland Sacramento		Phoenix	
+1.5		Orlando		Houston	
+2.0		Jacksonville			
+2.5					
+3.0		San Diego	San Francisco –Oakland –San Jose		
+3.5			Seattle		
+4.0				Dallas	Atlanta
+4.5			Honolulu		Washington, D.C.
+5.0					
+5.5					
+6.0				Miami Los Angeles	

SOURCES: Tables 6.2 and 6.3.

tional metropolis.[21] Three decades later, it was matched by Miami and surpassed by Los Anegles. Other cities that experienced major development of international roles included Honolulu, Washington, D.C., Dallas, and Atlanta. Most of the nine cities that did not show any change are located in the interior South and Great Plains.

Both factors were combined to array the cities based on overall change (see Table 6.4). Los Angeles, Washington, D.C., Dallas, Atlanta, and Miami achieved substantial growth along both axes. Five other cities had substantial increases in international roles but little change in the prominence of their information industries; five showed the reverse. Thirteen cities felt little effect of either trend. They may have grown, but they did not change.

Global Reach and Local Initiative

These comparative data indentify the Sunbelt cities that have experienced substantial economic change, but not how they have changed. Brief summaries of several development paths can serve as suggestions or hypotheses for fuller investigation of local economic strategies, decision processes, and their results.[22]

Atlanta, Dallas, and Washington, D.C., relied until the 1970s on transactional roles within the domestic economy. Since the 1970s, their educated workers, distribution and communication systems, regional banks, business services, and federal administrative agencies have allowed them to capitalize on the revolution in air travel and telecommunications and become hubs for international business.

Through the 1950s and 1960s, Atlanta and Dallas had remarkably similar economic profiles as the leading metropolitan centers of the southeastern and west–south central states. Each was a "regional metropolis" whose warehouse workers and paper pushers provided transportation, finance, distribution, and administrative services for multistate regions. Both cities were products of the American railroad system and each secured a central position in the new network of interstate highways. They were, in short, cities whose identities were formed and expressed as American regional cities.[23]

The idea of global roles arrived to considerable bemusement in the mid-1970s. Atlanta's business leaders proclaimed in 1972 that "Forward Atlanta [the action program of the chamber of commerce] is going international." Ads touting the advantages of the "world's next great city" were targeted at western European readers of the *Economist* and the *International Herald Tribune*. The advertising campaign was followed by persistent marketing of Atlanta and Georgia as attractive locations for foreign businesses by George Busbee, former governor of Georgia (1974–1982); the Georgia Department of Industry; and Andrew Young, former mayor of Atlanta (1982–1989). The selling point was the existence of a centralized transportation, wholesale, and banking network that made Atlanta an attractive location for overseas firms that wanted access to U.S. markets. By the end of the 1980s, thirty foreign banks operated in Atlanta, nineteen nations operated trade offices or consulate generals, and Europeans owned one-quarter of downtown office space.[24]

Economic development leaders in Dallas adopted the same sales pitch. With a diversified economic base that has weathered the Texas depression of the 1980s in relatively good condition, the Dallas Partnership currently talks about a future as "a preeminent center of world commerce in the twenty-first century." The quintessentially American city of Dallas cooperates with Fort Worth ("where the [American] West begins") to publish maps showing the "metroplex" as the navel of the world. Its publicists define a list of continental rather than regional rivals—Mexico City, Chicago, Los Angeles, and New York rather than Houston and New Orleans. Nevertheless, Dallas's entry point into the global economy has continued to be its role as the transactional hub of the Central Southwest.[25] Foreign corporations employ 35,000 workers. Like Atlanta, Dallas–Fort Worth is trying to acquire the critical mass of foreign firms, trade offices, and business agents to support an international infrastructure of translation services, specialized retailers, schools, and social organizations that can make life easier for non–Americans. Dallas–Fort Worth currently is a second-level center of international banking.[26]

To the undoubted confusion of most Americans, the big story about Washington, D.C., since the 1970s has been the declining importance of the federal payroll relative to the private sector. Washington's boom since the mid-1970s has been fueled by the expansion of private activities that feed off the vast quantities of information produced and used by federal administrators. Attorneys, accountants, consultants, trade associations, and lobbyists feed on the flows within the Washington information network. Major corporations like Mobil and Xerox have decided that proximity to federal regulators and politicians is more important than instant access to New York investment bankers.[27]

In the mid-1970s, local leaders began to argue that Washington was growing into an international business city. The *Washington Post* supported the new image with stories on foreign real estate investment, foreign residents, and even the proportion of Washingtonians holding passports (twice that of Detroiters). The same factors that made Washington a national business and information center have worked as well in the international scene. The Washington Board of Trade promotional brochures argue that Washington is the place to be for companies engaged in world markets. "For American firms," argue the boosters, "Greater Washington offers a community of worldwide investment and trade organizations which create an entree to the far corners of the earth. For international firms, Washington offers the

U.S. base of operations close to the government regulatory agencies which oversee import/export trade."[28] The result is currently the denial that Washington has any North American rivals except New York and possibly Los Angeles. "The most important city in the world" is a common phrase around town.

In all three cities, new airports are the symbols and supporters of globalization. Dallas–Fort Worth Airport opened in 1974 in a bid to take a midcontinent hub function away from Chicago. Boosters like to point out that it covers more land than Manhattan Island. Airport expansion in Atlanta was a central political issue of the 1970s, resolved by a massive expansion of Hartsfield Airport. It has been relatively easy to add international flights to these superairports that originally were conceived as domestic hubs. In Atlanta, increased investment from Germany, the Netherlands, and Japan followed the opening of direct Lufthansa service to Frankfurt, KLM service to Amsterdam, and Delta service to Tokyo.[29] Washington National Airport, within a quick cab ride or easy subway trip of Capitol Hill, represents the city's roles in domestic networks. Dulles International, built at the end of the 1960s but not fully used until the 1980s, represents its complementary roles in overseas networks.[30]

The international dimension of Atlanta and Dallas is still most apparent in board rooms and banking offices. The international dimension of Miami and Honolulu is obvious on the street. With limited and isolated commercial hinterlands, they developed significant foreign connections at the "mass market" level through tourism and immigration. These foreign ties, including social and linguistic support for Latin American or Japanese businesspeople, have helped to attract information businesses that the cities previously lacked. Honolulu's mix of native Hawaiians, Chinese, Japanese, and Anglo-Americans sets it instantly apart. European and Japanese tourists, Japanese banks, Japanese and Hong Kong investment in hotels and office buildings, and Japanese holdings of residential property add to the mismatch with other American cities.[31] Miami in the 1980s was commonly depicted as an actively "unAmerican" metropolis. Joel Garreau detached it from the Southeast in his *The Nine Nations of North America* and reassigned it as the capital of the Carribean Basin. The city's current image has been formed by a mix of Cuban and Haitian immigrants, Venezuelan investors, and Mexican shoppers. Americans may have grown accustomed to Spanish in the neighborhood stores of San Antonio, Chicago, and New York, but not in expensive downtown shops. Joan Didion's characterizations are typical of the Anglo-American judgments. On one page of her urban profile, Miami appears as "a Latin American capital, a year or two away from a new government. . . . There were too many shoe stores for an American city." On another page, the very real metropolis is "not a city at all but a tale, a romance of the tropics, a kind of waking dream."[32]

The data suggest that it is these street-level connections that paved the way for evolution into international information centers. Honolulu's Asian populations have made it an attractive destination not only for Japanese tourists and hotel builders but also for Japanese seeking to invest in second homes. Japanese real estate investments of $6 billion by the end of the 1980s put Honolulu third to New York and Los Angeles as a Japanese investment target.[33] Executives of multinational corporations place a high value on Honolulu's quality of life and infrastructure for head or regional offices. State development strategy after the election of Governor John Waihee in 1986 touted Honolulu as the economic center of the Pacific. The state planned to build on existing information exchanges such as the East–West Center, the Pacific Forum, and the Japan–America Institute of Management Sciences. Goals have included encouragement of air hub operations and development of stock market operations to take advantage of the trans–Pacific time lag.[34]

Miami is another example of the interaction between location and the possession of social and linguistic supports. Miami and adjacent Coral Gables in the early 1970s began to attract large numbers of "Edge Act" banks, that is, subsidiaries of U.S. banks that are authorized to engage in international lending and financing of foreign trade. After changes in state and federal banking legislation during the late 1970s, Miami also added numerous agencies of Latin American banks. It currently rivals Los Angeles and Houston in breadth of banking representation. The same factors that have attracted bankers also make the city a good location for Latin American headquarters of U.S. businesses and for initial U.S. offices of Latin American companies.[35]

Los Angeles represents a third pattern in which a major port and regional center has built on both sorts of globalization. If Los Angeles is currently "one of the preeminent economies of the world," its prominence has been built from the ground up. The city originated as a local market center for southern California farmers in the nineteenth century. It grew into a regional production and distribution center for the American Southwest in the first half of the twentieth century before finally emerging as a major world city in the 1970s. Despite the presence of several national and international market industries—particularly aircraft, electronics, and motion pictures— development at each stage has been driven by the city's regional roles and markets.[36]

Although Los Angeles's ambitions as a world port date to the opening of the Panama Canal, the city as late as the 1960s was chiefly a factory and warehouse for the Pacific Southwest. It supplied western markets with food, furniture, automobiles, and clothing.[37] In-migration from the desert Southwest, the southern plains, and northern Mexico reinforced its regional orientation. As the American economy shifted toward international exchange and toward the Pacific Basin, however, Los Angeles built new global roles directly on these established regional functions. In one example, Los Angeles and Long Beach since the 1970s have emerged as one of the premier port complexes of the United States. In 1967, they loaded and received essentially the same value of goods ($2 billion) as did San Francisco Bay Area ports. In 1986, the $63.8 billion value of Los Angeles–Long Beach shipments and receipts was 3.5 times that of the Bay Area. Other West Coast ports find it difficult to compete for import trade because the rich southern California market draws overseas shippers and shipping lines. What used to be the straightfoward Port of Los Angeles currently styles itself "WorldPort LA."[38]

The huge job market of greater Los Angeles has become extraordinarily attractive to foreign immigrants and investors. The popular press characterizes Los Angeles as the "new Ellis Island," implying an ethnic variety comparable with that of New York in 1900. Foreign-born residents of Los Angeles fill the full range of economic roles—low-skill service workers, low-wage garment workers, skilled electronics assemblers, small entrepreneurs in retailing and manufacturing, scientists, and professional workers.[39] Census data confirm the importance of Los Angeles as a key destination in the new American immigration. Between 1970 and 1980 alone, the number of foreign-born residents in the consolidated Los Angeles metropolitan area more than doubled. Observers noted an upturn in foreign investment in the second half of the 1970s. Canadian, Japanese, and other Asian investors have become major downtown building owners and speculators in downtown fringe land. Several major Los Angeles banks have passed into the control of Japanese and British interests.[40]

Ironically, Los Angeles's rising global role, as keyed off its regional base, has helped to make the city a major national center for finance and control functions. Edward Soja and colleagues have pointed out that eleven of the twelve largest U.S. banks headquartered outside California have their primary branch office in Los Angeles.[41] Los Angeles has similarly increased its share of major corporate headquarters by two-thirds since 1960 and has passed San Francisco–Oakland-San Jose.[42]

New Cities and a New Sunbelt

Theorists of the new economy disagree about its spatial effects. A number of writers make the case for strong centralizing tendencies, citing the established world cities that have acquired a richer and richer mix of information activities and international services. Examples include New York and London at a truly global scale, and Sydney and Toronto at a continental scale. Other writers argue that the rise of a new economic sector opens opportunities for smaller cities to find specialized international roles. Jean Gottmann has offered the example of Edinburgh, a historic regional capital at substantial remove from the center of British economic and cultural power that has nevertheless enjoyed increasing employment in research, technology development, and international finance.[43] Brussels, Luxembourg, and Geneva have specific European and world roles precisely because they are not London or Paris. Montreal has continued to serve as Canada's international city because it has lost national dominance to Toronto.

The exploration of metropolitan growth in the American Sunbelt supports this second suggestion that smaller cities currently have a special chance to elbow their way into the international system. In particular, the interaction of international and informational activities has provided one way in which semiperipheral U.S. cities have begun to work their way out of the shadow of the Northeast as part of the accelerating evolution of the Sunbelt. For the entire century after the Civil War and the completion of the first transcontinental railroad—from the mid-1860s to the mid-1960s—the South and West read their own character in the mirror of the northeastern industrial core. As late as 1950, the intensively developed corridor from Boston and Philadelphia west to St. Paul and St. Louis contained only 7 percent of the nation's land area but 43 percent of its population, 50 percent of its income, and 70 percent of its manufacturing employment.[44] Southerners and westerners produced food, fibers, and minerals for northeastern factories and repurchased the same raw materials as finished products. In the world-system model of Immanuel Wallerstein, the United States mirrored the division of labor in the larger world economy. Core nations or regions have specialized in capital-intensive production by skilled, high-wage workers. Peripheral nations or regions have been relegated to labor-intensive, low-wage production. Unequal terms of exchange have allowed the central accumulation of wealth at the expense of the periphery.[45]

Regional consciousness in the West and South reflected this economic subordination. Efforts to take regional control of economic change through the Populist movement and militant farm and labor organizations failed between 1880 and 1920.[46] In policy making and politics, regional spokespeople by the 1920s and 1930s identified themselves as lacking what the Northeast possessed. Westerners tended to emphasize their colonial economic status as a "plundered province" whose wealth accrued to eastern investors and corporations. The southern version focused on regional backwardness in economy and society, at some times as a gap to be closed and other times as a difference to be cherished.[47]

Since the 1970s, the idea of a Sunbelt has shouldered aside older images of a backward South and a plundered West. The Sunbelt's rise is sometimes explained as a natural rebalancing of population and economic activity in response to shifts in the relative costs of production—especially abundant and cheap labor, cheap land, cheap energy, and low costs from public regulation (the "good business climate"). Other experts focus their attention on the ability of the periphery to capture large shares of the "sunrise industries" of aerospace, defense, electronics, and leisure.[48] Whichever the driving force, the Sunbelt has remained a region that is understood as beating the core at its own game. The image of the Sunbelt still is structured within the domestic dialectic. It reverses the older idea of a colonized and exploited South and West, but it takes its meaning from a regional contrast with the Snowbelt, Frostbelt, and Rustbelt.[49]

The growth of the international and informational sectors, however, may be operating outside this biregional system. The essence of commerce in ideas is their extreme portability and the potential of their users to break free of regional limits. For air passengers or fax users, Paris is as close to Atlanta as it is to New York. Transactional cities themselves are partly the products of a globalizing economy with its needs for coordination at a distance. For cities in the historic core, participation in the new economic trends has meant an effort to retain past preeminence. In the periphery, it has meant a continuation of regional redefinition.

These patterns of change have divided the "hot" Sunbelt from the "slow" Sunbelt. The location of the fast-changing cities supports previous findings that the economic development of the American periphery has focused on its Southeast and Southwest corners. Lines drawn Northeast and Northwest from New Orleans carve out a triangular territory in the middle South and Great Plains, where major cities have changed much more slowly than along the South Atlantic Coast or the Texas–California axis (see Figure 6.1).[50] This pattern has the

FIGURE 6.1
Degree of Change as Global Information City

■ **Substantial**

▲ **Moderate**

● **Limited**

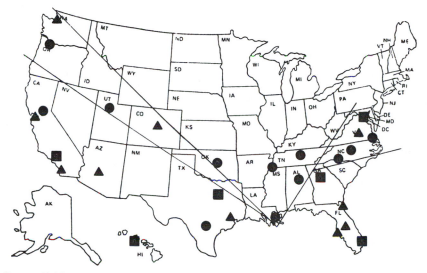

Source: Table 6.4.

troubling potential to exacerbate a regional division in U.S. politics between the rapidly changing "rimland" along the eastern, southern, and western borders and a stable (or even stagnant) interior of old factory cities, agricultural states, and mining communities. As scholars such as Richard Bensel and Ann Markusen have pointed out, regional economic differences remain an important source of political division in the United States.[51] Protectionism and immigration regulations are likely to be potent issues that pit the interests of a new set of globally oriented "haves" against domestic "have-nots."[52]

At the same time, the more ambitious and successful of the Sunbelt cities are breaking out of the old national framework in which the standards of comparison were always New York and Chicago. Dallas currently measures itself against Mexico City, Washington, D.C., against Paris and Moscow, and Los Angeles against London and Tokyo. As its leading cities go, the identity of the Sunbelt may follow—

from peripheral region in its first stage of development to internal rival in its second and perhaps to direct player on the world scene in its third stage.

The growing ability of major Sunbelt cities to bypass older cities by establishing direct roles in national networks and direct overseas contacts gives historical content to the transition from peripheral or semiperipheral status to core status. World-system theory recognizes the possibility of such dependency reversal but gives limited attention to the specific mechanisms and processes.[53] Within the United States, the apparent erosion of dependency reaffirms the importance of local policy and decisions. Many recent opportunities for urban economic change have been the unplanned consequences of federal policies with distinctly different aims. Such policies have included the promotion of free trade, loosening of banking regulations, detachment of the U.S. dollar from fixed exchange rates, and liberalization of immigration law. Exploitation of the new opportunities has been explicit at the state and local levels through facility development and trade promotion. This essay has examined differences in the impacts of new economic trends and the policy responses in selected metropolitan areas. The next step is to fill out the comparative framework with detailed historical analysis of individual communities. Such studies of the reformulation and implementation of strategic economic plans over the past generation will provide a necessary complement to our current understanding of urban growth programs that have been directed at the domestic economy.

NOTES

1. C. Vann Woodward, *The Burden of Southern History* (Baton Rouge: Louisiana State University Press, 1960), 6. Publicists for Boeing Commercial Airplanes reported that 755 Boeing 747s had been delivered for service by the beginning of 1990 and 196 more were on order.

2. John Friedmann and Goetz Wolff, "World City Formation: An Agenda for Research and Action," *International Journal of Urban and Regional Research* 6 (September 1982), 309–344; R. B. Cohen, "The New International Division of Labor, Multinational Corporations, and Urban Hierarchy," in *Urbanization and Urban Planning in Capitalist Society,* ed. Michael Dear and Allen J. Scott (New York: Methuen, 1981), 287–315; Saskia Sassen-Koob, "Capital Mobility and Labor Migration: Their Expression in Core Cities," in *Urbanization in the World-Economy,* ed. Michael Timberlake (Orlando, Fla.:

Academic, 1985), 231–265; John B. Goddard, "The City in the Global Information Economy," in *The Rise and Fall of Great Cities*, ed. Richard Lawton (New York: Bellhaven, 1989), 154–167; John Goddard and Andrew Gillespie, "Advanced Telecommunications and Regional Economic Development," in *Information and Regional Development*, ed. Maria Giaoutzi and Peter Nijkamp (Brookfield, Vt.: Gower, 1988), 121–146; C. P. Kindleberger, *The Formation of Financial Centers* (Princeton, N.J.: Princeton University Press, 1974).

3.   Jean Gottman, "Office Work and the Evolution of Cities," *Ekistics* 46 (January–February 1979), 4–7; Thomas M. Stanback, Jr., "The Changing Fortunes of Metropolitan Economies," in *High Technology, Space, and Society*, ed. Manuel Castells (Beverly Hills, Calif.: Sage, 1985), 122–142; Peter Hall, "Regions in the Transition to the Information Economy," in *America's New Market Geography*, ed. George Sternlieb and James Hughes (New Brunswick, N.J.: Center for Urban Policy Research, Rutgers University, 1988), 137–159; David Harvey, "The Geographical and Geopolitical Consequences of the Transition from Fordism to Flexible Accumulation," in *America's New Market Geography*, ed. George Sternlieb and James Hughes (New Brunswick, N.J.: Center for Urban Policy Research, Rutgers University, 1988), 124–125.

4.   In the western Pacific, for example, officials in Osaka hope to use an expanded airport to compete with Tokyo as a global center. The government of New South Wales is promoting Sydney as a finance center for the Pacific Rim. The mayor of Brisbane has tried to sell that city as a center for Asian tourism and investment in direct rivalry with Sydney.

5.   Carl Abbott, "International Cities in the Dual System Model: The Transformation of Los Angeles and Washington," *Urban History Yearbook 1991*, vol. 18 (Leicester, United Kingdom: Leicester University Press, 1991), 41–59.

6.   A voluminous literature has accumulated during the 1980s on post–World War II urban growth coalitions and their efforts to implement development programs. With a few exceptions, these studies have focused on land conversion, renewal of central business districts, use of federal aid, and competition for corporate investment. For collections of representative essays, see Susan Fainstein et al., *Restructuring the City: The Political Economy of Urban Redevelopment*, rev. ed. (New York: Longman, 1986); Clarence N. Stone and Heywood T. Sanders, eds., *The Politics of Urban Development* (Lawrence: University Press of Kansas, 1987); Scott Cummings, ed., *Business Elites and Urban Development* (Albany: State University of New York Press, 1988). For case studies, see Clarence Stone, *Economic Growth and Neighborhood Discontent: System Bias in Urban Renewal* (Chapel Hill: University of North Carolina Press, 1976); Chester Hartman, *The Transformation of San Francisco* (Totowa, N.J.: Rowman and Allanheld, 1984); John Mollenkopf, *The Contested City* (Princeton, N.J.: Princeton University Press, 1983); Todd Swanstrom, *The Crisis of Growth Politics: Cleveland, Kucinich, and the Challenge of Urban Populism* (Philadelphia: Temple University Press, 1985); Philip Trounstine and Terry Christensen, *Movers and Shakers: The Study of Community Power* (New York: St. Martin's Press, 1982). For one of the few examples that deals explicitly with the international dimension, see Spencer C.

Olin, "Globalization and the Politics of Locality: Orange County, California in the Cold War Era," *Western Historical Quarterly* 22 (May 1991), 143–162.

7. U.S. Bureau of the Census, *Historical Statistics of the United States from Colonial Times to 1970* (Washington: U.S. Department of Commerce, 1975), 887.

8. U.S. Bureau of the Census, *Historical Statistics*, 105–109; U.S. Bureau of the Census, *Statistical Abstract of the United States: 1989* (Washington: U.S. Department of Commerce, 1989), tables 7, 9, 12; Elliott Barkan, "New Origins, New Homeland, New Region: American Immigration and the Emergence of the Sunbelt, 1955–1985," in *Searching for the Sunbelt: Historical Perspectives on a Region,* ed. Raymond A. Mohl (Knoxville: University of Tennessee Press, 1990), 124–148.

9. U.S. Bureau of the Census, *Statistical Abstract,* tables 685 and 1369; Christopher Paul Beshouri, "The Global Economy: A Closer Look," *Economic Review* 70 (August 1985), 49–53; Daniel Vining et al., "A Principal Axis Shift in the American Spatial Economy," *Professional Geographer* 34 (August 1982), 270–278.

10. Ingo Walter, *Global Competition in Financial Services: Market Structure, Protection, and Trade Legislation* (Cambridge, Mass.: Ballinger, 1988), 10–11; B. P. Holly, "Regulation, Competition and Technology: The Restructuring of the U. S. Commercial Banking System," *Environment and Planning A* 19 (May 1987), 633–652; John Langdale, "Electronic Funds Transfer and the Internationalization of the Banking and Finance Industry," *Geoforum* 16 (1985), 1–13.

11. U.S. Bureau of the Census, *Historical Statistics,* 871; U.S. Bureau of the Census, *Statistical Abstract,* table 1359; Wilbur Zelinsky, "Coming to America," *American Demographics* 12 (August 1990), 44–47, 56.

12. Douglass C. North and John J. Wallis, "Measuring the Transaction Sector in the American Economy, 1870–1970," in *Long-Term Factors in American Economic Growth,* ed. Stanley Engerman and Robert Gallman (Chicago: University of Chicago Press, 1986), 95–108; Alfred D. Chandler, *The Visible Hand: The Managerial Revolution in American Business* (Cambridge, Mass.: Harvard University Press, 1977); Daniel Bell, *The Coming of Post-Industrial Society* (New York: Basic Books, 1973); Fritz Machlup, *The Production and Distribution of Knowledge in the United States* (Princeton, N.J.: Princeton University Press, 1962).

13. "Technology Gives the U. S. a Big Edge," *Business Week,* 30 June 1980, 102–106; M. E. Hepworth et al., "The Spatial Division of Information Labour in Great Britain," *Environment and Planning A* 19 (June 1987), 793–806. The British philosopher Bertrand Russell summed up the process when he wrote that "work is of two kinds: first, altering the position of matter at or near the earth's surface relatively to other such matter; second, telling other people to do so. The first is unpleasant and ill paid; the second is pleasant and highly paid. The second kind is capable of indefinite expansion; there are not only those who give orders, but those who give advice as to what order should be given." See Bertrand Russell, "In Praise of Idleness," in *Mass Leisure,* ed. Eric Larrabee and Rolf Meyerson (New York: Free Press, 1958), 97.

14. Jean Gottmann, "Urbanization and Employment: Toward a General Theory," *Town Planning Review* 49 (July 1978), 393–401; Jean Gottmann, *The Coming of the Transactional City* (College Park: University of Maryland Institute for Urban Studies, 1983); Kenneth Corey, "Transactional Forces and the Metropolis," *Ekistics* 49 (November–December 1982), 416–423; Thomas Stanback et al., *Services: The New Economy* (Totowa, N.Y.: Allanheld, Osman, 1981); Ronald Abler and John S. Adams, *The Industrial and Occupational Structure of the American Labor Force* (State College: Pennsylvania State University, 1977); Mark Porat, *The Information Economy: Definition and Measurement,* Special Publication no. 77-12 (Washington, D.C.: U.S. Department of Commerce, Office of Telecommunications, (1977).

15. Richard Barnett and R. E. Muller, *Global Reach: The Power of Multinational Corporations* (New York: Simon and Schuster, 1974).

16. This situation is the reverse of the international dimension of the urban economy, which plays a prominent role in local development schemes but has occasioned little systematic or theoretical analysis at the local level.

17. Hepworth et al., "Spatial Division of Information Labour," 793–806; Mitchell Moss, "Telecommunications, World Cities, and Urban Policy," *Urban Studies* 24 (December 1987), 534–546.

18. Washington Board of Trade, *A Capital Link* (Washington, D.C.: Washington Board of Trade, 1987); "Houston: A World Class City," advertising supplement, *Fortune,* 1 October 1982, 143–151; Andrew Young, "Why Cultivate International Markets and Investments?" *Economic Review* 71 (January 1986), 12.

19. The transactional dimension of an urban economy is usually measured either by its share of major corporate headquarters or its share of white-collar occupations. For examples, see Regina B. Armstrong, "National Trends in Office Construction, Employment and Headquarter Location in U.S. Metropolitan Areas," in *Spatial Patterns of Office Growth and Location,* ed. P. W. Daniels (Chichester, United Kingdom: Wiley, 1979), 61–93; Robert A. Harper, "Metropolitan Areas as Transactional Centers," in *Modern Metropolitan Systems,* ed. Charles Christian and Robert Harper (Columbus: Charles E. Merrill, 1982), 87–109; John D. Stephens, "Metropolitan Areas as Decision-Making Centers," in *Modern Metropolitan Systems,* ed. Charles Christian and Robert Harper (Columbus: Charles E. Merrill, 1982), 111–146; Cohen, "New International Division of Labor," 301–310.

I use these indicators in addition to two others—(1) role as center for regional offices of the federal government and (2) prominence of relatively narrowly defined set of decision-making jobs in Finance, Insurance, and Real Estate (FIRE) and Central Administrative Offices and Auxiliaries of manufacturing firms (CAO&A). Corporate headquarters are taken from *Fortune* magazine lists of the 500 largest industrial corporations and 250 largest service corporations in 1960 and the 500 largest corporations in both categories in 1988. White-collar employment comprises the professional managerial, and clerical–sales categories from the U.S. Bureau of the Census, *Census of*

Population, 1960: Characteristics of the Population, table 74, and U.S. Bureau of the Census, *Census of Population, 1980: General Social and Economic Characteristics,* table 121. Employment in FIRE is combined with data on CAO&A employment from the U.S. Bureau of the Census, *U.S. Census of Manufactures: 1958,* vol. 3: *Area Statistics,* table 1, and U.S. Bureau of the Census, *1982 Census of Manufactures: Geographic Area Series,* table 1. Point assignments are as follows:

Corporate headquarters: An equal distribution of 750 headquarters among 50 cities in 1960 would have given 15 points to each city. Cities in the target group therefore received 1 point for 9 to 18 headquarters, 2 points for 19 or more. An equal distribution of the 1,000 headquarters in 1988 would give 20 points to each of 50 cities. If one of the target cities gained 5 to 9 headquarters, it gained 1 point. It gained 2 points for an increase of 10 headquarters or more.

White-collar employment: The percentage for all metropolitan areas combined in 1960 was 45.6. A city received 1 point if its own percentage fell between 44 and 46.9, 2 points for a percentage between 47 and 49.9, and 3 points for a percentage of 50 or more. Between 1960 and 1980, the proportion for all U.S. metropolitan areas increased from 45.6 to 56.4 percent. A city gained 1 point if its own percentage increased by 12 percentage points or more.

FIRE/CAO&O Employment: The proportion for all metropolitan areas in 1960 was 5.5. A city received 1 point if its own percentage was 5 to 6.9, and 2 points for a percentage of 7 or more. Between 1960 and 1980, the proportion for all metropolitan areas increased from 5.5 to 7.2 percent. A city therefore gained 1 point if its own proportion increased by 2 percentage points or more.

Federal office center: Officially designated regional office centers received 1 point, whereas Washington, D.C., received 2 points. There were no changes from the 1960 point assignments.

    20.   Few researchers have defined the full set of factors that make a city "international." Two of these few are Max Barlow and Brian Slack, "International Cities: Some Geographical Considerations and a Case Study of Montreal," *Geoforum* 16 (1985), 333–345. They described a range of economic, governmental, and sociocultural factors that support international roles.

For the current analysis, foreign-born population by metropolitan area was taken from U.S. Bureau of the Census, *Census of Population, 1960: Characteristics of the Population,* table 32, and U.S. Bureau of the Census, *Census of Population, 1980: General Social and Economic Characteristics,* table 118. Foreign trade was taken from U.S. Department of Commerce, *United States Waterborne Exports and General Imports* for 1964 and 1986. Foreign banks were taken from "Financial Center–New York," *Banker,* 138 (March 1988), 37–61. Metropolitan roles as international information centers, the importance of foreign markets for local businesses, and foreign investment were based on a synthesis of secondary descriptions of each city. Point assignments were as follows:

Foreign-born population: The percentage for all metropolitan areas in 1960 was 5.4. Cities received 1 point for a percentage between 5 and 6.9 and 2 points for a percentage of 7 or more. Between 1960 and 1980, the proportion for all metropolitan areas increased from 5.4 to 5.8 percent. Cities gained 1 point if their own proportion increased between 1 and 2.9 percentage points and 2 points for an increase of 3 percentage points or more.

Foreign trade: Cities received 1 point if they accounted for 2 to 5 percent of total U.S. trade in 1964 and received 2 points if they accounted for a larger proportion. They gained 1 point for an increase of at least 1 percentage point in their share of the U.S. total and 2 points for an increase of 10 percent or more. The other international factors drew on a variety of quantitative and narrative sources for assignment of points or half points.

21. The leading position of San Francisco in 1960 confirms the findings of R. B. Cohen, "The Changing Transactional Economy and Its Spatial Implications," *Ekistics* 46 (January–February 1978), 7–15.

22. Barlow And Slack, "International Cities," offer a cross-sectional classification based on the number of a city's international activities and the extent of its global reach. Their examples include New York (large number, long reach); Geneva (small number, long reach); and Los Angeles (large number, short reach). The typology of development sequences outlined can be viewed as an explanation of shifts from one to another of the Barlow–Slack categories.

23. Rupert Vance and Sara Smith, "Metropolitan Dominance and Integration in the Urban South," in *The Urban South,* ed. Rupert Vance and Nicholas Demerath (Chapel Hill: University of North Carolina Press, 1954), 114–134; Otis D. Duncan et al., *Metropolis and Region* (Baltimore: Johns Hopkins University Press, 1960); Omer Galle and Robert N. Stern, "The Metropolitan System in the South: Continuity and Change," in *The Population of the South,* ed. Dudley R. Posten, Jr., and Robert H. Wells (Austin: University of Texas Press, 1981), 155–174; Martin Melosi, "Dallas–Fort Worth: Marketing the Metroplex," in *Sunbelt Cities: Politics and Growth since World War II,* ed. Richard M. Bernard and Bradley R. Rice (Austin: University of Texas Press, 1983), 163–173; Fred Vetter, "Atlanta's Economic Development: Past and Future," in *The Future of Atlanta's Central City,* ed. Edwin Gorsuch and Dudley Hinds (Atlanta: Georgia State University College of Business Administration, 1977), 52–80; Bradley Rice, "If Dixie Were Atlanta," in *Sunbelt Cities: Politics and Growth since World War II,* ed. Richard M. Bernard and Bradley R. Rice (Austin: University of Texas Press, 1983), 33–44.

24. Dana White andd Timothy Crimmins, "How Atlanta Grew: Cool Heads, Hot Air, and Hard Work," *Atlanta Economic Review* 28 (January–February 1978), 7–15; "The Big Name Hunt," *Atlanta* 16 (July 1976), 57–58, 114; Frank McCoy, "International Business: Ready for the World," *Black*

Enterprise 19 (June 1989), 162–176; Ralph D. Griffin and Maryjane Sutherland, "Atlanta's Emergence as an International City," *Global Trade,* 108 (September 1988), 20–24; "State Export Series: Georgia," *Business America,* 7 January 1985, 21–24; Stanley Topol, "Corporate Export Policies Provide the Competitive Edge," *Economic Review* 71 (January 1986), 24–26; Atlanta Chamber of Commerce, *Atlanta Consulates, Trade and Tourism Offices, and Foreign-American Chambers of Commerce* (Atlanta: Atlanta Chamber of Commerce, 1990); Rice, "If Dixie Were Atlanta," 44.

25. "Dallas/Fort Worth, the Southwest Metroplex: A New World Capital," advertising supplement, *Fortune,* 89 (October 1973), 50–82; *New Goals for Dallas* (Dallas: Goals for Dallas, 1977), 20; Dallas Partnership et al., *The Metroplex: Dallas–Fort Worth* (Dallas: Dallas Partnership et al., 1990).

26. "Worldly Concerns: Dallas Is Looking for International Attention," *Dallas Magazine* (April 1984), 24–30; Alan Cook, "The Canadian Connection," *Baylor Business Review* 3 (Winter 1985), 2–8; "Here They Come Again," *Dallas Magazine* (June 1987), 10–11.

27. Carl Abbott, "Perspectives on Urban Economic Planning: The Case of Washington, D.C., since 1880," *The Public Historian* 11 (Spring 1989), 18.

28. Greater Washington Board of Trade, *Board of Trade News,* 41 (December 1986), 10–11A; Greater Washington Board of Trade, *A Capital Link* (Washington Board of Trade, 1986), 7.

29. Adolph Reed, Jr., "A Critique of Neo-Progressivism in Theorizing about Local Development Policy: A Case from Atlanta," in *The Politics of Urban Development,* ed. Clarence N. Stone and Heywood T. Sanders (Lawrence: University Press of Kansas), 199–215; Betsy Braden and Paul Hagan, *A Dream Takes Flight: Harsfield International Airport and Aviation in Georgia* (Athens: University of Georgia Press, 1989); Griffin and Sutherland, "Atlanta's Emergence."

30. From the 1860s to the 1970s, Denver's development shadowed that of Dallas as a regional finance, service, and distribution center. The energy boom from 1974 to 1982 drew the city toward a narrower economic base centered on technical and business services for a single industry. Currently, civic leaders are interested in moving back to the Dallas model. In particular, the 1989 decision to build a new airport that will explicitly rival Dallas–Fort Worth is a self-conscious effort to add a new transactional and possibly international dimension to an essentially static continentally oriented economy. See Thomas J. Noel, "Unexplored Western Skies: Denver International Airport" (paper delivered at the 29th Annual Meeting of the Western History Association, Tacoma, Washington, October 13, 1989).

Although excluded from standard definitions of the Sunbelt, Kansas City competes with Denver and Dallas as a regional metropolis for the central United States. It too has actively promoted itself as an international city on the basis of its transportation and communication networks. A large foreign trade zone dates from 1976, and European investment grew during the 1980s.

31. Anthony Downs, "Japanese Capital Invades Hawaiian Market," *Na-*

tional Real Estate Investor 29 (October 1987), 40–46, 283–284; Lawrence Bacow, "A Localized Business Goes International," *Real Estate Today* 22 (June 1989), 60–61.

32. Joel Garreau, *The Nine Nations of North America* (Boston: Houghton Mifflin, 1981), 167–206; Joan Didion, *Miami* (New York: Simon and Schuster, 1987), 27, 33; David Reiff, *Going to Miami: Exiles, Tourists, and Refugees in the New America* (Boston: Little, Brown, 1987).

33. John Heins, "A Mixed Blessing," *Forbes,* 22 February 1988, 63–65; John Heins, "Island Hopping," *Forbes,* 21 March 1988, 44–46; K. Leventhal and Co., *1988 Japanese Investment in United States Real Estate* (Los Angeles: K. Leventhal and Co., 1989).

34. David A. Heenan, "Global Cities of Tomorrow," *Harvard Business Review* 55 (May–June 1977), 92; Alfred G. Edge and Mike French, "Management Development at the Japan–American Institute of Management Science," *Journal of Management Development* 5 (1986), 51–54; Nigel Holloway, "Nothing like a Dime: Hawaii Aims to Promote Belief in Business," *Far Eastern Economic Review,* 3 August 1989, 51–53.

35. Emmanuel N. Roussakis, "The Edges Come to Miami," *The Bankers Magazine* 164 (May–June 1981), 82–90; Raymond A. Mohl, "Miami: The Ethnic Cauldron," in *Sunbelt Cities: Politics and Growth since World War II,* ed. Richard Bernard and Bradley R. Rice (Austin: University of Texas Press, 1983), 72–77; Mira Wilkins, *Foreign Enterprise in Florida* (Gainesville: University Presses of Florida, 1979); Mira Wilkins, *New Foreign Enterprise in Florida* (Miami: Greater Miami Chamber of Commerce, 1980); Brookes McIntyre, "The Foreign Bank Presence in the Southeast," *Economic Review* 71 (January 1986), 36–39; Heenan. "Global Cities," 79–92.

San Diego also shows similarities to the Miami model. It has developed mass-market ties to Mexico as a magnet for migration through two-way tourism and shopping and through *maquiladora* manufacturing (manufacturing facilities located in districts of extreme northern Mexico that can import components from the United States and export finished products to American markets without paying Mexican or American tariffs). Its amenities could support development as a world research, information, and tourist city.

36. Abbott, "International Cities," 45–49.

37. Mel Scott, *Metropolitan Los Angeles: One Community* (Los Angeles: Haynes Foundation, 1949); Jane Jacobs, *The Economy of Cities* (New York: Random House, 1969), 150–155.

38. U. S. Department of Commerce, *United States Waterborne Exports and General Imports,* annual series; Manalytics, Inc., *The Competitive Position of the Bay Area Container Ports* (San Francisco: Manalytics, Inc., 1987).

Comparison of faster and slower growing port cities has suggested that diversified container cargo ports such as Seattle–Tacoma, Los Angeles–Long Beach, and San Francisco–Oakland have had a competitive advantage over bulk shipment ports such as Portland, New Orleans, and Norfolk–Newport

News. Bulk export of grain, lumber, or coal is a relatively routine process that makes few demands on local decision makers. Comprehensive ports that handle a wide variety of commodities, in contrast, develop more sophistication in international business and more elaborate commercial connections within the domestic economy. Such connections lead relatively easily into additional trasactional functions that, in turn, attract greater global roles. For a critical discussion, see K. O'Connor, "The Location of Services Involved with International Trade," *Environment and Planning A* 19 (May 1987), 687–700.

39. Kurt Anderson, "The New Ellis Island," *Time,* 13 June 1983, 18–25; Ivan Light, "Los Angeles," in *The Metropolis Era: A World of Giant Cities,* ed. Mattei Dogan and John Kasarda (Beverly Hills, Calif.: Sage, 1988), 56–59; Allen J. Scott, *Metropolis: From Division of Labor to Urban Form* (Berkeley and Los Angeles: University of California Press, 1989), 93–105.

40. U.S. Bureau of the Census, *1970 Census of Population,* Vol. 1: *Characteristics of the Population,* table 81; U.S. Bureau of the Census, *Census of Population, 1980: General Social and Economic Characteristics,* table 118; Security Pacific National Bank, *The Sixty Mile Circle: The Economy of the Greater Los Angeles Area* (Los Angeles: Security Pacific National Bank, 1981); Gilda Haas and Allan Heskin, "Community Struggles in Los Angeles," *International Journal of Urban and Regional Research* 5 (1981), 546–564; Joel Kotkin and Yoriko Kishimoto, *The Third Century: America's Resurgence in the Asian Era* (New York: Crown, 1988), 201–202; Walter, *Global Competition in Financial Services,* 12; Leventhal and Co., *Japanese Investment.*

41. Edward Soja el al., "Urban Restructuring: An Analysis of Social and Spatial Change in Los Angeles," *Economic Geography* 59 (April 1983), 222–226.

42. Seattle's career essentially has been that of Los Angeles written small, following the same growth sequence on a more limited regional base. Growing first as a regional distribution and export center, Seattle developed new roles within national networks beginning in the 1960s. Examples include the development of the University of Washington as a nationally competitive institution, successful competition for federal research and development contracts, and the capture of substantial diversified import cargo for national markets. These initiatives helped Seattle pass Portland as the principal metropolis of the Pacific Northwest in the 1960s and 1970s and to take initial steps as the regional access point for international travel, banking, and trade.

Houston is a greater puzzle. Both journalists ("Houston: The International City," *Fortune,* 14 July 1980, 38–50) and academics (Joe Feagan, *Free Enterprise City: Houston in Political and Economic Perspective* [New Brunswick, N.J.: Rutgers University Press, 1988]) have identified Houston as an international city. However, the city combines two different roles within the global economy. It has been a major exporter of bulk commodities such as cotton, grain, wood products, and mineral products since the nineteenth century. It also has become a center for worldwide exchange of petroleum technology and for transactional functions relating to the petroleum industry. Its international participation therefore has been longstanding and substantial, but also narrowly based in comparison with Los Angeles.

43. Gottmann, "Office Work and the Evolution of Cities," 5–6; John Fernie, "Office Activity in Edinburgh," *Ekistics* 46 (January–February 1979), 25–33; Heenan, "Global Cities," 79–92.

44. Edward Ullman, "Regional Development and the Geography of Concentration," *Papers and Proceedings of the Regional Science Association* 4 (1958), 179–98. See also David R. Meyer, "The Emergence of the American Manufacturing Belt: An Interpretation," *Journal of Historical Geography* 9 (April 1983), 145–174.

45. For a systematic summary of the world-systems model, see *World Systems Analysis: Theory and Methodology,* ed. Terence K. Hopkins and Immanuel Wallerstein (Beverly Hills, Calif.: Sage, 1982).

46. Lawrence Goodwyn, *Democratic Promise: The Populist Movement in America* (New York: Oxford University Press, 1976); John Thompson, *Closing the Frontier: Radical Response in Oklahoma, 1889–1923* (Norman: University of Oklahoma Press, 1986); Melvin Dubofsky, *We Shall Be All: A History of the Industrial Workers of the World* (Chicago: Quadrangle Books, 1969).

47. Michael O'Brien, *The Idea of the American South, 1920–1941* (Baltimore: Johns Hopkins University Press, 1979); William G. Robbins, "The 'Plundered Province' Thesis and the Historiography of the American West," *Pacific Historical Review* 55 (November 1986), 577–598; Gene Gressley, "Regionalism and the Twentieth Century West," in *The American West: New Perspectives, New Dimensions,* ed. Jerome O. Steffan (Norman: University of Oklahoma Press, 1979), 197–234.

48. For theoretical explanations for the rise of the Sunbelt, see Kirkpatrick Sale, *Power Shift: The Rise of the Southern Rim and Its Challenge to the Eastern Establishment* (New York: Random House, 1975); W. W. Rostow, "Regional Change and the Fifth Kondratieff Upswing," in *The Rise of the Sunbelt Cities,* ed. David C. Perry and Albert Watkins (Beverly Hills, Calif.: Sage, 1977), 83–103; Albert Watkins and David Perry, "Regional Change and the Impact of Uneven Urban Development," in *The Rise of the Sunbelt Cities,* ed. David C. Perry and Albert Watkins (Beverly Hills, Calif.: Sage, 1977), 19–54; Bernard L. Weinstein and Robert Firestine, *Regional Growth and Decline in the United States* (New York: Praeger, 1978); James Cobb, *The Selling of the South: The Southern Crusade for Industrial Development, 1936–1980* (Baton Rouge: Louisiana State University Press, 1982); Carl Abbott, *The New Urban America: Growth and Politics in Sunbelt Cities,* rev. ed. (Chapel Hill: University of North Carolina Press, 1987).

49. Carl Abbott, "New West, New South, New Region: The Discovery of the Sunbelt," in *Searching for the Sunbelt: Historical Perspectives on a Region,* ed. Raymond A. Mohl (Knoxville: University of Tennessee Press, 1990), 7–24.

50. Abbott, *New Urban America,* 24–35; Carl Abbott, "The End of the Southern City," in *Perspectives on the American South: An Annual Review of Society, Politics and Culture,* vol. 4, ed. James C. Cobb and Charles R. Wilson

(New York: Gordon and Breach Science Publishers, 1987), 187–218; William K. Tabb, "Urban Development and Regional Restructuring: An Overview," in *Sunbelt/Snowbelt: Urban Development and Regional Restructuring,* ed. Larry Sawers and William K. Tabb (New York: Oxford University Press, 1984), 9–12; Hall, "Transition to Information Economy," 147.

51.   Richard F. Bensel, *Sectionalism and American Political Development, 1880–1980* (Madison: University of Wisconsin Press, 1984); Anne Markusen, *Regions: The Economics and Politics of Territory* (Totowa, N.J.: Rowman and Littlefield, 1987); Anne Markusen, "Industrial Restructuring and Regional Politics," in *Economic Restructuring and Political Response,* ed. Robert Beauregard (Newbury Park, Calif.: Sage, 1989), 115–147.

52.   Goddard and Gillespie, "Advanced Telecommunications," 121–146, describe a similar division between information "haves" and "have-nots" in Great Britain.

53.   The possibility of "dependency reversal" or transition from semiperiphery to core is discussed from a variety of viewpoints. See Charles F. Doran et. al., eds., *North–South Relations: Studies in Dependency Reversal* (New York: Praeger, 1983), and see especially the following essays in that book: Charles Doran, "Structuring the Concept of Dependency Reversal"; George Modelski, "Dependency Reversal in the Modern State System: A Long Cycle Perspective"; Christopher Chase-Dunn, "Inequality, Structural Mobility and Dependency Reversal in the Capitalist World Economy."

7

SAM BASS WARNER, JR.

Eco-Urbanism and Past Choices for Urban Living

A CONCERN for environments, the public settings of human and non-human nature that surround family life, has long been a major focus of urban history and urban policy. Therefore, for a historian, it is not the novelty of people's circumstances that lends urgency to current environmental debates, rather it is the universality of what had formerly been understood as a special case: crowded, dirty cities. Had Americans been paying attention in the 1820s or the 1920s, they could have seen the links between U.S. urban and rural environments, but people did not view the world that way, nor did they value the nurture of humans sufficiently to attend to the environment required for their livelihood. Instead, Americans consumed human and nonhuman nature with a prodigal hand. The environment crisis is not new for Americans. Instead Americans are suffering, as they have been for centuries, from inadequate values and unstable economies and environments.

Urban Environmental History

A convenient entry into urban environmental history can be made by viewing urban nature. Imagine a pleasant school-yard scene. Imagine two third-grade girls running hand-in-hand through a public school doorway.[1] Here is urban nature in action, and whatever the picture in the reader's mind, it focuses on the species that currently is the most significant environmental challenge. A school-yard scene also calls up an essential human characteristic that often is neglected or forgotten: Running children are children expressing their pleasure and feeling in being creatures of nature. Although people are all creatures who breathe and move about like other mammals, it is hard to feel part of nature sitting and watching television or sitting behind the wheel of a car. When people run and jump, shout, and sing, they experience the pleasure of being creatures of nature.[2] It is vital that city dwellers never forget that they are creatures of nature, lest they neglect elements in their lives and surroundings that are necessary to sustain them.

The metropolis is a place where humans live in the midst of other living things, and if it is a well-built and well-managed metropolis, the humans will thrive, and so will a great variety of other creatures. Until the twentieth century, no large U.S. or European city afforded a sufficiently safe environment to allow the urban human population to even reproduce itself, never mind reproduce itself in good health and well-being.

The imagined school-yard scene also contains a vital urban component. The two children, formerly strangers, saw each other as fellow humans. They played together. Presumably they had become playmates since coming to school. Perhaps the two children represent the extremes of American social distance: one is black, the other is white. This meeting of strangers is the very essence of urbanity. It is a crucial urban value that must not be overlooked. A city is above all else a place where strangers come together to meet, play, trade, and work in peace and safety. The sociability and cooperation of strangers is the heart of urban life.

Such a scene also represents an approach to politics. It is perfectly clear in these days of international air and oceanic pollution, and third-world poverty and suffering that there are several different scales that demand appropriate environmental action. For air and oceanic pollution, people require international policies and international cooperation; for poverty, both national and international efforts; for water and soil pollution, regional policies to control systems such as the Mississippi River; and for many more energy, air, water, and health issues, the international and regional policies must be supplemented by appropriate metropolitan programs. Unless there is a good deal of local awareness, however, as well as local input into the regional and international programs, the programs will neither be good nor appropriate. Therefore, it is essential that environmental and urban values be discussed in the context of families and their modes of urban living.

Policy Goals

If the overall goal is to sustain and encourage both human and nonhuman nature in a modern American metropolis such as New Orleans, specific issues ought to be pursued.

Race

Surely Americans must redouble their efforts to build a multiracial society. Currently, racial animosities levy a terrible toll against U.S. cities and suburbs. Each year produces another crop of untrained and underemployed young people, and every year is still marked by poverty, bad health, drug abuse, and crime. How can one say U.S. cities are urban places if people are afraid to go out on the streets alone, or at night, if strangers are attacked when they stray into unfamiliar neighborhoods? If in American public policies and programs race, poverty, and the natural environment seem not to be joined, this separation is only the result of narrow specialization. A brief visit to any poor city block will quickly yield a simple census of the vegetation growing there. Compare that census to a richness of varieties found in any suburban block and the link between impoverished people and impoverished nature will appear dramatically.[3]

Housing

U.S. housing costs are inflated beyond the reach of citizens' incomes and savings. The structures currently being built are destructive of both the nearby and the regional environment. They are expensive to maintain, they guzzle energy, spew out waste and isolate one family from another. For all these costs, they make only a small fraction of U.S. residents comfortable.[4]

Land Use

Currently, national practice isolates economic activities, classes, races, sexes, and ages from one another because Americans are in the habit of using land antisocially. Businesses harass their neighbors with noise, smoke, fumes, and traffic; big businesses do all these things and also build towers to shut out their neighbors' sunlight. In their homes, people huddle together in enclaves of class and race and separate themselves from their neighbors because they lack the manners to share common space with other families, and their

children, and automobiles. Moreover, American suburban families
are isolated from all manner of educational, medical, and social institutions whose services they require. Surely for the needs of human
sociability and support and for the needs of a nonhuman environment, new construction and urban rebuilding must cluster housing,
and promote the development of common spaces, service spaces, and
service institutions within residential neighborhoods.[5]

Education

Both public and private systems of education currently are failing to
nourish either humans or the metropolitan nonhuman environment.
Many children are not learning basic skills in the schools, many adolescents are dropping out of school untrained, and many families are
finding that they cannot afford to pay for higher education for their
children. Still others, who need or would like further education as
adults, cannot afford the additional training. A few families are establishing and maintaining private schools for purposes of class and
racial segregation. All these schools fail to teach sufficient science to
the children so that they can later make informed decisions about the
qualities of their natural environments. Surely if a sensible public
goal is the nurture of humans, the United States needs a citizens
education program that, like the GI Bill of World War II, would allow
every American to pursue education throughout a lifetime. Moreover,
because the cultures within American metropolises are so numerous,
and their citizens so varied, variety must be fostered within city and
suburban school systems. Variety also must include activities other
than schoolwork, as well as training for those young people who are
dropping out and who seek employment. Youth crews of boys and girls
could be immediately useful planting and tending trees, building community parks and constructing walking and bicycle corridors through
our suburbs and cities, in building small neighborhood nursery and
elementary schools, and in reconstructing streets so that they would
slow traffic and reduce runoff. They could also be trained to care for
children and old people and to work in such care-giving teams. The
maintenance and improvement of the metropolitan environment is
obviously one of the most available and appropriate activities for non-
schoolwork training.[6]

Employment

Employment is the means for sustaining the population and is the
necessary means for raising children and caring for sick, disabled, and

old people. Therefore, it is essential in setting employment policies to remember that the people of the metropolis are the end products of labor, not the items for sale listed in the Yellow Pages. Americans do not make shoes to do it cheaper than the Brazilians, or snazzier than the Japanese, or more elegantly than the Italians, for example. They manufacture shoes to support their families. Americans should work in their own ways, ways that will sustain them; the qualities of every-day living are not something to be wagered in an international economic football game.

Employment policies must match the sequences of human life to enable Americans to reach such a goal. Citizens require learning time, paid leave time for birth, infant care, home nursing, and a wage structure that supports high-quality social, medical, and educational services.

Currently, U.S. wage structures draw much needed time away from young parents and away from poor families. They do so to deliver that time to businesses and to well-to-do families. The low wages in food services, nursing, hospital care, and human services of all kinds draw scarce time from low-income families and poorly paid peoples. The harvest is child neglect and family pathologies of all kinds. Let the machines do the dirty work of business, and let people pay each other well for caring for each other.

These five policy goals are obvious commonsense statements suitable to contemporary metropolitan living. They, of course, are not representations of the values that have governed American human and nonhuman environments since Europeans first settled on the continent. Because these statements are at once so obviously sensible and yet so at odds with American traditions, their meanings can best be appreciated by holding them up against the traditional best practice.

Urban Tradition Versus Metropolitan Requirements

Two past examples that represent America's prosperous and comfortable urban environmental behavior sharply illustrate the differences between people's best urban tradition and current metropolitan requirements. The first case reviews the arrangements for urban living of a merchant during the 1820s; the second reviews the urban living arrangements of a businessperson during the 1920s.

Merchant Family Life-Style
during the 1820s

The first case recalls the nostalgia decades for New Orleans, the years
from the late eighteenth century to the 1850s: the Seignouret House
at 520 Royal Street (1816–1817), the Tricou House at 711 Bourbon
Street (1834), many French Quarter row houses, and the Pontalba
Buildings at Jackson Square (1849–1950).[7] Imagine a handsome row
of federal houses built in the early nineteenth century in what was
then the national urban style of row houses with Georgian details, an
imitation of preceding London fashions.[8] As a dense cluster style, this
old way of building met two 1990 environmental criteria by not
spreading over the land and by providing a high population density
without tall structures. By so doing, the style occasionally allowed
some public space—a park—to be created out of the land saved from
private lots. The site design was such that there were no street trees
and no house lot trees to shade the houses so that they were unnecessarily hot in summer and unnecessarily cold in winter. The only good
energy feature of these buildings was their row design: it produced
warm party walls on two sides of each house.

Because these row houses were laid out in rectangular grids, as in
the 1811 Manhattan plan of numbered streets and avenues and 25 by
100 foot lots, this site design did not respect the inherited land forms
of hills and valleys, nor did it orient the houses so that they caught
the winter sun and fell into shade in summer. Also, because most
American cities were surveyed in grids with an eye to maximum
development profit, few public squares were inserted into the grid.
The frequent parks and squares that made London's Bloomsbury section so attractive, were generally omitted, and, instead, block after
block of continous housing went up.

Two decades later, such overbuilding provoked an outcry for green
space. The country park movement of Andrew Jackson Downing
(1815–1852) and Frederick Law Olmsted (1822–1903) was a specific
reaction to the brick confinement of this relentless building. Just
because the demand for a country park to relieve the monotony of the
city, as opposed to redesign of house lots and streets, the country park
movement fostered Americans' antiphony between the built city and
the open green environment.

The sanitary arrangements of these houses soon brought disaster.
When built in the 1820s, such houses had chamber pots in the rooms,
and privies in the basement or in the small rear yard. Near the privy
stood the family well, so that it was only a matter of time before the
well became polluted. In New York, as in New Orleans, the local

groundwater tasted so bad that carters sold homeowners *tea water—* fresh water from large casks on wagons. When American cities reached a threshold population of about fifty thousand, they turned lethal. That is, the levels of groundwater pollution rose high enough so that periodic epidemics of typhoid, yellow fever, malaria, and cholera accompanied the regular killing from dysentery and tuberculosis. Philadelphia suffered the first such epidemic in 1793. It lost four thousand inhabitants in one summer of yellow fever.

Despite the subsequent introduction of public water (unfiltered) and the later building of sewers, American cities and their European counterparts remained lethal human habitats until the twentieth century. To even maintain a level population, they required the importation of thousands of young European immigrants. The best current historical assessment says that the repeated importation of fresh diseases from Europe, overcrowded housing, inadequate sanitation, and spoiled milk and food together created an environment that year after year killed more children and adults than it allowed infants to grow to adulthood.[9] In short, these handsome merchants' houses stood in the same relation to the epidemics of their day as suburban houses currently stand in relation to the drug, crime, and acquired immune deficiency syndrome epidemics of our time: they deny the urban interconnectedness in which they exist.

The family economy of these houses differed a great deal from the current family economy. The husband generally was the sole money-earner, the only family member who worked in the cash economy. He walked to work to a nearby desk in a small office located on a street of shops and warehouses. Then he returned to eat his dinner at home about 3 P.M. or 4 P.M., after taking coffee, or a drink, at noon with his business associates at a nearby coffee house or tavern.

Despite its size and obvious luxury, the merchant's house did not contribute to the social or economic segregation of the city. It, and its immediate block of neighbors, were an island of wealth in an urban pudding of shops, barns, wharves, and homes of every degree of comfort and squalor. Communications among houses and families depended on family visiting and on notes and letters carried about the city by children and servants.

The national and international economy that sustained the merchant's business was highly unstable: it depended on the ebbs and flows of European capital and labor and on the mining of American resources. The husband's goal was to accumulate property, to build up his business, and to buy real estate. He was to assemble property for the security of his family, as insurance against illness and death, as a dower for his daughters, and as an inheritance for his sons. Although life insurance and fire insurance could be purchased, there was no public safety net for families without wealth who were stricken with accidents, disease, or death. The good fortune of personal health and the rapid growth of the economy were American families' best hopes for comfort and prosperity. However, accidents and business failures were frequent and only were offset by the ease with which a person could start over again in a fast-growing city.

Education, formal training, corporate career ladders, were not the supports or barriers they are currently. Merchants' families used the public schools, so family education costs were low. The sons were expected to finish high school, but college was optional. Afterschool recreation for older children often meant mischief because there were no organized sports at schools. Putting children to work at chores and as helpers to men and women was the common way of managing adolescents. A grammar school education sufficed for most daughters.

The wife presided over a team of resident and nonresident servants who tended the house. As in late twentieth-century America, personal servants to families, whether resident or nonresident, were poorly paid, such personal services drew time and resources from young and poor people and applied the time and resources to the well-to-do employer. Most of the house servants were married and unmarried women, young girls, and widows. Often these servants were poor relatives of the merchant's family, people who traded labor for shelter in the home. The nonresident workers, the wood splitters, livery stable workers, delivery boys, and women who came in to wash and to sew, also were at the bottom of the economic ladder.

Most of the clothing was made, washed, and repaired within the home itself. The wood and coal fireplaces consumed enormous amounts of fuel so that in the winter smoke hung over the city and the nearby forests were quickly denuded. In a well-to-do home, cooking was done in a large brick and cast iron stove located in a basement kitchen. People shopped daily for food because food could be preserved only by drying, smoking, and salting. Canning was a midnineteenth century invention. All the nursing and health care was given in the home. Babies were born and people suffered illnesses and injuries, and were attended by a physician and the family women as nurses. Everyone except very poor people and the vagrant died at home. As a family economy, these 1820s merchants houses were dense, formal, mannered, labor intensive, and enormously dangerous and destructive to human life.

Such houses placed in their urban environment present a picture of order in the midst of tempos of change that resembled chaos. The 1820s was the opening decade of the era of America's most rapid rate of urbanization. The invention and perfection of machines of all kinds and the harnessing of water and steam power transformed traditional ways of work and travel. American cities boomed with interlinked regional and national economies built on vast imports and money and human capital and massive exports of raw materials. England, in particular, shipped pounds sterling, manufactures, and English people, Irish people, and Germans, whereas America sent back lumber, wheat, tobacco, and especially cotton. It was cotton that built New Orleans and New York.[10]

The forest from Maine to the Ozarks were cut down, and the soils mined for crops. Tobacco, cotton, wheat, and corn are notorious for their soil depletion when pursued as monocultures, but less remarkable soil destruction went on everywhere. For example, in Thoreau's Concord, the suburban farmers had cut down all the town's trees in search of hay land. They had so carried on their business that one-third of their cleared fields by 1850 already had been abandoned to junipers and wild shrubs.[11] It was no accident that the pioneering work by an American on the state-of-the-world's environment appeared in 1864.[12]

In 1820, most of what a wealthy merchant's family needed were changes outside itself, changes in the urban and public realm. The family was missing such public goods as decent land planning, public water and sewers, and progress in science and medicine that could ensure decent food preservation and food handling and force the abandonment of dangerous medical practices. Families without the merchant's accumulated wealth also needed safe savings banks and varieties of social insurance. An early nineteenth-century balance sheet clearly demonstrated that subsequent changes in the urban and social setting of the family were the most important life-enhancing gains.

The urban balance sheet was also environmental. The cities of the early nineteenth century surely were growing in population, jobs, housing, and tax base—all the elements that are indicators of prosperity. Only the panics brought about by the sudden flows of capital back to Europe cloud a conventional portrait of the American economy in these years. However, in such an accounting should not the massive pollution and destruction of regional land, water, timber, and soil be considered? What of the destruction of immigrants, women, and children?

Suburban Family Life-Style during the 1920s

The situation a century later is easier to bring to mind because the physical evidence stands all about in well-to-do suburban neighborhoods. Examples are the houses and streets of the Fairway section of the "Country Club District" of Kansas City. The streets and district had been laid out by the J. C. Nichols Company in 1928. This subdivision of single-family houses matched the best design principles of its day: one housing type only, detached single-family houses, uniform setbacks, streets with sidewalks and trees, no fenced front lawns, and a neighborhood unit plan for parks, playgrounds, and schools. Both zoning and covenants on the land enforced strict segregation against nonwhites, poor people, and often Jews as well. A golf club served as the focus of the subdivision: there were peripheral boulevard streets, a shopping center with streetcar public transportation, and parking for automobiles. Indeed, the shopping center was the the famous Country Club Plaza. In such settings, one can easily imagine George Babbitt's Floral Heights or his Glen Oriole, styles for living that were as important to American city development as the earlier Georgian row houses.[13]

The developer, Jesse Clyde Nichols, was a national leader in the movement for carefully planned suburban development, an early advocate of city planning, a founder of the National Association of Real Estate Boards, and one of the group who succeeded in getting what it regarded as good practice written into later federal mortgage guidelines.[14] These exemplar suburban streets and houses solved many of the environmental problems of the early nineteenth century. Streets could be, and often were, laid out to conform to the shape of the land, and the lots were large enough so that they supported street and yard trees to shelter the houses. The site planning, however, did not orient the houses for sun and wind, but presented the houses formally to the street behind the continuous front-lawn expanse that was the pride of a well-to-do neighborhood. Although the lot was large enough to process the household wastes, this was a heavy, public infrastructure design. There was metropolitan gas, water, telephone, and electric service to the house, and a double sewer system—one for household wastes and the other for surface runoff.

The streets were always graded and paved in such a way that it facilitated high-speed automobile and truck traffic. Therefore, like all modern suburban streets, these streets in Kansas City were an unnecessary hazard to children. Also, their impervious asphalt or concrete surface shed water and thereby created serious runoff problems in storms, and contributed heavy pollution to regional rivers and groundwater. Also, lead had just been added to gasoline in 1922 so that massive street, air, and water poisoning was underway when this subdivision was laid out and the street paved.[15] However, particle pollution—the old coal and wood smoke from the home fireplaces—was declining in the 1920s with the use of furnaces and the introduction of oil burners. Because coal, oil, and natural gas were cheap during those years, the houses were not insulated, nor were their windows and doors designed to stop heat loss. Such houses were the typical twentieth-century American energy guzzler.

The husband in such a suburban family during the 1920s commuted downtown by automobile, but some bus and streetcar transportation was still available on the the main streets of the city. Imagine, in this case, that the husband worked in a large manufacturing or wholesaling firm. He was career oriented, not a property accumulator, so that his house, minus the mortgage, and a little insurance represented all the family wealth. His goal was not to accumulate wealth for his children, but to pay off his debts, build up his insurance for his wife's benefit, see his children through high school, and help a bit if the sons wished to go to college. The daughters were to be given nice clothes and sent out to forage for husbands. The father, in such a family, moved from company to company if he wished to improve his salary, and the J.C. Nichols Company stood by to market his house for him if he needed to sell and to move on.

This suburban house design assumed that the wife was not in the wage labor market, but worked at home without pay. She cooked and tended the children when they were not in school. Indeed, such a neighborhood, which was filled with at-home mothers, gained safety for children and strangers because of the many eyes that looked out from the houses on to the street and yards. Another woman came in a day or two each week to help the mother with the housework and with minding the children.

Such a suburban family served as the import center for the entire urban economy. Almost all the products and services of the home were purchased and brought to the house: groceries were delivered, department stores delivered, and the milk route worker and dry cleaner came by regularly. The hospital was used occasionally for births and surgery, but physicians made house calls, trained nurses worked in private homes, and most Americans suffered illnesses and died in their homes.

The family was expected to socialize with relatives by telephone and by visiting regularly on Sundays. The wife and children also were likely to make friends through the children's school and neighborhood acquaintances, and the wife was expected to find an outside life in clubs. The early twentieth century was an era of golf clubs, and men's and women's clubs of all kinds. If all else failed, there was a lot of card playing. Overall, the abundance of products and services and the liberalization of manners freed the family considerably from its former constraints, but all the systems both within and without the family were unstable and out of balance.

The well-being of the wife and her children still depended on the income and behavior of the husband, whereas the proper functioning of the home depended on the unpaid labor of the wife. The many services to the home, in turn, depended on a pool of low-wage workers who were paid something less than a *family wage,* that is, a wage that would allow one person to support a family. Thus, there was a constant transfer of human time and effort up the racial and class ladder to sustain the middle-class suburban home. Also, because the child care and home care services of the wife were neither paid nor recorded in the economic accounts of city, region, or nation, the costs of the goods and services produced by the predominantly male-paid work force were artificially lowered, and the gross national product and other such measures of productivity were artificially inflated. The contemporary valuation of prosperity and the valuation of human well-being remained, as they still do currently, totally divorced from each other.[16]

The husband's urban, regional, and national money economies continued to be out of balance and highly unstable. All the former practices of exhausting natural resources and polluting water, air, and land continued, only on the larger scale of big farms and modern corporate enterprise. Inventions and fashions crowded one upon the other as business reached out toward the consumer with ready-made clothing, washing machines, vacuum cleaners, and radios. The marketing strategy was always the same: *skimming,* that is find and sell a product that will reach large affluent market, and never mind the consumers' costs—get them to trade up. Above all, the automobile dominated the era. It was a great gain in convenience in transportation, but it required a vast city, state, and federal investment in roads, and it disadvantaged poor people, women, and children by bankrupting urban public transportation and by making the streets of the city and suburbs dangerous.

Just as the dynamic new economy stranded millions of farmers and rendered obsolete whole industries and regions, like the textiles of New England, so it continued to express itself as a steep hierarchy of income and benefits. Such was the pace of change that, by the late 1920s, the economies of Europe and the United States had overwhelmed the private banking system and it collapsed in the Great Depression. Consequence: "I see one third of a nation ill-housed, ill-clad, ill-nourished," Franklin D. Roosevelt declared in his 1937 inaugural address.[17]

Current Values

The look from the 1990s backward toward these two previous examples of American urban family life places the elements of contemporary urban and environmental problems clearly in focus. The economies of the United States currently are still way out of balance. The family economy is by every measure unsettled: single-headed households multiply, two-wage-earner households are commonplace, parents of infants are working, and many men and women are working overtime. Another large group is ill-educated and almost unemployable; children are neglected; taxpayers and families say they cannot afford decent day care, decent schools, or college tuition; and medical and social services to families are in crisis. Inflation has overtaken housing, transportation, and many natural resources, whereas pollution of air, water, and land is approaching dangerous levels.

Clearly, the kind of economic growth that propelled urban America since 1820 is proving more and more costly and more and more dangerous to human life. To alter the circumstances in the United States, Americans need to begin to think clearly about what they value: the values will suggest the remedies.[18]

Value 1:
Humans

The test of the success of the city is the quality of the people it nourishes. How many people did the police have to put in jail? How many children do not read? How many people are sick and injured? How many people are working at dangerous jobs and dead end jobs a machine could do better? How many people who need good social services cannot get them? Is the housing safe and cheap? Can people get around the city easily and cheaply? Is this a city where strangers can meet safely and join together in common interests? Even strangers of different races and sexes?

Value 2:
The Nonhuman Natural Environment

Is clean air, water, and land getting scarcer or more plentiful? Are the nonhuman environments getting more or less various? Do they sustain humans in more ways or fewer? Is the metropolitan species list growing ever shorter? Is the city getting hotter, despite air-conditioning? Is it getting drier despite the metropolitan water system? If the trend is toward sharp species limitation, and if the climate is getting more and more like a desert, then this metropolis, like all American metropolises, is coming to be a less-satisfying place for humans to live in, and also it is becoming a biologically more dangerous place.

The human and environmental issues overlap in policy because the remedies for both lie in redesigning the city so that it will be cheaper to maintain, will be more suitable for the nurture of family life, and will be more sustaining of the sociability of urban life. For example, cluster housing will save open land and make public transportation and services to families easier; the closing of streets to fast cars and trucks and their repaving with porous surfaces will make streets safer for children and less hostile to the natural environment. Flexible career sequences, child care leaves, shorter hours, and lifetime education credits will enable adults to work and grow through life at a pace that fits the stages of human development, and therefore they will not have to tear up the landscape seeking quick escapes from their urban lives.[19]

An economic planning that totes up the full social and environmental costs of building, making, and marketing will find modes of doing business that are much cheaper and more humane than those currently used. Such an accounting will demonstrate that investments in clean air, water, soils, and plant covers within the metropolis itself are ways to increase public wealth—they are not just painful short-run costs.

The test of the prosperity of any American city is the health, liveliness, creativity, and sociability of its citizens, and the richness of the supporting nonhuman environments among which they live. If these tests are considered, then American city dwellers can look forward to more progress in the twenty-first century than in all the years that have gone before.

NOTES

1. See the photograph taken in New Orleans in 1961 during the celebration of integration of the city's schools in Anthony Lewis, *Portrait of a Decade: The Second American Revolution* (New York: Random House, 1964), photo section, page III.

2. Harold F. Searles, *The Nonhuman Environment in Normal Development and in Schizophrenia* (New York: International Universities Press, 1960).

3. For a promising study that examines urban class and vegetation issues, see Joan M. Welch, "An Assessment of the Land-Use and Socio-Economic Histories that Influence Urban Forest Structure" (Ph.D. diss., Department of Geography, Boston University, 1990). For recent data on school desegregation that indicate the effectiveness of using incentives with families to get them to behave in ways that reduce segregation, see Christine H. Rossell, "The Carrot or the Stick for School Desegregation Policy?" *Urban Affairs Quarterly* 25 (March 1990), 474–499.

4. For a fine ecological analysis of home building, see Malcolm Wells, *Gentle Architecture* (New York: McGraw-Hill, 1981). For issues of social appropriateness of contemporary housing styles, see Dolores Hayden, *Redesigning the American Dream: The Future of Housing, Work, and Family Life* (New York: W. W. Norton, 1984).

5. Colin Ward, *The Child and the City* (London: Architectural Press, 1978), 96–105, 116–125; Ray Oldenburg, *The Great Good Place* (New York: Paragon House, 1989).

6. William J. Spring, "Youth Unemployment and the Transition from School to Work," *New England Economic Review* (March–April, 1987), 3–16; Elizabeth F. Fideler, "A Second Chance: Meeting the Needs of Adult Learners," *New England Journal of Public Policy* 3 (Winter–Spring 1987), 89–109.

7. New Orleans Chapter of the American Institute of Architects, *A Guide to New Orleans Architecture* (New Orleans: American Institute of Architects, 1974).

8. See an exemplary merchant's row—State Street, overlooking Battery Park, 1864—in Mary Black, *Old New York in Early Photographs, 1853–1901* (New York: Dover Publications, 1973), plate 6.

9. Robert Williams Fogel, "Nutrition and the Decline in Mortality since 1700: Some Preliminary Findings," in *Long-Term Factors in American Economic Growth,* ed. Stanley L. Engerman and Robert E. Gallman (Chicago: University of Chicago Press, 1986), 439–555.

10. Robert G. Albion, *The Rise of the New York Port: 1815–1860* (New York: Charles Scribner's Sons, 1939).

11. Brian Donahue, " 'Damned at Both Ends and Cursed in the Middle'; The 'Flowage' of the Concord River Meadows, 1798–1862," *Environmental Review* 13 (Fall/Winter 1989), 62–65.

12. George Perkins Marsh, *Man and Nature; or, Physical Geography as Modified by Human Action* (New York: Charles Scribner's Sons, 1864).

13. Sinclair Lewis, *Babbitt* (New York: Grosset and Dunlap, 1922).

14. Marc A. Weiss, *The Rise of the Community Builders: The American Real Estate Industry and Urban Land Planning* (New York: Columbia University Press, 1987).

15. David Rosner and Gerald Markowitz, "A 'Gift of God'?: The Public Health Controversy over Leaded Gasoline during the 1920's," *American Journal of Public Health* 75 (April 1985), 344–352.

16. Hayden, *Redesigning the American Dream,* 149–155.

17. *Inaugural Addresses of the Presidents of the United States from George*

Washington in 1789 to George Bush in 1989, Bicentennial ed. (Washington, D.C.: U.S. Government Printing Office, 1989), 277.

18.   Martin Ryle, *Ecology and Socialism* (London: Century Hutchinson, 1988).

19.   Lewis Mumford wrote an eloquent program for the design of a city based on the life-stage needs of its inhabitants. See Lewis Mumford, "Planning for the Phases of Life," *Town Planning Review* 20 (April 1949), 5–16; reprinted in *The Urban Prospect* (New York: Harcourt, Brace and World, 1968). See also Michael Laurie, "Ecology and Aesthetics," *Places* 6 (Fall 1989), 48–51, who suggests the shift in values required for appropriate urban open space design.

Index